PRAISE FOR *TINSELTOWN GANGSTERS*

"Jeffrey Sussman presents a riveting picture of the most degenerate, immoral characters in the movie industry. Included are the sexual behavior of actors and executives, along with their relationships with members of organized crime over numerous decades. *Tinseltown Gangsters* is concise and well done. Bravo to Mr. Sussman!"

—**S. M. Chris Franzblau**, former federal prosecutor and criminal defense attorney for alleged organized crime figures and professional boxers, in a career that has spanned more than fifty years

"Tinseltown, implying a shiny, soft place, was an easy target for organized crime. Sussman again takes us on a harrowing journey, showing how gangsters preyed on the soft targets, big and small, in Tinseltown, USA."

—**Joseph Giannini**, Esq., former criminal defense attorney for members of organized crime and retired captain of the U.S. Marines Corps

"Sussman has established himself as one of the premier writers on La Cosa Nostra and organized crime. *Tinseltown Gangsters* is another opus that enhances this reputation."

—**Ron Chepesiuk**, author *Bad Henry: The Murderous Rampage of the Taco Bell Strangler* and other books, two-time Fulbright scholar, and host of the podcast *Crimebeat*

TINSELTOWN GANGSTERS

TINSELTOWN GANGSTERS

The Rise and Decline of the Mob in Hollywood

JEFFREY SUSSMAN

ROWMAN & LITTLEFIELD
Lanham • Boulder • New York • London

Published by Rowman & Littlefield
An imprint of The Rowman & Littlefield Publishing Group, Inc.
4501 Forbes Boulevard, Suite 200, Lanham, Maryland 20706
www.rowman.com

86-90 Paul Street, London EC2A 4NE

British Library Cataloguing in Publication Information available

Library of Congress Cataloging-in-Publication Data

Names: Sussman, Jeffrey, author.
Title: Tinseltown gangsters : the rise and decline of the mob in Hollywood
    / Jeffrey Sussman.
Description: Lanham : Rowman & Littlefield, [2024] | Includes
    bibliographical references and index.
Identifiers: LCCN 2023026540 (print) | LCCN 2023026541 (ebook) | ISBN
    9781538173565 (cloth) | ISBN 9781538173572 (ebook)
Subjects: LCSH: Gangsters—California—Los Angeles—History—20th century.
    | Motion picture industry—Employees—Labor unions—California—Los
    Angeles—History—20th century. | Extortion—California—Los
    Angeles—History—20th century. | Hollywood (Los Angeles,
    Calif.)—History—20th century.
Classification: LCC HV6439.U7 L776 2024 (print) | LCC HV6439.U7 (ebook) |
    DDC 364.106/60979494—dc23/eng/20231027
LC record available at https://lccn.loc.gov/2023026540
LC ebook record available at https://lccn.loc.gov/2023026541

To Barbara, my wife and best friend

Contents

ACKNOWLEDGMENTS

FIVE PEOPLE WERE INSTRUMENTAL IN THE BIRTH AND NURTURING of this book. I thank them all: Steven Spataro, chief reference librarian at the East Hampton Library, who proved himself ever resourceful in locating magazine articles and news stories going as far back as the 1920s. Becca Beurer, editor for three of my mob books, whose support has given me free rein to achieve my goals. Elizabeth Von-Buhr, assistant acquisitions editor. Tricia Currie-Knight, production editor. And my wife Barbara, who has read every page of this book and offered valuable suggestions.

INTRODUCTION

LIKE SHARKS TO BLOOD IN THE WATER, THE MOB ARRIVED IN Hollywood greedy and ready to tear off huge chunks of cash. Opportunistic mobsters saw labor unions as the means for muscling into the movie industry and extorting millions of dollars from studio bosses. Control the unions to which projectionists, art directors, cinematographers, electricians, scene designers, stagehands, extras belong, and you control the whole industry. Call a strike, and the cameras cease. But studio costs keep rising.

This book is a history of the mob's tactics for controlling the movies throughout much of the twentieth century. It paints colorful portraits of numerous mobsters, producers, actors, and directors. It begins with Joseph Kennedy, father of President Kennedy. Though not a member of any mob, Joseph Kennedy had numerous dealings with a wide assortment of mobsters beginning during Prohibition, when he partnered with Frank Costello, the prime minister of the underworld. Costello was a powerful mobster in Vegas and Hollywood during Prohibition. In the 1950s, he was instrumental in getting Frank Sinatra his career-changing role in *From Here to Eternity*.

But before organized criminals could get their teeth into the unions, Joseph Kennedy made his own sharklike attack. He was hired by FBO (Film Booking Office of America) to find a buyer for the company. It was not an easy sell; FBO was primarily an import and distribution company that also made low-budget genre movies, such as westerns and costume dramas. FBO was losing money, unable to compete with larger companies. Kennedy saw an opportunity; rather than sell the company, he would buy it. However, he lacked the necessary funds, so he borrowed money from his father-in-law, Honey Fitzgerald, and Louis Kerstein, boss of Filene's department store; however, the bulk of the money came from the Chicago Outfit. Its gangster principals had partnered with Kennedy during Prohibition. Having acquired the necessary funds and several unsavory partners, Kennedy bought FBO and immediately began producing a movie a week; each one was a low-budget movie that was rapidly distributed. FBO's profits quickly soared. Kennedy seemed to operate on the same principles as Henry Ford: turn out product as quickly and as cheaply as possible. Movies came off Kennedy's assembly line and were quickly shipped to theaters.

It was during this time that Kennedy courted, seduced, and began a three-year affair with the tiny, five-feet-tall Gloria Swanson. She was one of the most popular and glamourous screen stars, a highly valuable commodity that Kennedy wanted to control. On their first date, he managed to step on one of her size 2½ shoes. He laughed and apologized and the next day sent her a pearl necklace. When he offered to manage her finances, she readily agreed, for she completely trusted him. He bought her luxurious jewels, fur coats, a magnificent automobile. He seemed completely devoted to her. He took her on ocean voyages to Europe and invited her to stay at his home. Kennedy's wife, Rose, either accepted that her husband was having an affair with Swanson and chose to ignore it or thought they had a business relationship only. Either way, she would have been partly correct. For Kennedy was milking the relationship for everything it was worth. Kennedy was Swanson's Svengali. And the affair ended only after Swanson discovered that all the lavish, expensive gifts that Kennedy had given her had been charged to her own accounts.

Swanson produced small profits for Kennedy compared to what he would make when he sold FBO to David Sarnoff, head of NBC. A happy Kennedy walked away from that sale with a $5 million profit and repaid his Outfit partners $1 million.

His next Hollywood investment would be pursued with all the ruthlessness of a gangster. He had decided to buy a chain of theaters owned by Alexander Pantages, who controlled or owned a total of seventy-two theaters. The owner of such a chain could make enormous financial demands on producers who wanted their movies shown in his theaters. Kennedy was salivating at the prospect of owning the chain, but Pantages refused to sell. Kennedy then got his friends and business associates in the movie industry to withhold first-run releases from Pantages's Los Angeles Theater; instead, the movies were shown in other theaters. By the time the movies were available to Pantages, they had been seen by thousands in LA. Yet Pantages still refused to sell. A desperate Kennedy sought the help of a shady theatrical agent named Dunaev, who lived with an aspiring actress named Eunice Pringle, who was ready to sell her charms for an any opportunity to advance her career. Kennedy paid the pair $10,000 to set up Pantages. He also promised Pringle a part in a movie he was producing. Pringle gained an audience with Pantages by attempting to sell a screenplay by Dunaev. The screenplay was so awkwardly and amateurishly written that it was not worth the paper it had been typed on. Pantages rejected it and told Pringle that it was obviously the work of an untalented hack. Pringle was not finished with Pantages. On August 29, 1929, she hid in a closet of the Pantages Los Angeles Theater. Dressed in a sexy low-cut dress, she burst out as soon as Pantages was in proximity of the closet. She began screaming that Panatages had attempted to rape her. Startled employees called the police, and Pantages was arrested. At trial, Pantages was found guilty and sentenced to fifty years in prison. However, his attorney Jerry Giesler (attorney for

Bugsy Siegel and other gangsters and celebrities) appealed the case, and the California Supreme Court overturned the conviction, noting that a conspiracy had resulted in the conviction of Pantages. By the time he was acquitted in 1931, Pantages had sold his theaters to Kennedy for less than Kennedy had originally offered, though he still made millions of dollars. Two years later, as Pringle lay dying from cyanide poisoning, she confessed to the conspiracy to set up Pantages. No one was ever investigated for her murder.

Kennedy's trajectory was aimed at even more profitable enterprises. He had decided it was time for him to bid goodbye to Hollywood. Tinseltown's moguls were not the right kind of people for a social climber to associate with: they were uneducated Jews, and Kennedy was a snob and anti-Semite who referred to studio owners as "pants pressers," kikes, and sheenies. He aspired to be accepted as part of the WASP establishment, not as a partner of vulgar nouveau riche movie magnates. It didn't matter that Kennedy may have been as greedy and ruthless as they were; he had worked assiduously to generate a polished image of himself as a highly successful man of the world. He was a gentleman. Yet Franklin Roosevelt correctly drew a bead on Kennedy's character when he appointed him as head of the Securities and Exchange Commission, because (as Roosevelt said) "it takes a thief to catch a thief."[1]

It wasn't until the outset of World War II, when Kennedy hobnobbed with pro-German lords and ladies in England, that his defeatism and anti-Semitism led to the perception that he was less a gentleman than an appeaser of a vicious dictator.

After Kennedy repaid his loan to the Outfit, the gangsters in Chicago realized there was more gold in the hills of Hollywood than they had previously realized. Though Al Capone had shown a tentative interest in the business of moviemaking, it was not until the end of Prohibition that the mobs saw Hollywood as a new source of illegal wealth. Among the first mobsters to enter the land of dreams was Bugsy Siegel, who—upon arriving—declared himself a sportsman (i.e., a professional gambler of independent means).

Siegel was movie-star handsome, a former killer for Murder Inc., and a man so prone to violence that he was referred to as Bugsy, a reference to being as crazy as a bedbug. Yet he could be the very essence of charm and kindness. He seduced some of the biggest stars in Hollywood, including Jean Harlow, Wendy Barrie, and Marie McDonald. (Harlow became the godmother to Siegel's daughter Millicent). He believed he was irresistible and so handsome that he should be a movie star like his friend from New York, George Raft.

Raft (né Ranft) had been a protégé of Hell's Kitchen gangster Owney "the Killer" Madden. Raft eventually became a ballroom dancer, then a gigolo, then an actor. From Broadway, he immigrated to Hollywood, where he became one of the highest paid movie actors of the 1930s and 1940s. Siegel wanted Raft to open doors to a Hollywood career. Siegel bought his own movie equipment, and Raft arranged for a Siegel screen test. It was professionally edited, but Siegel never bothered to show it to any producers or directors. Though he had an overblown ego, it was as thin and fragile as the skin of an overinflated balloon. If he were rejected, Siegel's ego would have quickly deflated, landing crumpled on the ground. He could not take the chance of being rejected, so the gangster's thespian ambitions remained unfulfilled. Yet Siegel watched his screen test over and over again in the security of his living room, never failing to marvel at his thespian abilities. He averred to whomever watched the screen test with him that he was as good as any actor on the silver screen. The one thing about which there was no doubt was his ability to extort the studios, which he accomplished through third parties while controlling the union for extras. As Tere Tereba writes in her biography of Siegel's aide-de-camp Mickey Cohen,

Following the lead of industrial racketeer Lepke Buchalter, a New York partner, Ben Siegel took a slice of the movie labor action. Nobody liked union troubles. The film moguls had no choice but to go along with the underworld's program. A crowd scene scheduled for the morning? Threats of a walkout by hundreds of extras? A call to Ben Siegel would smooth things over: everyone knew he was the power behind central casting.[2]

While surreptitiously extorting Hollywood studios, Siegel had managed to befriend the biggest stars in Hollywood, numerous directors, and producers. According to John William Touhy,

Siegel took over the Screen Extras Guild and the Los Angeles Teamsters, which he ran until his death. With control of the Screen Extras Guild, Siegel was able to shake down Warner Brothers Studios for $10,000, with a refusal to provide extras for any of their films. He also shook down his movie star friends for huge loans that he never paid back, and when he came back for another loan, he always got it, because they were, justifiably, terrified of him. He once bragged to Lansky that he had fleeced the Hollywood crowd out of more than $400,000 within six months of his arrival. He was a one-man terrorist campaign.[3]

In addition to his extortion rackets, Siegel collected $100,000 annually from Los Angeles brothels that bought protection from the mob, which—in turn—guaranteed a hands-off policy from the local vice squad. However, Siegel's primary sources of income were the Transcontinental Racing Wire (to which bookies in three states were forced to subscribe) and various high-class gambling enterprises that attracted the crème de la crème of Hollywood society, whose members gambled away fortunes faster than they had acquired them.

One of those who gambled away huge sums and had been a lover of such leading Hollywood stars as Gary Cooper and Clark Gable was the Countess Dorothy di Frasso. She was a rich heiress who had married an Italian count for his title. She and Siegel became lovers, and she subsequently invited him to visit her villa in Italy. Since there was tremendous anti-Semitism in Europe in the 1930s, she altered Siegel's pedigree with the snap of her fingers. He became a British baronet named Sir Bart. When the pair arrived at her husband's villa, they discovered that the count had invited two Nazi houseguests: Joseph Goebbels and Hermann Göring. Siegel was furious. He referred to Goebbels as "that weaselly cripple" and Göring as an "overfed pig" whose belly would nicely accommodate a barrage of .45 slugs. He told the countess that he planned to bump off the two Nazis. The countess became alarmed and beseeched him not to take such foolish actions. If he did, she and her husband would wind up in a concentration camp—if not worse—and Siegel might not get out of Italy alive. Siegel relented and the two packed their bags and traveled to the south of France. There, the ersatz baronet and the countess partied with rich expatriates. Back in LA, Siegel's life expectancy became dangerously truncated.

It wasn't his aborted assassination plans or retribution for any of the many murders he committed that got Siegel killed. It was stealing from his mob partners back East who had financed the building of his Las Vegas casino, the Fabulous Flamingo. Siegel had originally assured his investors that the cost would amount to no more than $1 million. When it rocketed to $6 million, Meyer Lansky, Lucky Luciano, Frank Costello, and Joe Adonis decided that they had to put an end to their thieving spendthrift partner. So Bugsy was ambushed one night while sitting on the couch of his wife/mistress Virginia Hill's rented Beverly Hills mansion. As he sat reading the *Los Angeles Times* and chatting intermittently with his pal, Allen Smiley, a fusillade of bullets tore into the back of Siegel's head. One of the great visionaries of Las Vegas died before he could see his vision of Sin City become a reality. Yet he had left his mark on Hollywood, paving a road for other mobsters, especially Willie Bioff and Mickey Cohen, to travel on.

Siegel's death had a profound effect on Raft, who had been invited to have dinner with Siegel the night of the assassination. Raft had told Siegel he had other commitments and would call him the next day. When he learned that his closest friend had been murdered, Raft said that he might have been collateral damage, if he had gone to Siegel's house that night. He ruefully reflected that banner headlines would have screamed, "Mobster and Star Murdered!" Though he was lucky to have declined Siegel's invitation, Raft felt such a deep sense of bereavement that he noted to a reporter that "when they shot Benny, they shot me."[4] Raft had regarded Siegel as an older brother, a replacement for Owney Madden. Raft had always agreed to carry out any favor that Siegel had asked of him. When Siegel requested a loan, Raft gave it, knowing that—at best—it would only be partially repaid. Once when Siegel was arrested on a gambling charge, Raft publicly testified on behalf of his friend. Raft had been warned by his studio that his testimony would be injurious to his career. But friendship to Siegel came before any loyalty to a studio. Not only did Raft testify for Siegel, helping to secure an acquittal, but he also posed with one arm around Siegel for a photograph on the courthouse steps. The photograph was reprinted in thousands of newspapers, not just in North America, but in Europe and South America too. One producer told Raft that he had committed career suicide. It didn't matter to Raft. He generally preferred the company of gangsters to that of Hollywood celebrities. Years later, he reminisced of the gangsters he had known: "I knew them all. They were guys I looked up to. They were interesting company and when you talked to them, as I did, you learned a lot. Over dinner at a nightclub or restaurant, they were more fun and laughs than any businessman or studio head I ever met."[5]

The memory of Siegel's friendship never left Raft. He knew that his admiration and fondness for Siegel had been sincerely reciprocated:

> *There was no question that "'Bugsy" Siegel admired—even envied—his pal George Raft. He often visited George on the sets of his pictures and had Raft photograph him with his own camera equipment acting out scenes he had just watched George performing, claiming that he could act better than his friend. Because the Raft image was so strong and his sartorial preferences emulated by many men in America, Siegel likewise took to dressing like his pal, and he, too, cut a fashionable figure around Tinseltown. . . . He made no secret of the fact that he considered George Raft the most authentic movie tough guy of them all.*[6]

For Raft, that was praise indeed. That he was thought of as a genuine tough guy pleased Raft. Even James Cagney said that Raft was the only true tough guy in Hollywood. Cagney had rebelled against the mob's shakedown of the Hollywood unions and so he was targeted for murder. When Raft learned of the threat, he contacted Owney Madden, who then contacted the Outfit in Chicago and arranged for the contract on Cagney's life to be rescinded.

It was not out of character for Raft to be associated with mobsters. He was raised in Hell's Kitchen and became a junior member of the Gophers gang, which was headed by his childhood mentor Owney "the Killer" Madden. Raft's delinquent past was part of his character. It showed up in various ways, the most consistent being his need to steal anything that was not nailed down, whether it was from stores, restaurants, a train, or a movie studio. He had collected silverware, knickknacks, clothing, movie weapons, haberdashery.

His admiration for larcenous individuals did not extend to Siegel's replacement, Mickey Cohen.

Cohen, who had been a violent delinquent since childhood, was Siegel's aide-de-camp and quick-tempered muscle. His audacious criminal career had begun at age nine, when he and several preteen gang members held up the box office of one of the biggest movie theaters in Los Angeles. Cohen, who was only about five feet five as an adult, was so small at age nine that he hardly appeared menacing. Yet he wielded a baseball bat with such ferocity that he terrified the female box office employee at the theater, who handed over all the money demanded by Cohen after he had threatened to bash in her skull. Years later, with the threat of violence and in some cases acts of violence, he took over Siegel's operations. He had none of Siegel's charm, good looks, or ability to hobnob with Hollywood royalty. Though he had abandoned his earlier career as a professional boxer, he maintained his trade as a killer, heist man, and extortionist. He not only used those skills to take over Siegel's Hollywood ventures, but he relied on them to squeeze ever more money out of his victims than Siegel had.

Always looking for new illegal means for increasing his power and the money he could amass, he introduced a unique blackmailing racket to the world of Hollywood crime: he made porno films using women who bore a close resemblance to famous movie stars. He would sell the movies back to studio bosses who wanted to maintain their investments in the popularity of their stars. In other cases, he used hidden cameras to film well-known actresses in flagrante then proceeded to blackmail them. Having milked the stars of thousands of dollars, he would then extort their bosses, who paid huge sums to Mickey for destroying the films and negatives.

There were certain stars, many of whom Cohen referred to as dumb whores, whose reputations he wanted to destroy. One such star was Lana Turner. Cohen was incensed that Turner's daughter took the rap for killing Turner's lover, gangster Johnny Stompanato, a friend of Cohen's. Cohen, along with numerous others, believed that Turner had killed Stompanato but that her lawyer convinced Cheryl Crane, Turner's daughter, to say that she accidentally stabbed Stompanato, who was beating up her mother. Cohen wanted the world to know that Turner stabbed Stompanato multiple times while he slept in their bed and that his friend had not beaten Turner. (The sheets on Turner's bed were drenched in blood, but the floor on which Stompanato lay dead was absent blood. Cohen believed the body had been dragged to the spot where Crane claimed she accidentally stabbed Stompanato.) Cohen told reporters that Stompanato never beat Turner. To prove his point, he released the Turner/Stompanato love letters to the press. He then provided a possible motive for Stompanato's murder. Cohen told the press that Stompanato was hired to buy films of stars having adulterous sex. Perhaps he was extorting his own lover, but that was certainly no cause for stabbing the guy multiple times while he slept. Cohen noted the case of MGM hiring Stompanato to buy a porno movie titled *Casting Couch*, which featured a young Joan Crawford. Stompanato was also instructed to buy the negatives. Large sums were spent to track down and buy copies of the movie. When Crawford left MGM, she had to repay that money. Tim Adler writes: "MGM's former head of security, Howard Strickling, told erstwhile colleague Samuel Marx that the studio had to buy up pornographic movies starring Crawford."[7] Studios did whatever was necessary to protect their investments in their stars. And that included protecting Lana Turner from being indicted and tried for murder, even if she could have proven self-defense. She never responded to Cohen's accusations. It didn't matter to Cohen. He had found a place for himself in the media spotlight. He loved the attention of reporters and was quick to offer his opinions on anything from murder to raising money for Israeli independence.

Though Cohen never shied away from the media, his top priorities remained extortion, gambling, loan-sharking, and drug dealing. And he never stopped killing people who got in his way. As he said in a TV interview conducted by Mike Wallace, "I didn't kill no men that, in the first place, didn't deserve killing."[8]

Though he killed numerous men, he did not kill women. It was not that he was chivalrous; he simply never ran into a woman who he felt deserved killing, not even prostitutes who may have run rackets that competed with ones that Cohen controlled. He did become tangentially connected to a celebrated prostitution case, but it had nothing to do with murder. It involved a high-class madam named Brenda Allen. She was a former streetwalker who organized a call girl ring of 114 beautiful women. Clients were wealthy businessmen, movie stars (such as Errol Flynn, Mickey Rooney, and Xavier Cugat), politicians, and corrupted cops who took partial payoffs in client services. Each client would call Allen's unlisted number, 5-255. Once the client was identified, he was offered a magnificent heroine of a novel. He was told that she had long, luxurious blonde hair, was five two or five three, and was draped in a full-length mink coat over a green low-cut silk dress. The client could pick up a copy of the "book" at 9:30 p.m. in front of a bookstore on Sunset Boulevard. The client would arrive at the designated time, and a few minutes later the prostitute whom Allen had described would emerge from a limo.

Allen herself was a beauty: she had red hair, a stunning figure, and movie-actress features. Her soigné appearance, however, did not protect her from the clutches of the law. A police wiretap had recorded her outgoing calls, one of which was about Cohen and corrupt cops. The bug had picked up a call between Allen and a vice cop named Sergeant Jackson, who not only provided her protection, but was also her lover. Jackson bragged that he was shaking down some of Cohen's gambling dens. The revelation of the attempted police shakedown freed Cohen of Jackson's coercion. Cohen laughed at the revelation and his good fortune. Unfortunately for Allen, however, the bug led to her arrest, indictment, and conviction for pandering. She was sentenced to a year in jail.

The following year, Allen was taken from jail to appear before a grand jury investigating police corruption. She was conservatively and expensively dressed in a sleek gray suit. Her face was slightly obscured by large sunglasses and a translucent black veil. Her shapely lips were blood red. She admitted that she operated her call girl ring with the help of LA cops.

"Allen swore that she paid $150 a week per girl for police protection and proceeded to inform the panel: 'I paid for everything that I got, and I paid plenty. If they [the cops] got into this mess, it was their own business not mine. Now it's everybody for himself.'"[9] Following her testimony, a number of cops were indicted, including Jackson and Police Chief C. B. Horrall. The exposure caused Horrall to resign; at trial, Jackson was acquitted. Though Jackson claimed he knew Allen only through his undercover work, it was reported that he had shot a holdup man who was necking with Allen in a parked car. The public was not only outraged by the reported level of police corruption, but also—following the trial—by the gruesome murders of several call girls who could have testified against the police.

Killing prostitutes was not part of Cohen's modus operandi, though he certainly killed plenty of people, most of whom were fellow mobsters. There was little profit in murder, other than eliminating competitors and rats. Cohen did profit, however, by creating an innovative venue for extorting movie stars and studio bosses. He succeeded in his new caper through the publication of *Hollywood Nite-Life*. Hank Sanicola, Frank Sinatra's manager, was named publisher of *Nite-Life*, but it was Cohen who financed and controlled the publication. Sanicola's name on the masthead, however, did not prevent Frank Sinatra from becoming a blackmail target. The magazine was prepared to print a story that Sinatra was having an extramarital affair with Ava Gardner. Sinatra paid to have the story killed, and Sanicola promised thereafter to protect his client. The men who attempted to extort Sinatra and other stars called themselves "salesmen" (one of whom was Robert Mitchum's manager). They were as voracious and persistent as piranhas. They informed vulnerable stars on their list of targets that their indecent acts would be featured in the publication unless each of them agreed to take out a substantial ad or series of ads. *Hollywood Nite-Life* was regularly delivered to the desks of studio heads, producers, directors, and major stars. It was read avidly, often with a sense of relief, disbelief, anger, or schadenfreude. Readers' emotions varied depending on who was being mocked as a hypocrite, a fraud, a thief, an adulterer, a lesbian, or a gay man. During its brief run, *Hollywood Nite-Life* made hundreds of thousands of dollars for Cohen.

When it came to extortion, Willie Bioff proved to have a more voracious appetite for extorted funds than Cohen. Bioff, a mean-spirited thug, had started out as a pimp and holdup man in Chicago then graduated to membership in the Outfit. There he honed his skills as a vicious, no-holds-barred extortionist. Capone's successor, Frank "the Enforcer" Nitti, sent Bioff to Los Angeles to run mob-controlled labor unions and to bring other unions into the fold. He was joined by another Outfit emissary, George Browne, who had become president of the International Alliance of Theatrical Stage Employees (IATSE). Joining the duo was Outfit member Johnny "Handsome Johnny" Rosselli, who would be the bag man, collecting extortion payments from Hollywood studio bosses.

Shortly after Browne and Bioff began running IATSE, they learned that the movie theaters were able to dictate to the studios what movies should be produced. Tim Adler writes: "IATSE members ran nearly every movie theater in the country. Nitti added that, contrary to popular belief, New York–based theater chains controlled movie production—not the other way around. MGM, for example, was a subsidiary of the Loew's theater chain."[10] Bioff told theater owners that his union demanded that each theater must employ two projectionists. The owners said they couldn't afford it, so Bioff said hire two and pay them less. Bioff collected the difference.

In addition to theaters, Bioff extorted hundreds of thousands of dollars from movie studios, each of which went along with Bioff's demands so that they would avoid strikes. He next forced technicians to join the union. Within three years, Bioff increased the union's membership from two hundred to twelve thousand. Those who had refused to join Bioff's union were threatened with death. If they argued against the union, their jaws were broken, their teeth knocked out with brass knuckles. With his union as leverage, Bioff made sure that each studio owner understood that a strike would be far more expensive than the cost of paying him. None of the studio heads resisted Bioff.

However, one who was threatened then permitted to avoid paying off Bioff was Harry Cohn, president of Columbia Pictures. Cohn was so well connected with the mob and such a close friend of Johnny Rosselli that he managed to rebuff Bioff without suffering the consequences that others would have endured. Cohn had complained to Rosselli that Bioff wanted a payoff of hundreds of thousands of dollars for labor peace. Rosselli then notified his bosses, who put Bioff on a leash regarding Cohn. Not only did they restrain Bioff, but they told him to apologize to Cohn. When Bioff visited Cohn in his office and offered his apology, Cohn simply grunted and refused to shake Bioff's hand. Bioff departed. Had he been a dog, his cowering tail would have been tucked up against his stomach.

Bioff soon reasserted his nasty aggressiveness and belligerence at other studio bosses, getting them to agree that only his union of stagehands would be recognized as legitimate representatives of all stagehands. Independent stagehands therefore had no choice but to join his union or face unemployment. To demonstrate to the independents that he wanted only the best for them, he offered them a 10 percent increase over their current salaries. Of course, Bioff would then receive a larger amount from the dues they paid his union. In addition, he took 2 percent of their salaries for a union strike fund. Of the $1.5 million that Bioff collected, he kept a few hundred thousand dollars for himself and sent the balance to his overseers in the Outfit. Bioff next told the head of the Eastman Film Company that if it wanted to continue selling film stock to Hollywood studios, Eastman would have to pay him a 7 percent commission on all of its sales. Eastman agreed.

Bioff thought that Hollywood would be his cash cow for as long as he lived. The government, however, had different plans. The stream of money pouring into Bioff's vaults began drying up when the government's investigation of his illegal practices swung into high gear. The government's attack caused guilty parties to run for cover, but they couldn't hide. Bioff and top members of the Outfit were indicted for extortion, tried, found guilty, and sentenced to ten years in prison. Among those convicted with Bioff were Nitti, Rosselli, Paul "the Waiter" Ricca, Phil D'Andrea, Nick Circella, Charles "Cherry Nose" Gioe, and Ralph Pierce. Nitti had no intention of rotting in prison. Desperate, he chose a quick alternative to incarceration by firing a bullet into his head. That left Paul "the Waiter" Ricca as the new head of the Outfit, a position he maintained for thirty years. While in prison, he was patient and stoical, but after being released he proved vengeful. He had learned that Bioff was an FBI informant who had testified against his compatriots in exchange for a reduced sentence. Bioff was living in Phoenix under the assumed name of Bill Nelson. He had become a close friend of Senator Barry Goldwater and went into business with one of the senator's nephews. For entertainment, Bioff often traveled to Las Vegas, where he was fingered by the mob. After his presence was reported to the Outfit, his days were numbered in single digits. In ignorant insouciance, he returned to Phoenix on Goldwater's private plane. He spent a peaceful evening at home with his wife. The next day, he kissed her goodbye, departed his house, and climbed into his pickup truck. He inserted and turned the ignition key and was immediately blown into a thousand pieces, spread over hundreds of yards in all directions. The thunderous blast blew out a few neighboring windows and soon brought siren-wailing police cars. Debris of glass and metal were scattered on the street. The FBI believed that Ricca, one of the few surviving members of the gang against whom Bioff testified, arranged for the truck bomb.

On November 9, 1955, the theatrical paper *Variety* headlined the event: "Willie Bioff's Last Shakedown: Hoodlum's Booby-trapped Demise Recalls Blackmail of Studios." The story continued with this sentence: "Thus ended the career of a Chicago racketeer who, with George Browne, extorted over $1,000,000 in shakedown money from the Hollywood film studios."[11]

One of Bioff's more talented cohorts was the charming and ruthless Johnny Rosselli, a gangster whose greed rarely exceeded his discretion. Whereas Bioff had been crude and coarse, Rosselli was smooth and diplomatic. He continued to extort the movie studios, but his implied threats came with a serpent's smile, not a gruff threat of murder. Of course, all threats had to be backed up with the possibility of murder, otherwise there was no force behind the threats. And those whom Rosselli extorted knew he represented the murderous Outfit.

Rosselli, who was born Filippo Sacco, chose his nom de guerre after reading about Cosimo Rosselli, the man who had completed the painting of the Sistine Chapel following the death of Michelangelo. But Handsome Johnny was no artist. Instead, he chose to follow in his stepfather's footsteps, becoming a prolific thief who graduated to membership in the Outfit. The Outfit bosses thought that Rosselli's charm, good looks, and smoothly gracious manners would go over well in Hollywood, where he was sent in the 1930s. He was given the mission of working with Bioff and Browne to increase revenue from gambling and labor racketeering. He became so much a part of the Hollywood scene that he was welcomed into the homes of stars, directors, and producers. Neither Bioff nor Browne, who were regarded by Hollywood elites as ill-mannered hoodlums, would ever have been invited to the swank Hollywood parties where Rosselli was often seen with a drink in one hand and a cigarette in the other while chatting with a lovely young star.

Rosselli proved to be an excellent choice for the Outfit. He conducted a strong stream of money to the Outfit. It came to an end when he was indicted and convicted of extorting the movie studios and sent to prison in February 1944. Unlike Bioff, he served his term without turning on his bosses. He was released in 1947 and soon went to see his old friend Harry Cohn at Columbia Pictures. Rosselli had done many favors for Cohn and expected Cohn to help him achieve solvency. He asked Cohn for a job, but Cohn said that his board of directors and the stockholders would never permit his hiring a confessed extortionist of movie studios. Rosselli, angered by Cohn's response, lost his temper, telling the unmoved Cohn how he had protected him from being extorted by Bioff and other mobsters. Cohn said he was sorry, but his hands were tied. Rosselli cursed him and departed.

Ever resourceful, Rosselli turned to his friend, movie producer Bryan Foy, who agreed to hire Rosselli as an assistant producer at Eagle-Lion Films, where Foy was celebrated as a master of low-budget gangster movies. Foy was the son of a well-known vaudevillian, Eddie Foy. As a boy, he and his brothers regularly appeared with their father in a vaudeville act, "Eddie Foy and the Seven Little Foys." As an adult and no longer performing vaudeville, Bryan went on to be a successful producer of more than two hundred movies and a director of forty-one other movies. He worked for such major studios as Warner Brothers, Columbia Pictures, 20th Century Fox, and Universal Pictures.

Together, Foy and Rosselli produced three film noir classics: *He Walked by Night*, *T-Men*, and *Canon City*. Foy could not have chosen a better assistant, for Rosselli provided the inside information of a seasoned gangster. As a result, the movies were critically acclaimed for scenes of harsh and gritty verisimilitude. Years later, Foy said of Rosselli: "We never saw the gangster side of him. He was a great guy. Half the people in this town were his friends. No one who ever had a drink or dinner with Johnny ever picked up [the] check."[12]

Rosselli divided his time between Las Vegas and Los Angeles. In Vegas, he helped to negotiate the sales of casinos and received substantial commissions. In LA, he participated in a scam that would send him back to prison. He had applied to join the Friars Club in Los Angeles, and his application was supported by Frank Sinatra, Dean Martin, and club founder George Jessel. The most attractive attribute of the club for Rosselli and others was its card room. There, a card player named Maurice Friedman organized a scheme to cheat a fellow card player named Harry Karl. Friedman's dislike of Karl was apparent to all who knew the pair. So that Friedman's scheme wouldn't seem solely directed at Karl, Friedman also planned to cheat various celebrities who also participated in the card games. To put his plan into operation, Friedman hired an ex-convict to drill a hole in the ceiling of the card room. From there, the cards of players could be seen and the information surreptitiously passed on to Friedman, who went on to win between $8,000 and $10,000 a night. The games were played every week for months. When Rosselli learned of the scheme, he confronted and threatened Friedman with exposure. To keep Rosselli quiet, Friedman dealt him in for 20 percent of the take.

The FBI, working with informants, learned of the scam, and on July 20, 1967, six agents raided the club. As the Christmas holiday season was about to start, Rosselli and five others who had been arrested were indicted in the Friars' cheating scandal. As if that wasn't bad enough, Rosselli was also being indicted as an illegal alien. That case could not only land him in prison, but upon his release, he could be deported to Italy. For the Friars Club scheme, Rosselli was sentenced to five years in prison and fined $50,000. He served three years and was then paroled. The government never pursued the immigration case, perhaps because Rosselli had found a way to ingratiate himself with the Department of Justice and the CIA.

He became involved in CIA plots, along with Mafia bosses Sam Giancana and Santo Trafficante, to assassinate Fidel Castro. It was known as Operation Mongoose. All of their plans failed, including an attempt to poison Castro and another that involved sending Castro exploding cigars. Their biggest failure was the Bay of Pigs attack in which a brigade of armed recruits, known as Brigada Asalto 2506, landed on the Bay of Pigs to bring down the Castro government. Under heavy counterattack, the brigade pleaded for air and naval support, which was refused by the highest US government officials. According to the CIA:

> *Without direct air support—no artillery and no weapons—and completely outnumbered by Castro's forces, members of the Brigade either surrendered or returned to the turquoise water from which they had come. Two American destroyers attempted to move into the Bay of Pigs to evacuate these members, but gunfire from Cuban forces made that impossible. In the following days, US entities continued to monitor the waters surrounding the bay in search of survivors, with only a handful being rescued. A few members of the Brigade managed to escape and went into hiding, but soon surrendered due to a lack of food and water. When all was said and done, more than seventy-five percent of Brigade 2506 ended up in Cuban prisons.*[13]

Eventually members of the US Senate decided to investigate the role of the CIA in its attempts to assassinate Castro. Rosselli was called to testify before the US Senate Select Committee on Intelligence on June 24 and September 22, 1975. Another person called to testify about the failed operations and possibly about the assassination of President Kennedy was Sam Giancana. Shortly before Rosselli testified, Giancana was in the basement of his home frying sausages and peppers for a late-night snack. He was scheduled to testify a few days hence, but he was shot seven times in the head and neck with a .22 caliber pistol. Giancana's murder unnerved Rosselli, who fled the West Coast and moved in with his sister in Miami, Florida.

On April 23, 1976, Rosselli was again called before the committee to testify, this time specifically about a conspiracy to assassinate President Kennedy. Three months later, the committee intended to recall Rosselli, but he couldn't be located, so the FBI began an investigation into his whereabouts. By this time, the Mafia was well aware that Rosselli had testified, but they did not have concrete information about what he said. He had not notified his Mafia bosses in advance of his testimony nor had he asked their permission. Yet he felt safe in Miami. His testimony was of deep concern to the mob, for Rosselli could testify about the mob's role in the assassination.

On July 28, Rosselli had dinner at the Landings Restaurant in Fort Lauderdale with Mafia boss Santo Trafficante. After dinner, Rosselli drove to a marina and boarded a cabin cruiser that was operated by one of his mob friends from Chicago. After the boat returned to the marina, a man left the boat, entered Rosselli's car, and drove it to Miami International Airport. A Mafia informer said that while Rosselli sipped a glass of vodka, his Chicago pal grabbed him from behind, holding one hand over Rosselli's mouth and pinching his nose with the other hand. Rosselli was unable to put up much of a struggle due to his emphysema. He soon suc-cumbed and collapsed onto the deck. Rosselli's arms and legs were sawed from his body to fit into a metal oil drum on the boat. The drum was tossed overboard and sank. The killers had drilled holes in the drum, thinking it would fill with water and sink. However, gases from Rosselli's decomposing torso caused the drum to bob to the surface of the water and float to a sandbar. Three fishermen spotted it and contacted the police.

Those who reported on Rosselli's death did not mention that the victim's erstwhile friend Harry Cohn had died in 1958. The two had been great friends until Cohn refused to hire Rosselli. Cohn felt so close to Rosselli that he wore an expensive friendship ring that Rosselli had given him. Rosselli had not only been a friend of Cohn, but he had been Cohn's emissary to various mobsters in New York, Chicago, and Las Vegas. He never failed to do a favor for Cohn. One of which involved contacting their mutual friend New Jersey mob boss Abner Longy Zwillman and suggesting that he invest $500,000 in Columbia Pictures so that Cohn could buy out one of his partners. Cohn offered to sign a loan agreement with Zwillman, who refused the offer, and instead insisted on $500,000 worth of Columbia Pictures stock. Cohn reluctantly agreed. More importantly, as noted earlier, Rosselli saved Cohn from being extorted and possibly murdered by Willie Bioff.

As much as Cohn liked and admired Rosselli, the man whom Cohn most admired in the world was Benito Mussolini. Having visited Il Duce in 1933, Cohn returned to his office in LA and had it completely redecorated so that it was a picture-perfect fac-simile of Mussolini's office. He even kept a large framed photo of Mussolini on the wall adjacent to his desk. As Mussolini terrified all those who came into conflict with him, so Cohn terrified all those who got in his way. He had a hair-trigger temper that would result in his haranguing actors, producers, and directors, often threatening to end their careers. He would call a director an ungrateful shit and yell at a writer that he was an overpaid hack. He was as tough and ruthless as any mob boss. One of his writers, the eminent Ben Hecht, referred to Cohn as White Fang. His angry aggressive personality was said to be the inspiration for the character of Jack Woltz, the movie producer in *The Godfather* who wakes up to find a horse's bloody severed head at the foot of his bed.

His mobster instincts shone forth to devastating effect in his relationship with Sammy Davis Jr. and Kim Novak. For years, Cohn had been grooming the young Novak to be Columbia's premier sexy blonde star, whose bedroom eyes, tentative come-hither smile, and cool allure were undeniable elements of her sexual desirability. In two movies (*Man with the Golden Arm* and *Pal Joey*) with costar Frank Sinatra, Novak looked so deliciously tempting one wonders why Sinatra didn't carry her off to the nearest bed during the first scenes in which they appeared. Reported romances with Sinatra, a host of other leading men, and international playboys all contributed to Novak's reputation as a sexual goddess of the silver screen. However, her romance with Sammy Davis Jr. drove Cohn into fits of anger. Interracial couples were verboten in Hollywood during the 1950s. Throughout the country, there were periodic reports of assaults against interracial couples. In some states, there were even laws against such couplings. As news stories about the romance between Davis and Novak proliferated across the country, Cohn was concerned that Novak would become box office death. He was not about to lose his investment in the hot beauty who enlivened the fantasies of male moviegoers.

He would do whatever it took to smash the romance. "Harry Cohn wanted [Davis] dead," said comic Jack Carter, Sammy's Broadway costar in *Mr. Wonderful*. "What he was cocking around with was the mob," said Jerry Lewis. "They had a lot of money in Columbia—namely Harry Cohn—and I knew it."[14] In other words, the mob would whack Davis as a necessary favor to Cohn.

All Cohn had to do was tell his mobster investors that their investment in Novak would be flushed down a toilet, and they wouldn't have hesitated to issue a contract on Davis's life. When Cohn's frustrations finally boiled over, he called on Mickey Cohen to deliver the coup de grâce message that would put an end to the Davis-Novak romance. Gus Russo, in *Supermob*, writes: "Davis's father was warned by LA mobster Mickey Cohen that Harry Cohn had put a contract on his son."[15]

Prior to ordering that hit on Davis, Cohn had called his old pal Frank Costello, the "Prime Minister of the Underworld," at his apartment in New York. Cohn allegedly told Costello he wanted Davis killed if the relationship with Novak could not be terminated. Costello told Cohn he would see what he could do. He then contacted Mickey Cohen, who

> *visited Sammy in Las Vegas to deliver a warning and offer advice. The warning was that someone was about to put a contract on his head. The advice was to dump Kim Novak and go find himself a nice black girl to marry. Panicked, Davis promptly called Sam Giancana in Chicago to plead for help. Giancana replied that there was only so much the Outfit could do on the West Coast. A fearful Davis broke off the relationship with Novak and abruptly married showgirl Loray White.*[16]

White and Davis divorced a few months later, after she had been paid $25,000 to agree to the marriage, plus another $10,000 for clothes.

As notorious as were Cohn's dealings regarding the Davis-Novak relationship, his role in giving Frank Sinatra the role of Angelo Maggio in *From Here to Eternity* has proven even more notorious, generating reams of speculation. In the movie *The Godfather*, a studio head refuses to cast Johnny Fontane (a Sinatra-like character) in a movie that the singer desperately needs to resurrect his dying career. When the studio boss refuses to give him the role, the godfather's consigliere arranges for the boss's prize-winning racehorse to be decapitated and the bloody head placed on the man's bed. Sinatra got the part of Maggio, but it was far less dramatic than portrayed in a manifestly fictional movie. (Mario Puzzo said that *The Godfather* is pure fantasy, and it would be impossible to put a bulky, bloody horse head under someone's bed covers without them knowing it. But it made for a shocking and memorable cinematic scene.)

Sinatra got the role he begged for through leverage and a little pressure. Again, Frank Costello was called upon, but not by Harry Cohn. "Frank Costello supposedly told friends over dinner at the Copacabana that he received a phone call [from Frank Sinatra] asking for his help. Although Costello was not particularly friendly with Sinatra, he telephoned Mafia associates who controlled Hollywood unions asking them to apply pressure."[17] A Costello associate, Jack Farrel, flew to LA where he met with Johnny Rosselli. The two men visited Cohn, "pointing out how much he owed the mob. By the early 1950s, Columbia employed 19,000 people and had an annual payroll of $18 million. . . . Rosselli and Farrell told him that without Mafia money there would no Columbia Pictures."[18] And so Sinatra got the part that resurrected his career.

While Harry Cohn threw Frank Sinatra's career a life preserver and saved his investment in Kim Novak, he often ended the careers of those who wouldn't cooperate with him. If, for example, Cohn attempted to seduce an ambitious but still unknown young actress who refused his sexual advances, he would kill the possibility of her having a career. Hardly a day passed when his casting couch was empty. From established stars, Cohn often had to accept rejection, but he brooded about it and never forgave any actress who rejected him. Neal Gabler writes:

> *Connie Calvet, a beautiful, amply proportioned French starlet, received a command from Cohn that she appear on his yacht to*

discuss a contract. That evening, Cohn in his pajamas, bullied his way into her room and attacked her. Calvet, who found him physically repulsive, managed to fend off his advances and hide until her boyfriend, actor Rory Calhoun, could arrive later that night to spirit her off the boat to safety.[19]

Another star not supinely devoted to furthering her already successful career beneath the body of Cohn was Jean Arthur. She quit Columbia rather than become one of Cohn's conquests. When her contract expired in 1944, she exultantly ran through the streets of the studio, shouting "I'm free, I'm free!"[20]

To suggest that Cohn was hated by many and loved by few would be exaggerating his popularity. When he died of a heart attack six weeks after the Davis-White wedding, his elaborate funeral was staged on a Columbia lot. More than one thousand people attended the event. Seeing the large number of people in attendance, Red Skelton remarked to a reporter: "Well, it only proves what they always say—give the public something they want to see and they'll come for it."[21]

Harry Cohn, when in need of top legal talent, relied on mob lawyer Sidney Korshak, the Outfit's most resourceful fixer in the city of angels. Korshak, in addition to being the Outfit's lawyer in LA, was also a man of such power and influence that no one who knew his reputation would venture to cross him, refuse to pay his bills, or challenge his advice. He was one of the most powerful, secretive, and discreet figures in Hollywood. When he asked someone to meet with him, whether a movie mogul, a senator, or a governor, he was never turned down. His reputation as a power broker was assured not only as a representative of the Outfit, but also by his representation of the most powerful people in Hollywood. The FBI named him the most powerful lawyer in the world, a lawyer who had obtained his power through a wide variety of criminal activities, such as bribery, extortion, fraud, and labor racketeering.

And racketeering meant being able to call upon mob muscle when needed. He seemed able to fix the outcome of every case in which he was involved, from murder to larceny to management-labor problems. He enabled his mob clients to gain powerful positions in unions and movie companies and helped others gain and maintain control of companies in the leisure and entertainment industries. Presented with a problem, he proved inventive and resourceful. For example, when Senator Estes Kefauver conducted a series televised interrogations of mobsters in Chicago, Korshak was able to terminate Kefauver's television performances, which could have subjected his mob associates to criminal indictments. Korshak had arranged for a prostitute to seduce Kefauver in his hotel room. The encounter was surreptitiously photographed, and the prints were made available to Kefauver. The price for not publishing the photos was for the senator to pack up his pads of questions and leave town. For public consumption, he pretended to be a straight-arrow marshal who cleaned up Dodge then rode into the sunset a hero.

When Korshak wasn't organizing blackmail schemes against politicians, he was instrumental in paying them off to do his bidding. And that included criminal court judges. But to ensure the cooperation of judges and to make their decisions look reasonable, he instructed his clients to follow a script he prepared for them. When Willie Bioff, for example, was on trial for extortion, he was told by his Outfit handlers to do exactly what Korshak instructed him to do. Bioff was made to understand that the Outfit placed a high value on Korshak and his instructions were commandments. If Bioff didn't do as he was told, he would be a dead man.

Regardless of the problem, Korshak achieved results that other lawyers envied. He pulled strings as if he were a master of marionettes. If the head of MCA, Lew Wasserman, couldn't get a luxurious suite on a liner sailing to Europe, Korshak got him three suites with one phone call. If a friend's daughter couldn't get into a certain Ivy League college, Korshak got her accepted along with a full scholarship. He never spoke about deals on the phone and told his clients to act as if their phones were tapped. If someone phoned and began venturing into dangerous territory, he would say, "let's take a walk."[22] According to *The Godfather* producer Robert Evans, "Sidney's first commandment was, the greatest insurance policy for continued breathing is continued silence."[23] Korshak operated behind locked doors and in the offices of others. When mobsters called and left messages for him, they identified themselves with the names for former US presidents. Korshak was as elusive as a ghost and could be as intimidating as a nightmare. Though his name came up in more than twenty investigations of mobsters, prosecutors were unable to lay a glove on him. The FBI regarded him as the most significant intermediary and consigliere for organized crime syndicates in Chicago, New York, Las Vegas, and California. And he also represented some of the largest and most respected corporations in America. As a man of such inestimable power and influence, he commanded the respect of the biggest names in the movie industry. He was the man they turned to when they were in trouble. With such power came prestige, not just for Korshak, but also for his clients. The only thing more prestigious than being a Korshak client was being invited to the Korshak's famous Christmas parties. People not invited claimed they were out of town and couldn't return for the party. One non-invitee told a gossip columnist that she couldn't attend because she was hospitalized at the time of the party.

Among the many A-list Hollywood celebrities whom Korshak represented was Robert Evans, who regarded the famed lawyer as a father figure. Evans, grateful for all that Korshak had done for him when he was a producer at Paramount Pictures, sang Korshak's praises as if singing hymns. Evans produced such hits as *Godfather I* and *II*, *Serpico*, *Chinatown*, *The Odd Couple*, and *Rosemary's Baby*, among various others. He later became an independent producer of such movies as *Marathon Man* and *Urban Cowboy*. But by the time he had begun producing *The Cotton Club*, he was nearly drowning in a swamp of trouble.

Prior to the movie's production, Evans had been introduced to a flamboyant New York theatrical producer named Roy Radin. The introduction had been effected by a former drug dealer named Karen Greenberger (aka Lanie Jacobs). Radin and Evans cemented a deal in which $2 million would be raised for the production of *The Cotton Club* and perhaps other movies. Radin offered Greenberger a $50,000 finder's fee, which she angrily turned down. She wanted to be a partner with Radin and Evans. But Evans and Radin would each own 45 percent of their company. There was no room for another partner. Even if Radin wanted to cut Greenberger in, the remaining 10 percent would not have satisfied her. And once production got underway, there was no money for Greenberger: *The Cotton Club* racked up huge costs, at one point, ballooning to $24 million, and future costs were projected to skyrocket. Evans was unable to rein in spending, and his inability to do so was aggravated by his excessive use of cocaine. Greenberger, meanwhile, was becoming increasingly angrier: she was not only furious about Radin's offer, but she suspected him of breaking into her home, from which $870,000 in cash and a large quantity of cocaine had been stolen. Following the theft, she phoned Radin and suggested they meet for dinner. He agreed. Following that dinner, Radin was never seen alive again. His body, with several bullet holes in his head, was discovered in the dry riverbed of a canyon about sixty-five miles north of Los Angeles. Evans was considered a possible suspect after police reports noted that two potential witnesses had implicated him in the murder, asserting that he had entered into a pact with Greenberger to hire three men to murder Radin. Detectives eventually decided that Evans was not a suspect and chose to believe that Greenberger alone had hired the hitmen to kill Radin.

Nevertheless, Evans needed a top lawyer to clear him; for years, he had followed the advice of Korshak, who also pulled levers to help Evans when he was producing hit after hit for Paramount Pictures. But this time, he couldn't hire Korshak to defend him at trial, because Korshak was not licensed to practice law in California. Instead, Evans hired another top-gun attorney, Robert Shapiro, who advised his client to take the Fifth Amendment when questioned. Behind the scenes, Korshak upbraided Evans, asking what kind of successful Jewish producer of major hits becomes a cocaine addict. In the past, Evans had promised Korshak that he would stop taking cocaine.

At trial, Karen Greenberger and three shooters were convicted of second-degree murder and kidnapping. Greenberger's motive was said to be anger about being denied a producer's role and being cut out of future earnings. She also testified that Evans was not involved in the murder and added that she had been Evans's lover. Wags said that Greenberger should have taken the $50,000 and been thankful, because she would have been the only person who made money from *The Cotton Club*. The movie was a commercial and artistic disaster.

In addition to these tales of murder, mayhem, and mendacity, *Tinseltown Gangsters* contains stories about the alleged murder of Hollywood star Thelma Todd and the mob's control of pornographic movies. From the silent movies and early talkies through the golden age of the studios to wild, iconoclastic, independent producers, this book provides a historic view of the mob's role in Tinseltown.

NOTES

1. www.professorbainbridge.com/professorbainbridgecom/2005/12 /it-takes-a-thief-the-first-sec-chairman.html (accessed March 1, 2022).

2. Tere Tereba, *Mickey Cohen* (Toronto, Canada: ECW Press, 2012), 49.

3. www.americanmafia.com/Feature_Articles_166.html (accessed March 1, 2022).

4. Stone Wallace, *George Raft* (Albany, GA: BearManor Media, 2008), 159.

5. Wallace, *George Raft*, 34.

6. Wallace, *George Raft*, 156.

7. Tim Adler, *Hollywood and the Mob* (London: Bloomsbury, 2007), 66.

8. www.youtube.com/watch?v=eqc7LA_jFG0 (accessed March 7, 2022).

9. Tereba, *Mickey Cohen*, 124.

10. Adler, *Hollywood and the Mob*, 58.

11. https://archive.org/details/variety200-1955-11/page/n85/mode/1up ?view=theater (accessed March 4, 2022).

12. www.nytimes.com/1977/02/25/archives/mafia-said-to-have-slain-ros selli-because-of-his-senate-testimony.html (accessed March 4, 2022).

13. www.cia.gov/stories/story/the-bay-of-pigs-invasion/#the-recruits (accessed March 4, 2022).

14. Gus Russo, *Supermob* (New York: Bloomsbury, 2006), 154.

15. Russo, *Supermob*, 156.

16. John Buntin, *L.A. Noir* (New York: Harmony Books, 2009), 246–47.

17. Adler, *Hollywood and the Mob*, 125–26.

18. Adler, *Hollywood and the Mob*, 125–26.

19. Neal Gabler, *An Empire of Their Own* (New York: Crown, 1988), 247.

20. www.criterion.com/current/posts/6930-jean-arthur-the-nonconformist (accessed March 4, 2022).

21. Russo, *Supermob*, 156.

22. Connie Bruck, *When Hollywood Had a King* (New York: Random House, 2003), 169.

23. Bruck, *When Hollywood Had a King*, 168.

CHAPTER ONE

Joseph Kennedy

The First Shark

JOSEPH KENNEDY, FOUNDER OF AN ABORTED POLITICAL DYNASTY, was one of corporate America's great sharks. He could smell blood in corporate waters when a company was drowning in debt, bleeding cash, and going down fast. He would lunge in, tear off what was healthy, and get rid of the rest. His appetite for power and profits was enormous. One bleeding company was FBO (Film Booking Office of America). The company was desperate to find a buyer before it sought safety in bankruptcy. However, there were no buyers to rescue the company. FBO had once been profitable, producing low-budget genre movies, such as westerns and costume dramas. That was no longer the case: its costs grew greater than its profits. It could not compete with the larger movie studios. Like any opportunistic shark, Kennedy circled the company, evaluating its weaknesses and strengths. He saw a chance to make a killing. He came to management with a friendly smile and presented his benign resume of financial accomplishments. He was soon hired to find a buyer. While looking for a buyer, he collected a weekly salary for his efforts, all the while realizing that he could make the company profitable if he bought it and slashed costs. As owner, he would not only fire employees to reduce labor costs, but he would also produce movies as cheaply and as rapidly as Henry Ford churned out inexpensive autos on an assembly line. The Henry Ford method of production could be applied to any manufacturing company. And movie studios were manufacturing companies. They manufactured movies that were distributed to theaters and sold to consumers. Kennedy would buy FBO and manufacture movies with the efficiency of a CPA and CFO. However, he did not have the funds to buy the company, so he borrowed money from his father-in-law, Honey Fitzgerald, and from Louis Kerstein, owner of Filene's department store in Boston. An additional chunk of the money came from the Chicago Outfit. Its gangster principals had partnered with Kennedy during Prohibition. Having acquired the necessary funds and several unsavory partners, Kennedy bought FBO and immediately began slashing costs: he fired those he considered either superfluous or hangers-on. He next cut salaries. He then began an ambitious program of producing a movie a week; each one was a low-budget movie that was rapidly distributed. Movies came off Kennedy's assembly line with clocklike regularity and were then quickly shipped to theaters. In 1926, he made a movie a week, each one for no more than $30,000. By contrast, the big studio movie of 1925, *Ben Hur*, cost $4,000,000 and took two years to film.

Although profitability was his governing principle, Kennedy unexpectedly offered to make a celebratory movie about Charles Lindbergh, whom he regarded as an exemplary Christian hero. Kennedy associate Joseph W. Powell commented that Kennedy was the only Christian in the moving pictures business to offer to do a good job for this very fine young gentleman."[1] Lindbergh turned Kennedy down. It didn't matter, because under Kennedy's business plan, FBO's profits continued to soar on relatively small budgets.

Among those assisting Kennedy were the cronies with whom he had been doing business for years. They were "Ed Derr, who served as a treasurer of FBO, and the ever-present John Ford, Eddie Moore, Pat Scollard, and Charles Sullivan. All were intensely loyal to Kennedy. All put their private lives on hold whenever their boss wanted them. And all of them were amoral enough to go along with anything Joe tried to do, no matter how questionable."[2]

Having turned FBO into a highly profitable company, Kennedy was eager to enlarge his holdings. He soon acquired the Keith-Albee-Orpheum (KAO) chain of theaters. He agreed to keep Edward Albee as president but soon told him he was worthless and should resign. "Albee was so crushed to be forced out of the business he loved that he died shortly thereafter."[3]

Next on Kennedy's menu was Pathé-DeMille, which he acquired through a clever stock deal. In keeping with his FBO modus operandi, Kennedy cut costs wherever he could. In fact, his cost cutting was so severe that Cecil B. DeMille felt he had no future working under Kennedy's tight-fisted control. DeMille packed up his brilliance and moved to MGM, where he felt his creativity would thrive without immoderate constraints.

Kennedy didn't care about losing DeMille. He was focused on a new dimension of moviemaking: the introduction of sound. If silent movies were soon to be replaced by movies with sound, he wanted in on the action. And he wanted in immediately. Success depended on getting in early. Kennedy approached David Sarnoff, head of RCA, who had developed Photophone in March 1928. Sarnoff wanted it to be the premier technology for sound in movies. Ever the shark, Kennedy could taste another opportunity to enrich himself. He agreed to use Photophone if Sarnoff bought $400,000 of FBO stock, which Sarnoff did. If Kennedy laughed about it, he did not let on to Sarnoff. Kennedy next made a deal with First National Pictures that put him in charge of multiple departments for which he would receive a weekly salary, and eventually he would be able to take over the company. But rather than utilizing Sarnoff's sound system at FBO, Kennedy began secret negotiations to bring the Western Electric sound system to First National. As Kennedy kept putting off using Sarnoff's sound system, Sarnoff grew suspicious. There he was with $400,000 of FBO stock, and he couldn't get the company to use Photophone. Sarnoff began hearing rumors that Kennedy was considering using Western Electric's system and not Photophone. "Sarnoff, fearing that Kennedy might double-cross him entirely and install Western Electric equipment in the FBO and Pathé Studios, demanded that he sign an exclusive agreement with RCA for both studios and start spending studio money to make sound films."[4] It would not happen. Neither Kennedy nor Sarnoff was willing to accede to the demands of the other. Their relationship was about to shatter on the rocks of a fierce disagreement. Though Kennedy thought he was sitting securely in the catbird's seat, he was in for a rude surprise. The board of directors of First National decided that Kennedy wasn't worth what he was being paid, so they terminated their company's relationship with Kennedy. Sarnoff may have experienced a well-deserved sense of schadenfreude. Kennedy's departure now opened a door for Sarnoff, who swooped in: RCA purchased KAO and FBO. The catbird seat had a new occupant. The *Los Angeles Times* reported that Sarnoff's deal would make RCA the General Motors of the entertainment business. The new company became known as RKO and quickly began producing sound movies. With the money he got for FBO, "Kennedy . . . repaid Chicago [the Outfit] the $1.1 million he had borrowed plus a healthy premium."[5]

Kennedy's wealth had grown substantially since he first arrived in Hollywood. And rather than buying another studio that was in trouble, Kennedy turned his fancy to a sexual conquest. There was no one more desirable, more famous, and considered the ne plus ultra of glamour than Gloria Swanson, silent movie star and a model for millions of women across the globe. On screen, she was a woman whom men found irresistible. When gazing at her male costars, her eyes widened and shone with sexual desire. Her lips parted and she looked ravenous and ravishing. Up close and in person, however, Swanson was not quite Aphrodite: she was a mere five feet tall and wore a little girl's size 2½ shoe. Her breasts were small and her ankles thick. Nevertheless, she would become Kennedy's lover during her third marriage to a French nobleman. The affair began with a dance when Kennedy stepped on her foot, laughed and apologized, then sent her a pearl necklace the next day. The two agreed to meet at the Palm Beach Hotel, where Kennedy launched his conquest, and their affair would become torrid. As Swanson's maid left her suite, Kennedy entered as softly as a cat, but he soon turned into a tiger, charging at Swanson lying on her bed. He threw himself on her, his mouth pressed on hers. His hands pulled off her torn kimono. Resistance, if even considered, would have been impossible for the tiny movie star. Naked under him, she returned his passionate kisses and embrace. She did not resist his penis penetrating her. They moved together, kissing passionately. When it was over, they lay side by side, breathing heavily. Swanson had not only found a new lover, far more passionate than her husband, but also a protector. That was what she wanted: a man who would love her and protect her from double-talking producers and agents whom she couldn't trust.

Soon thereafter, Kennedy offered to manage her finances, and Swanson readily agreed, for there was no one she trusted as much as Joe Kennedy, her knight in shining armor and amour. Swanson turned over her financial affairs to Kennedy. They became not just intimate as lovers, but also as mutual confessors. They exchanged confidences as if pledging fungible assets. Ted Schwarz writes in his biography of Kennedy,

Gloria quickly discovered Joe Kennedy's secret for success. He understood his limitations, that he was not a particularly intelligent man. The same would be true for at least two of his sons, Jack and Ted. However, he hired the most brilliant staff he could find, made certain they lacked ambition other than to anonymously serve their employer, and taught his sons to do the same.[6]

Though Kennedy seemed as transparent to Swanson as a window, he was really holding a mirror before her. She followed it as ardently as she followed her own publicity. Reflected back to her was an image of her own wisdom in choosing such a devoted protector. Now that he controlled her finances, Kennedy secretly spent her money, buying her expensive bracelets, rings, necklaces, fur coats, a magnificent automobile. Swanson's narcissism led her to believe that Kennedy was completely devoted to her. Otherwise, why would he lavish so many gifts on her? He took her on ocean voyages to Europe and invited her to stay at his home. He regularly brought her into the presence of his wife, Rose. Completely devoted to her husband, Rose either accepted that her husband was having an affair with Swanson and chose to ignore it or thought they had a business relationship only. Either way, she would have been partly correct.

Now that he had full control of Swanson—her finances as well as her career—Kennedy followed his precept of hiring the best people. He hired the brilliant Erich von Stroheim to direct his first movie for Swanson. The movie was to be called *The Swamp*. The title was later changed to *Queen Kelly*. As filming progressed, its costs stampeded like a herd of cattle that had broken through a financial corral. This would not have happened at FBO. Kennedy blamed von Stroheim for the runaway costs and quickly fired the headstrong egotistical director. Kennedy replaced him with the disciplined Edmund Goulding. With financial matters under control, Kennedy decided to finance two additional Swanson movies (*The Trespasser* and *What a Widow*), before ending his affair with Swanson. Swanson, in awe of what Kennedy had accomplished for her, was shocked to learn that her accounts had often been surreptitiously invaded by Kennedy. For example, Kennedy was so pleased with the script for *What a Widow* that he gave its screenwriter, Sidney Howard, a bonus: a new Cadillac. Howard profusely thanked Kennedy for his generosity, not knowing that Kennedy had charged the cost of the car to one of Swanson's accounts. That fact, along with information that jewels, fur coats, and other luxuries that Kennedy gave her had been purchased with her own money, was brought to Swanson's attention by her accountant, Irving Wykoff, a man whom Kennedy had failed to control. "Many of the gifts Joe Kennedy lavished on his lover had been paid for out of her accounts. He had robbed her in ways so subtle that there was no full determination of how many hundreds of thousands of dollars he cost her."[7]

In addition to being robbed by Kennedy, Swanson learned that he was having an affair with her chief screen rival, Constance Bennett. Angry and disappointed, Swanson thought she would return to her titled husband, James Henri Le Bailly de la Falaise, marquis de la Coudraye. He had been a director of several travelogues and occasionally acted. However, his true career had been as a husband-in-waiting, standing in the shadow of one of the world's most luminous movie stars. Unfortunately, the role meant pretending to be unaware of behind-his-back snickers and snide whispers. It was a humiliation that he found difficult to ignore. He and Swanson divorced. However, he could not break himself of his way of life. Shortly after his divorce from Swanson, Henri made the acquaintance of Bennett. The two had what movie columnists call a whirlwind romance. While those newspapers had been selling carrions of gossip about the de la Falaise–Swanson divorce, Bennett and her new lover married, generating new feasts of gossip for gluttons of celebrity news. Swanson, no longer part of a sexual charade, playing musical chairs, decided not to play the role of a scorned wife and lover. Subtly prowling for a new lover, she soon found an overeager partner named Michael Farmer; he was handsome, charming, and popular with society women (with and without titles) and regarded as a debonair man-about-town. The two became lovers, and Swanson soon became pregnant. Farmer suggested to Swanson that they marry. She put him off. He became insistent. She said no.

She enjoyed his company and his skills as a lover, but marriage was out of the question. She didn't have to be a detective to learn that Farmer was a professional gigolo and known as such in the world of high society. Swanson, not willing to become a target of society's ridicule, especially after being victimized by Kennedy, refused Farmer's proposal. She would not go from robber baron to titled dilettante to gigolo. Yet Farmer would not let up. He was not about to lose the opportunity of being married to the most popular and glamorous movie star in the world. In addition, her earning power as a screen siren was enormous. With the instincts of blackmailer grasping his main chance, he warned Swanson that he would go to the press with the news that she was about to bear an illegitimate child. Swanson flew into a rage and called him hateful and a bastard but finally capitulated. They married on August 16, 1931, then divorced two years later.

Of the Kennedy-Swanson affair, David Nasaw writes, "The inescapable truth was that for Joseph P. Kennedy, Swanson was another sexual conquest, one of many he would fit into his busy life. That he wandered from the marriage bed was inconsequential to him. Adultery was a sin, but one easily forgiven."[8] The end of the Swanson-Kennedy affair meant little to Rose Kennedy. There would always be women for Joe Kennedy to seduce, even in the homes he shared with his wife. Rose knew that as Catholics she and Joe would never divorce. Their marriage bed was sacred ground. To present an elegant picture of herself to Joe and to show the world that she was a stylish woman of considerable wealth and taste, she spent large sums of money on the latest fashions, attended important charity balls, and took pride in appearing—year after year—on many of the best dressed lists.

Kennedy was indeed proud that his wife was recognized for her keen sense of style, but he focused the majority of his attention on more important goals. His next venture was not a seduction of a famous movie star, but an investment that became a target of his sharklike appetite. He pursued his goal with an intensity that typified his hunger for power and money. Several movie producers who had less than pleasant encounters with Kennedy said that he was nearly as ruthless as some of the gangsters they had to deal with. Kennedy's new target was a chain of theaters owned by Alexander Pantages, a Greek American who controlled or owned a total of eighty-four theaters. Kennedy understood that the owner of such a chain could make enormous financial demands on movie studios if they wanted their movies shown in his theaters. Kennedy salivated at the prospect of owning the chain, but Pantages adamantly refused to sell. He had devoted years to acquiring his empire of theaters—the second largest chain of theaters in California—and he was not about to sell it to Kennedy or anybody else. But Kennedy was relentless. He wanted those theaters as if his life depended on the acquisition. Kennedy offered to buy the chain for $8 million in February 1929. Pantages brushed aside the offer as if swatting away a fly. Ever persistent, Kennedy made another offer. That, too, was rejected. A third attempt at an offer was submitted, and Pantages said he wasn't interested.

Pantages didn't realize that after three strikes, he was about to be put out of the game. Kennedy's first move was to get the major studios to deny Pantages the opportunity to screen any first-run movies in his Los Angeles theater. Although the freeze-out hurt Pantages's bottom line, he still reaped profits from his many other theaters. He would not give in to Kennedy, who was growing increasingly frustrated and angry. Kennedy called on a sleazy character named Nicholas Dunaev, a failed screenwriter, minor theatrical agent, and possible pimp. He was promoting a wannabe starlet named Eunice Pringle, not exactly a name to be put in lights. Agent and ambitious actress lived inexpensively in the Moonbeam Glen Bungalow Court, a name right out of a Raymond Chandler mystery. Kennedy quickly sized up the pair and paid them $10,000 to set up Pantages on trumped-up criminal charges. As an added incentive, Kennedy promised an important role to Pringle in one of his movies. Pringle was now eager to nail Pantages, with whom she had a previous humiliating run-in: she had brought him a play written by Dunaev, but Pantages dismissively returned it. Ted Schwarz writes: "Apparently Dunaev and Pringle thought Pantages might be able to help them either produce it or have it turned into a film. Instead he rejected it as 'vulgar.'"

"Again according to Pantages, Pringle returned to the theater after receiving the rejection of her lover's work. She became irate, attacking him with such force that she tore his shirt. Then she clung to his legs until he could get rid of her."[9]

Pringle was now ready to attempt another hackneyed technique: though she had visited many casting couches, she had never yelled rape, even though her trysts brought her no movie roles. Now she would emote vociferously to attract a crowd, yelling rape as loudly as a police siren. Her screams would arouse dozens of people who would come running to her defense. She would make Pantages suffer for all the rejections she had suffered. Pantages would also suffer on behalf of Kennedy.

On August 29, 1929, Pringle, dressed in a sexy low-cut dress, hid in a closet of Pantages's Los Angeles Theater. As soon as Pantages was in proximity of the closet, she tore her dress and burst out, screaming that she was being attacked. Pringle claimed that Pantages had attempted to rip off her dress, bite her breasts, and rape her. Employees called the police, and Pantages was arrested. No one doubted Pringle. No one commented that she could have successfully fought off Pantages and perhaps even have overpowered him. She was, after all, a strong athletic young woman, and Pantages was sixty-two years old, weighed 126 pounds, and was five feet six. No one commented that she had neither bruises nor bite marks on her breasts. Pringle was the perfect picture of an innocent victim, and neither she nor the police requested a medical examination. Casting directors should have been present, for Pringle had given her finest performance. At trial, the prosecutor, the jury, and the judge all believed her. Poor, pitiful Pantages was found guilty and sentenced to fifty years in prison.

However, he was not as defeated as Kennedy and others might have assumed, for he retained the services of Jerry Giesler (a slick mob attorney for Bugsy Siegel and other gangsters and several celebrities), who appealed the case to the California Supreme Court, which overturned the conviction. The court noted that a conspiracy had resulted in the conviction of Pantages. By the time he was acquitted in 1931, Pantages had already sold his theaters to Kennedy for $3.5 million, which was considerably less than the $8 million Kennedy had originally offered. Two years later, as Pringle lay dying from cyanide poisoning, she confessed to the conspiracy to set up Pantages. No one was ever investigated for her murder. It was rumored that the Outfit had tied up loose ends.

Having achieved his goals, Kennedy decided it was time to bid goodbye to Hollywood. His trajectory was now aimed at conquering other profitable enterprises back East. Tinseltown's moguls were not the right kind of people for a social climber to associate with: they were uneducated Jews, and Kennedy was a snob and anti-Semite who referred to studio owners as pants pressers, kikes, and sheenies. He aspired to be accepted as part of the WASP establishment, not as a partner of vulgar nouveau riche movie moguls. It didn't matter that Kennedy may have been as greedy and ruthless as they were. He had worked assiduously to generate a polished image of himself as a highly successful man of the world. He was a gentleman. He knew which fork to use at elegant dinner parties; his grammar was correct; his manners were smooth and correct; his bespoke suits implied the handcrafted work of expensive Savile Row tailors. He had been accepted in the best boardrooms on Wall Street, where he manipulated stocks like a magician. In fact, it was his experience as an unethical manipulator of stocks that caused President Roosevelt to appoint

Kennedy chairman of the Securities and Exchange Commission. When asked why he made the appointment, Roosevelt smiled and said, "it takes a thief to catch a thief."[10]

Even as a stock manipulator, Kennedy refused to associate with Jewish brokers. To gentiles who associated with Kennedy, his anti-Semitism was apparent not only from his use of derogatory epithets, but also by his actions. When in Palm Beach, for example, Kennedy could not join an exclusive club because he was Catholic. Jews, knowing they were excluded from joining restricted Palm Beach country clubs, formed their own golf and beach clubs. Being targets of discrimination, they welcomed all those who were not accepted by WASP clubs. In the Jewish clubs, Catholics, blacks, Hispanics, and Asian Americans were all welcomed. For Kennedy to play golf at such a club was to accept the humiliation delivered unto him by the snobbish Boston Brahmins. Kennedy would rather not play golf if it meant playing with a bunch of Jews, no matter how wealthy they were.

Kennedy used his anti-Semitism to further his business and political goals. On one occasion, he attempted to gain control of Paramount Studios by telling its board of directors that President Roosevelt was worried about anti-Semitism in America. So that Paramount would not become a target of anti-Semitism, Kennedy told the Paramount board that he should be appointed the company's president. However, when board members checked with Roosevelt, they learned that the president had no idea that the studio was owned by Jews and furthermore had never endorsed the proposal that Kennedy should be made president of the studio.

As if that were not sufficiently offensive to Jews, Ben Hecht reports in his memoir *Child of the Century*, "The movie chieftains, nearly all Jews ... told me that Ambassador Joseph Kennedy, lately returned from beleaguered London, had spoken to fifty of Holly-wood's leading Jewish movie makers in a secret meeting in one of their homes. He had told them sternly that they must not protest as Jews, and that they must keep their Jewish rage against the Germans out of print.

"Any Jewish outcries, Kennedy explained, would impede victory over the Germans. It would make the world feel that a 'Jewish War' was going on."

Hecht continued: "I argued that the sound of moral outrage over the extinction of the Jews would restore human stature to the name Jew. In silence this stature was vanishing. We Jews in America were fast becoming the relatives of the garbage pile of Jewish dead. There would be no respect for the living Jew when there was no respect for a dead one."[11]

The general public did not know of Kennedy's anti-Semitism when he was appointed ambassador to the Court of St. James. It may be why he kept his conversations with Nazis and Nazi sympathizers sub rosa. One Nazi with whom Ambassador Kennedy often met was Herbert von Dirksen, the ambassador representing Nazi Germany. After numerous discussions with Kennedy, von Dirksen said he

> *felt that Kennedy understood why the Germans wanted to get rid of the Jews. . . . He later related that Kennedy told him that getting rid of the Jews was not harmful to the Nazis. It was "rather the loud clamor with which we accompanied the purpose. He himself understood our Jewish policy completely; he was from Boston and there in, one golf club, and in other clubs, no Jews had been admitted for the past . . . years." Joe allegedly added that there was little anti-German sentiment in the United States except in the East, where the majority of America's 3.5 million Jews were living."[12]*

Kennedy went on to claim that the suffering of German Jews was the result of their own actions.

The more Roosevelt learned of Kennedy's anti-Semitism and proselytizing for an alliance with Germany, the angrier Roosevelt became. He compared Kennedy's attitudes to those of the Cliveden set, a British aristocratic group who favored a policy of appeasing the Nazis. In addition to the Cliveden set, there was the Anglo-German Fellowship, whose goal was to build a strong friendship between the United Kingdom and Nazi Germany. It existed from 1935 to 1939. The group regularly hosted magnificent dinners to which high-ranking Nazis were invited to speak about the need for a German-British alliance. That was one thing, but some members of the group could not condone the Nazi's treatment of German Jews. Finally, the organization's chairman, Lord Mount Temple, resigned in November 1938 to protest the Nazi treatment of German Jews. Following his resignation, he released a statement that appeared in the London *Times*:

Although I have resigned from the chair of the Anglo-German Fellowship, I still remain a member of the fellowship. I wrote my letter of resignation yesterday, to be read at the council meeting this morning. In the letter I stated that I was resigning from the chairmanship because of the treatment of the Jews in Germany and the attitude of the Germans towards the Catholic and Lutheran communities. One hopes that times may become better in the future and that the good work of building up friendship between the two nations may be resumed.[13]

The Fellowship responded with the following statement:

The Council deeply regrets the events which have set back the development of better understanding between the two nations. The Council will, however, steadily prosecute its efforts to maintain contact with Germany as being the best means of supporting the Prime Minister in his policy of appeasement, and as being the most useful way of encouraging those friendly relations upon which peace depends.[14]

There were many in Britain, however, who found appeasement to verge on treason. And as Kennedy's support for appeasement became well known, he came to be seen by the Roosevelt administration as an embarrassing apologist for the Nazis. He further alienated Roosevelt by commenting to journalists that Britain would be defeated by the Nazis and the United States should therefore limit its aid to Britain. Why support a country that would soon be defeated? It made sense for the United States to accept the inevitability of a Nazi victory and be prepared to engage in business with victors. It was apparent to Roosevelt and others in his administration that the opportunistic shark, following a Nazi victory, had plans to further enrich himself by doing business with a murderous Nazi regime. It was too much. Roosevelt angrily demanded Kennedy's resignation as ambassador. The flame of Kennedy's ambition to one day run for president of the United States had been extinguished. As a result, he later invested all his ambitions in the political careers of his sons.

When John Kennedy ran for the presidency of the United States in 1960, he explained that he did not share his father's defeatism and anti-Semitism. But many in and out of Hollywood and Great Britain would neither forget nor forgive Joe Kennedy, who departed the United Kingdom a failed ambassador who had tarnished his own reputation. And when President Kennedy made his famous "Ich Bin Ein Berliner" (I am a Berliner) speech on June 26, 1963, many who had been aware of Joe Kennedy's pro-Nazi stance were appalled by the echo. It didn't matter to them that books and editorials poked fun, writing that citizens of Berlin did not refer to themselves as Berliners, for the name referred to jelly donuts.

Back in the United States, Joe Kennedy did not return to Hollywood, but his earlier departure from the land of moviemaking had opened the eyes of the Chicago Outfit to the golden opportunities that awaited them in Tinseltown. The ease with which Kennedy earned the money to repay the Outfit's loan tipped them off that there was plenty of gold in them thar hills.

Though the Outfit, under boss Al Capone, had shown only a tentative interest in Hollywood, the post-Prohibition mobsters viewed the studios as ripe for organized labor to squeeze them for millions of dollars. But before the Outfit could dispatch a hotshot gangster to put together a plan that would force the studios to disgorge millions of dollars, the East Coast mob dispatched its movie-star-handsome gangster Bugsy Siegel, who—upon arriving—claimed he wasn't a gangster. He was just a colorful sportsman (i.e., a professional gambler of independent means). He flashed his famous smile, befriended famous actors, and began dating the crème de la crème of Hollywood beauties. He was a dream come true for the Hollywood gossip columnists.

NOTES

1. David Nasaw, *The Patriarch* (New York: Penguin, 2012), 102.
2. Ted Schwarz, *Joseph P. Kennedy* (New York: John Wiley, 2003), 119.
3. Schwarz, *Joseph P. Kennedy*, 132.
4. Nasaw, *The Patriarch*, 124.
5. Tim Adler, *Hollywood and the Mob* (London: Bloomsbury, 2007), 26.
6. Schwarz, *Joseph P. Kennedy*, 151.
7. Schwarz, *Joseph P. Kennedy*, 168.
8. Nasaw, *The Patriarch*, 147.
9. Schwarz, *Joseph P. Kennedy*, 169.
10. www.professorbainbridge.com/professorbainbridgecom/2005/12 /it-takes-a-thief-the-first-sec-chairman.html (accessed March 1, 2022).
11. Ben Hecht, *Child of the Century* (New York: Simon and Schuster, 1954), 520.
12. Schwarz, *Joseph P. Kennedy*, 240.
13. *Times* (London), "German Treatment of Jews," November 19, 1938, 7.
14. *Times* (London), "Anglo-German Fellowship," November 22, 1938, 11.

CHAPTER TWO

Bugsy Siegel

Dream City Gangster

FOR BUGSY SIEGEL, HOLLYWOOD WAS A CITY OF DREAMS. FOR the movie stars who befriended Siegel, he was dream city's perfect gangster. He had the looks, the charm, the wardrobe, and the sinister reputation for murder and thuggery that was a magnet for all the fake silver screen gangsters and the femmes fatales who either betrayed their cinematic lovers or went down in a storm of bullets with them.

Siegel started out on the Lower East Side with his boyhood chums Meyer Lansky and Lucky Luciano. They were soon joined by Frank Costello (né Francesco Castiglia). Though the four had formed an alliance, Siegel and Lansky independently operated as the bosses of an all-Jewish gang known as the Bugs and Meyer Gang. According to Ralph Salerno, former organized crime detective, the gang was the most vicious in the city. For the right price, they committed murders, arson, beatings, and robberies. Eventually, the gang evolved into the Jewish Italian organization known in the media as Murder Inc., which was controlled by Albert "Mad Hatter" Anastasia and Louis "Lepke" Buchalter. The latter was the only mob boss to end his days in the electric chair (aka Old Sparky) at Sing Sing prison.

Lansky and Siegel wanted more than to be killers for hire, so with Luciano and Costello they formed the National Crime Syndicate (NCS), which managed to organize gangs throughout the country. Each gang, though independent of other gangs in the syndicate, operated as a subsidiary of the syndicate. There were member gangs from Chicago, Buffalo, Cleveland, Detroit, Philadelphia, Miami, New Orleans, Los Angeles, New Jersey, Rhode Island, and even in Canada. The syndicate had its own board of directors, known as the commission, and the head of each gang had a seat on the commission. Luciano and Lansky operated as joint CEOs and presidents, and their decisions were final. The members of the commission, each of whom had a vote, included the heads of the five New York Mafia families and the heads of all member gangs. As a result of its ethnic diversity and national membership, the NCS was more powerful than the five Mafia families of New York. Each gang member had to abide by the decisions of the commission.

Lansky and Luciano, the commission's two leaders, decided that Siegel should go to Los Angeles, organize the racing wire there, and absorb into his sphere of influence the local Mafia family run by Jack Dragna, whose family—due to its ineptness—was known as the Mickey Mouse Mafia. Dragna was warned, prior to Siegel's arrival, that he would be a secondary figure: Siegel was the mob's designated West Coast boss. As expected, Dragna was resentful of Siegel, but he swallowed his anger and accepted his diminished position. If he hadn't, he would have been a target for a mob hit. It wasn't until after Siegel's death that Dragna attempted to assert himself, going to war with Siegel's successor, Mickey Cohen.

Siegel arrived in LA like a king without a country, but one who would soon be the reigning mob potentate. He would control and run several labor unions, hundreds of bookies, and a pair of racetracks and invest in several gambling casinos—including offshore ones—all the while extorting movie studios for hundreds of thousands of dollars.

To the Hollywood elite, he presented himself as a wealthy sportsman (i.e., a gambler), whose lavish parties would be attended by only the most important people. A Siegel "invitation" may be a euphemism, for those who received such invitations were expected to attend, no excuses accepted. Initially his parties were held in an imposing mansion that Siegel had rented on McCarthy Drive in Beverly Hills. To impress his newly minted friends, he joined the classy Hillcrest Country Club and signed up his daughters, Millicent and Barbara, for riding lessons at the exclusive DuBrock Riding Academy. He also enrolled them in an expensive private school attended by the children of movies stars, producers, and directors.

He increased his allure by squiring Jean Harlow to fancy restaurants, where the crème de la crème of Tinseltown took notice of the star and her gangster companion. When gossip columnists asked if he and Harlow were romantically involved, he winked, smiled, and said that he was a gentleman who respected a woman's reputation. Nevertheless, the two were such close friends that Harlow was perceived by Millicent Siegel as a family member, and she declared to reporters that Harlow was her godmother. Indeed, Millicent developed such a warm friendship for Harlow that she kept autographed photos of the star in her bedroom.

But Siegel's reason for being in LA was to advance the business interests of his mob partners, not to become a socialite. He began by buying a 25 percent interest in a company that ran gambling in various restaurants and bars in Los Angeles. He followed that up by purchasing a 15 percent interest in a dog racing track in Culver City. He took over Dragna's control of the local bookies, splitting his take with Dragna (though Dragna received a smaller share), and he forced professional gambler and casino owner, Tony Cornero, to sell him percentages in his offshore gambling boats. The racing wire that he would control would be one of the mob's greatest western sources of income.

Though Siegel secretly controlled a number of gambling operations, he presented himself to Tinseltown as a customer of gambling joints, just a lucky bettor who managed to pick an inordinate number of winners. Because he, like his gambling cohorts, knew that the odds always favor the house and bettors sooner or later part with their money, Siegel only betted on sure things: fixed boxing matches, fixed horse races, and sports events whose outcomes had been decided in advance of the final scores. With such knowledge, Siegel bet from $2,000 to $5,000 a day and walked away with the loot. He also learned a valuable lesson from the fate of Al Capone: never live beyond your reported earnings. Otherwise, the IRS will nail you. Siegel reported his gambling winnings without causing suspicious agents to wonder how one man could be so lucky.

With all the money Siegel was raking in, he decided that he needed a bigger, more impressive mansion than the one he had been occupying. He invested $180,000 of his gambling winnings in a new home for himself and his wife, Esta (short for Estelle). The mansion was built at 250 Delfern Avenue in Holmby Hills. Numerous movie stars, such as Humphrey Bogart, Bing Crosby, and Judy Garland, were neighbors. Because he enjoyed swimming, he had an Olympic-size pool installed behind the house. (On the internet, there's a brief video of Siegel romping with his daughters in that pool.) Beside the pool, he had an architect design a pool house that served as a guesthouse that could comfortably accommodate a family of five. As he would do years later when overseeing the building of the Flamingo in Las Vegas, Siegel visited the site daily and badgered the construction foreman. He changed designs, materials, and even the landscaping plans. Budgets were torn up, thrown out, and replaced with new ones. Costs soared. All the while, he told the construction workers to work harder and longer without making the slightest mistake. They also had to meet the original deadline for completing the project, regardless of the changes that Siegel demanded. The house, constructed of luxurious materials such as rare marble smuggled from Italy, boasted twenty-three rooms and contained secret compartments, hiding places for his many guns, and a concealed escape route.

When he wasn't overseeing the construction of his dream house, he devoted hours every day to maintaining his physical fitness. He lifted weights, did push-ups, sit-ups, and chin-ups, and swam laps in his pool. He maintained a Cary Grant–like tan. Because he considered himself something of a pugilist, he regularly shadowboxed and attempted to induce his pals to spar with him. His boyhood friend, George Raft, refused, since he had suffered a broken nose years earlier when he had attempted to become a professional boxer. That was years before becoming one of Hollywood's leading tough guys. Raft consistently wanted to maintain his Rudolph Valentino–like profile. Other potential sparring partners, however, could not refuse Siegel's commands, but they were careful not to throw the kind of punches that might ignite Siegel's explosive temper. As part of his health and fitness routine, Siegel rarely drank liquor, but he often puffed on a long Cuban cigar. He slept with an elastic band tied under his chin to prevent the skin from sagging. He was obsessed with his thinning hair and worried that one day he would have to wear a toupee. The only person allowed to kid him about his hair was Raft, but such kidding could not take place in front of others. Like most narcissistic sociopaths, Siegel did not permit anyone to kid him about his insecurities. He was intent on presenting an image of himself as a self-confident, suave, man of the world who was well read and politically astute.

God forbid someone should call him Bugsy, a nickname appended to several low-life criminals back in New York. Many people thought the sobriquet referred to insects. Others, however, knew that the name originated from Siegel's teenage years back in New York when his murderous rages were so out of control that his neighbors said he was as crazy as a bedbug. If a waiter or doorman or a hotel clerk was foolish enough or insufficiently enlightened to call him Bugsy, the offender would be the recipient of a lightning right cross to the jaw. Looking up at the snarling Siegel, the supine offender might ask what offense he had committed or simply close his eyes and hope that Siegel would be gone when he attained a vertical position. Sometimes Siegel would tell his victims that perhaps they didn't know better and were ignorant of his actual name. He would clearly enunciate "Benjamin Siegel," then warn the victim not to make the same mistake again. "Yes, Mr. Siegel" was often the apologetic response. He might add that his friends may call him Benny, but "you're not my friend."

As part of his self-improvement agenda, Siegel worked diligently to expand his vocabulary, pronouncing new words over and over again, just to make sure that his pronunciation was correct and not affected by his New York accent. As an aspirant to Hollywood society, he did not want to sound like a thug from the Lower East Side. He worked hard to develop a Midwestern accent common to many actors. When an acquaintance misused the word "fortuitous," Siegel would explain that that word meant accidental, not fortunate. He would say that "disinterest" did not mean uninterested; it means impartial. He would explain the differences between "complacent" and "complaisant." Had he gone to college, he would have been one of the world's great pedants.

To help him maneuver his way through Hollywood society and the world of movies, Siegel often relied on George Raft, who enormously admired Siegel and the gangster overlords who controlled the National Crime Syndicate. Raft even stated that he would have preferred being a gangster to being a movie star. He told an interviewer,

When I became a movie star and was asked about tough guys I knew, I said: "I think they're the greatest guys in the world. These fellows—Siegel, Costello, Adonis, Luciano and Mad-

*den—were gods to me. They all had 16-cylinder Cadillacs, and,
like somebody said, when there is money around you might step
on it. Wherever they went there were police captains and politicians bowing to them. I thought, these fellows can't be really
doing anything wrong. Why shouldn't I be like them? I wanted
to follow them."*[1]

Raft was only one of the numerous admirers who presented
themselves to Siegel. Jo-Carroll Silvers, the wife of comedian Phil
Silvers, said,

*"Phil and Frank [Sinatra] admired and adored Bugsy Siegel
so much. When we were in Chasen's [for dinner] and saw him,
Frank and Phil would immediately stand up when he passed
and, with real reverence in their voices say, "Hello, Mr. Siegel.
How are you?" They were like two children seeing Santa Claus,
or two little altar boys standing to pay homage to the pope. . . .
Bugsy was handsome, charming, and very pleasant, but he also
had an aura of danger that Frank would later cultivate. . . . I
will always remember the awe Frank had in his voice when he
talked about him. He wanted to emulate Bugsy.*[2]

Silvers and Sinatra would even brag about how many men Siegel
had killed.

Although other stars, such as Cary Grant, Gary Cooper, and
Clark Gable, loved rubbing shoulders with Siegel, some refused
to associate with Siegel. One such star was Jimmy Stewart. Siegel
regularly threw lavish parties and invited the crème de la crème
of Hollywood to attend. Those who refused to attend were never
invited again. If any of them called out greetings to Siegel at a racetrack, restaurant, or another venue, Siegel acted as if he hadn't heard
them and would not even deign to look at them. Jimmy Stewart

was a special case. He not only announced to friends that he would not attend a Siegel party, but he did so vociferously, arguing with other actors that they too shouldn't attend the "monster's" party.

The "good guy" in so many films, Stewart even once denounced Siegel to his face. Bugsy's temper instantly flared and a worried Raft rushed in to calm him down.

"If Siegel wants to try his luck with me, let him take his best shot," retorted Stewart, who was perhaps in danger of believing his own on-screen persona. "If he takes his best shot, it'll be the last shot you hear," Raft advised him.

However, as Stewart's wife Gloria observed, Jimmy's quest was pointless for, as far as most movie stars were concerned, "the only people who could be remotely more glamorous were royalty and big-time gangsters."[3]

Hollywood columnist Florabel Muir agreed, observing how Siegel was "one of the most fabulous characters' ever to pitch up on the LA social scene."[4]

While many of Siegel's movie star friends primarily sought the excitement of being in the presence of a real-life gangster, Raft was a genuine friend, loyal and reliable. Perhaps it was their backgrounds: they both grew up in poor immigrant neighborhoods, where the only people carrying rolls of money were the gangsters, the guys who kids admired. Siegel became a hoodlum when he was a teenager. Raft, however, never became a hoodlum: he merely liked associating with them, especially the members of a local gang known as the Gophers, so called because they planned their numerous robberies in the bleak, dark basements of tenements. The leader of the Gophers was Owney "the Killer" Madden. Raft (né Ranft) so admired Madden that he imitated his walk, his talk, his gestures. Flattered, Madden treated Raft as a younger brother. Raft, who did not get along with his strict German father, viewed

Madden as a father figure and followed him on many of his illegal ventures. He particularly enjoyed standing on rooftops as he and Madden dropped bricks and flowerpots on policemen.

Madden, without assistance from Raft, graduated to more profitable crimes than those carried out by the Gophers. He worked assiduously to become one of the most powerful bootleggers in the city, converting a one-square-block building into the biggest brewery in the city. Enlarging his market for his booze, he forced numerous speakeasy proprietors to sell him their joints, the most well-known being the Cotton Club in Harlem. Madden also took over a fleet of taxicabs. An entrepreneur with an eye for new opportunities, he entered the world of fixed boxing matches by forcefully taking over the contract of naive heavyweight boxer Primo Carnera, all of whose earnings Madden stole. Raft himself spent two years as a boxer, attempting to work his way up the ranks of club fighters before becoming a successful dancer on Broadway. According to *Ring Magazine*, Raft had fourteen fights, won nine, lost three, and had two draws. However, he was more skilled at maneuvering speeding Cadillacs than at pulverizing boxing opponents, and he became Madden's chauffeur. One of the gangsters who occasionally accompanied Madden on his nightly visits to collect payoffs from speakeasies was Siegel. After speaking with Siegel and seeing his impressive wardrobe, dash, and the roll of hundred-dollar bills that he carried, Raft was smitten. He had found a new idol. He soon looked upon Siegel as an older brother, though Raft was five years older than his hero. He so admired Siegel that he adopted many of Siegel's gestures when playing silver screen gangsters. During the filming of *Manpower*, Raft let Siegel act out his own scenes off camera. Raft said that Siegel easily could have become an actor, but he didn't have the drive to achieve that goal. And when Siegel began building his Vegas dream casino, the Fabulous Flamingo, Raft said he wished he could be Siegel's partner. But Raft had to wait eight years after Siegel's death before he was able to buy a 2 percent interest in the Flamingo for $65,000. At the Flamingo, Raft felt close to his deceased friend. His admiration for those from the underworld never left him.

James Cagney, a costar and friend of Raft, said: "[Raft] was of the underworld, yet not in the underworld. From Al Capone down, he knew them all. The worst hoods you could imagine."[5] In 1942, after Cagney was named president of the Screen Actors Guild, he attempted to thwart the mob's ambition to take over the Guild. The mob then put a contract on Cagney's life. When Raft learned of the plan to kill Cagney, he called his pals and had the contract rescinded. Cagney would always remain grateful to Raft.

Although close friendships with mobsters allowed Raft to ask for their favors, his friendships had a downside too. So, for example, when Raft was invited to manage a casino in London, the British government refused him entry into the country. He was perceived as having mob connections.

Friendships with mobsters also meant that one was expected to return favors, to be at hand to carry out missions that bordered on the illegal or that might make one an accessory to a crime. If, for example, a gangster was collecting a loan-sharking debt or extorting a storeowner for protection, he might ask a friend to stand guard outside, not letting anyone enter. He might also be expected to be a lookout, giving a signal if a cop approached. I know of one friend of a mobster who was asked to hold a package for a week without looking inside. The friend did as he was asked. The favor was repaid when the friend informed the mobster that a tenant in a building he owned had refused to pay his rent for several months. The mobster visited the tenant and inserted a .32 caliber pistol into the tenant's trembling mouth. "Bite the barrel and stop whining," demanded the mobster. The tenant not only paid the rent that was in arrears, but also paid two additional months in advance. When the mobster departed, he noticed that the tenant had wet himself.

Raft, however, as far as anyone knows, never had to carry out illegal activities for Siegel. Instead, he had to be prepared to lend Siegel money. Siegel occasionally borrowed money from Raft and either never repaid the loan or paid small portions of it over a period of many months. When Siegel opened the Flamingo Hotel and Casino in Las Vegas, Raft was on hand on opening night and made sure that he lost more than $60,000. On another occasion, Raft was impolitic and it almost cost him his friendship with Siegel. The actress Wendy Barrie, who was having an affair with Siegel, asked Raft if he thought the affair might hurt her career. Raft said it probably would. She reported Raft's judgment to Siegel, whose temper flared into a burning rage. He grabbed a pistol and sped off in his yellow Buick convertible to Raft's house. He banged on the door, and when it opened, he pushed aside Raft's friend Mack Gray and ran up a flight of stairs. Siegel flung open Raft's bedroom door, rushed inside, pulled off Raft's bedcovers, and shouted: "I'll kill you, you bastard." Raft, at first startled, immediately attempted to cool Siegel's hot temper. When he learned the cause of Siegel's rage, he apologized, saying the two should not forget their close friendship spanning years. He concluded by calling Siegel "Baby Blue Eyes," a nickname that always caused Siegel to mellow. The friendship resumed as if it had never been interrupted. So intense were Raft's feelings for Siegel that when his friend was murdered, Raft told Los Angeles investigators, "When they shot Benny, they shot me."[6]

Throughout their friendship, Raft served whatever purpose Siegel required, including creating guest lists for Siegel's parties. Though numerous stars were eager attendees, they didn't realize until late in the evening that Siegel often levied a subtle cover charge on them. During cocktails, Siegel would chat with each of several enthralled stars, now and then asking for small loans from $500 to $1,000. Fearful of what could happen if they refused, the stars graciously gave Siegel checks or cash before departing. Over the years, Siegel claimed to have borrowed more than $400,000 from his Hollywood pals and admirers. He also bragged that he didn't repay one penny of those loans. And, as might be expected, no one asked for repayment. Such a request might result in a fate similar to that of Harry "Big Greenie" Greenberg.

Greenberg had long been associated with mobsters in the East, particularly Lepke Buchalter. Greenberg was often employed as a strong-arm thug in labor disputes. When Buchalter wanted a union to call off a strike against one of his extorted garment center clients, he sent in his thugs to club the strikers into capitulation. Greenberg was known for fiercely clubbing his victims, leaving them sprawled on sidewalks with fractured, bloodied heads. When the government caught up with Greenberg, who had jumped ship from Poland and entered the United States illegally, they deported him back to Poland. From there, Greenberg made his way to Germany, where he got a job as a deckhand on a freighter bound for Canada. After several weeks in Canada, he ran out of money and sent a letter to Buchalter via a third party, demanding money. If Greenberg didn't receive the money, he threatened to become a rat and testify against his former boss. Such a threat was certain to elicit a death sentence. Buchalter dispatched Albert "Tick Tock" Tannenbaum and Jack "Cuppie" Migden to Canada, where they were to ensure that no one would find Greenberg's corpse.

Unfortunately for the two hitmen, Greenberg, having realized the stupidity of his threat, rapidly departed Canada and was on his way to Los Angeles. He hoped that his old pal Siegel would intervene and perhaps give him some money. When he visited Siegel, he was told to lay low, then handed a few hundred dollars. Greenberg found a small apartment in a rooming house at 1804 Vista Del Mar in Hollywood. Siegel notified Buchalter of Greenberg's address. There was to be a meeting in New York, the subject of which was who would take charge of eliminating Greenberg. Siegel left for New York, where he met with Buchalter and other members of Murder Inc.: Albert "Mad Hatter" Anastasia, Mendy Weiss, and Longy Zwillman, who was known as the Al Capone of New Jersey and who had been a former lover of Jean Harlow.

Tick Tock Tannenbaum, a Murder Inc. hitman, was given the commission for the hit. One of Zwillman's gofers picked up Tannenbaum at his Brooklyn home and drove him to Philadelphia. There, Zwillman gave Tannenbaum two guns, a .38 revolver and .45 Colt automatic, and money for his airfare to California. Tannenbaum was met at the Los Angeles airport by Frankie Carbo, also a hitman with Murder Inc. and later known as the czar of boxing. The two drove to Carbo's apartment and were met there by Siegel, who examined the two guns as if appraising fine merchandise and said that he might like to do the hit himself. He hadn't killed anyone since leaving New York. Carbo insisted that he and Tick Tock had been chosen for the job and then warned Siegel that if he did this piece of work, he would be the first person the cops would suspect. Siegel agreed and handed back the two guns.

The next day, Siegel ordered one of his underlings, Whitey Krakower, to steal a getaway car. After hours spent looking for a car, he spotted a black Mercury. The doors were unlocked, and he was able to cross the ignition wires, start the engine, and drive back to Carbo's apartment. Once there, the car's license plates were switched with ones from another Mercury.

Later that night, Siegel, driving his yellow Buick convertible, led Carbo and Tannenbaum in the black Mercury to the rooming house where Greenberg had been living. Siegel parked his Buick a hundred feet or so from the rooming house, while Tannenbaum and Carbo parked in front of the residence and waited. The headlights were off, and there was no lamplight from the street to illuminate their faces. They sat in the Mercury with their hats pulled down and guns in their hands. About a half hour later, Greenberg arrived, driving a noisy old Ford convertible with yellow wire wheels and a busted muffler. He exited the car, a local newspaper folded under his right arm. Carbo leapt from the Mercury, one gun in each hand, and fired several shots, each one hitting Greenberg, who slumped to the sidewalk. Siegel, Tannenbaum, and Carbo sped away, head-lights still off. Several blocks away, the two cars were met by a third car driven by Champ Segal (whose brother invented the ubiquitous Segal lock). Tannenbaum was told to get into Segal's car; he would be driven north to the airport in San Francisco and from there flown east to Philadelphia. Carbo would hide out in his apartment for several days.

Having heard multiple shots while waiting for her husband to return to their small apartment, Greenberg's wife, Ida, ran out outside. There, lying in a puddle of blood on the sidewalk, was her husband's bloody body. He had been shot in the head five times. Kneeling on the sidewalk, she screamed that she would avenge her husband's murder; however, when cops arrived, she told them that she didn't know who killed her husband. When Siegel was later indicted for the murder, Ida had nothing incriminating to say. She averred that she had no knowledge of her husband being an associate of mobsters and added that she did not know that he had demanded $5000 from Buchalter to keep his mouth shut. That was one piece of luck for Siegel. A more important event played out in Brooklyn.

A Murder Inc. killer named Abe "Kid Twist" Reles had been arrested. It was his forty-second bust. He thought he might beat the rap but then heard that some of his colleagues were prepared to rat him out. The first to make a deal with prosecutors invariably gets the best terms, so Reles had his wife inform the Brooklyn DA that her husband was willing to talk about his crimes and those of others, such as the murder of Big Greenie Greenberg. For twelve days, he talked and talked. He was a verbal encyclopedia of crimes. A stenographer filled twenty-five notebooks with the Reles's nar-rative. He revealed for the first time the existence of Murder Inc., which he called "the combination." He claimed that hundreds of men filled its ranks and committed murders for hire from New York to California. He told the DA that Lepke Buchalter had ordered the murder of Greenberg and that Buchalter, Siegel, Zwillman, and Weiss had organized it. He added that Frankie Carbo was the triggerman.

The DA was next able to flip Tannenbaum, who confessed that he had delivered the murder weapons supplied by Zwillman and had been part of the hit team.

Now there were two turncoats who had fingered Siegel, who looked as if he were a candidate for life in prison or a hard seat in the gas chamber. A police raiding party proceeded to Siegel's mansion; a butler reluctantly let them in, and the cops walked from one baronial room to another. They were surprised by the lavish accoutrements that Siegel had assembled and installed. It was during the Great Depression, and Siegel was living like he was a member of British royalty. The cops proceeded to Siegel's bedroom, where they found footprints on the rumpled silk sheet on the bed. Above the bed was a trapdoor; several cops pushed it open and hoisted themselves above the ceiling and into Siegel's hideout, where they found him in his monogrammed silk pajamas. He giggled, saying he was hiding from someone who may have wanted to kill him.

Siegel was arrested but spent little time in jail. He often had lunch with his mistress, British movie star Wendy Barrie and was driven around town by a deputy sheriff. He was dropped off for a haircut or to exercise at the local Y. He refused to eat prison food and arranged to have specially prepared meals delivered to him from Chasen's, the Brown Derby, Ciro's, and Perino's, among various others. During this time, Siegel sent a wire to former congressman and new DA John Dockweiler, asking him to return $30,000 that Siegel had contributed to his congressional election campaign. The embarrassed DA quietly returned the money, and Siegel used it to hire famed defense attorney Jerry Giesler. On December 11, 1940, deputy DA Vernon Ferguson requested that charges against

Siegel be dropped. Forthwith he was released. It happened because Brooklyn DA William O'Dwyer refused to let Reles go to LA and testify against Siegel. O'Dwyer, a potential mayoral candidate, was suspected of being paid off by Frank Costello. But negative editorials and public outrage about Siegel's release caused O'Dwyer to change course: Siegel was rearrested, and Tannenbaum was taken to LA to testify against Siegel. But the DA needed the corroboration of Reles, who was being held as a protected witness in the Half Moon Hotel in Coney Island.

Reles was being guarded by five New York City cops. Frank Costello, ever resourceful, paid the five cops a total of $100,000 to fling Reles out of the six-story window. The case against Siegel also went out the window. The cops claimed that Reles had attempted to escape by tying two sheets together and skittering like a squirrel down five stories, but it made no sense. There was a contract on Reles's life; by escaping, he would wind up in the hands of the mob. Furthermore, a pair of sheets was hardly sufficient to descend five stories.

> *Lansky and Luciano reported to associates that Costello had spent $100,000 to bribe the five policemen. . . . All five were subsequently demoted, but they each deposited $20,000 into their individual safe deposit boxes. That was considerably more than their salaries, which were not more than $3,000 annually. For Costello, it was money well spent. . . . [Albert "Mad Hatter"] Anastasia commented to a crony that "the canary could sing, but he couldn't fly." Of course, his singing career flopped too.*[7]

Siegel, before the elimination of a corroborating testimony, had been put on trial for the murder of Greenberg. Newspapers revealed Siegel's past and referred to him as "Bugsy." When he read those stories that used his nickname, he fumed and cursed, often tearing the papers to shreds. Siegel was finally acquitted when Tannenbaum could no longer serve as a witness to corroborate Reles's story about Greenberg's murder. The notoriety heaped upon Siegel by the press during his incarceration did not disturb or discourage his movie star pals; shortly after Siegel was freed, he and his celebrity pals attended horse races and boxing matches; they joined him for dinner at his favorite restaurants, and—of course—attended his lavish parties. They even invited Siegel to the sets where they were filming their latest movies. The studio bosses, however, tried to discourage such associations. They warned the stars that being associated with a well-known mobster could hurt their careers. However, when their concerns proved unfounded, the studio bosses shrugged away their concerns and focused on more pressing matters. However, their anxiety was reignited when Siegel was arrested for bookmaking in 1944. It didn't matter to Raft. He was Siegel's good friend, and at that time, he was indulging Siegel's fantasy of becoming a movie star. He helped Siegel choose the right movie equipment to film a few scenes of Siegel imitating Raft in *Manpower*, a 1941 movie starring Marlene Dietrich, Edward G. Robinson, and Raft.

The clips were professionally edited, but Siegel never showed them to any producers or directors. Though he had an overblown ego, it was as thin and fragile as the skin of an overinflated balloon. If Siegel were rejected, his ego would have quickly deflated, landing crumpled on the ground. He could not risk rejection, and so the gangster's thespian abilities remained untested. Yet Siegel watched the test over and over again in his living room, never failing to marvel at his abilities. He averred to whomever watched the screen test with him that he was as good as any actor on the silver screen.

The one thing about which there was no doubt was his ability to extort the studios, which he accomplished through third parties while controlling various unions, such as the Screen Extras Guild. The studio bosses felt compelled to give in to mob demands. If not, the costs could be enormous. For example, if a studio scheduled scenes in which numerous extras were required to be on set, a studio couldn't afford a strike. Better to pay a few hundred thousand dollars to avoid a strike than spend millions on cost overruns. Though studio bosses knew that Siegel was behind the protection racket, none of them said a word about it to him at any of his lavish parties. Siegel not only took over the Screen Extras Guild, but also the Los Angeles Teamsters. With such control, he was able to shake down all the studios, big and small. Siegel loved shakedowns: it was part of his character since his early days on the Lower East Side of New York, where he and Lansky extorted money from newsdealers, small shop owners, and street peddlers. His first larcenous payoff whetted his appetite for a lifetime of larcenous activities. Those larcenies included skimming money from his mob investors while building the Flamingo Hotel and Casino. In addition to his extortion rackets, Siegel collected $100,000 annually from Los Angeles brothels that bought protection from the mob, which in turn guaranteed a hands-off policy from the local vice squad. However, Siegel's primary sources of income were the Transcontinental Racing Wire (to which bookies in three states were forced to subscribe) and various high-class gambling enterprises that attracted the crème de la crème of Hollywood society, whose members gambled away fortunes faster than they had acquired them.

Though the studio bosses obediently paid for union peace, they were unhappy that Raft continued to associate in public with a man they regarded as a notorious gangster. It was one thing to play gangsters in the make-believe world of movies, but it was quite another to announce one's admiration and friendship for a gangster. Raft was undeterred. He not only testified on behalf of Siegel during the bookmaking case, but he was then photographed on the courthouse steps with an arm around Siegel's shoulder. That photograph was syndicated around the world. When one producer saw the photograph, he told Raft that he had just committed career suicide. Raft didn't believe him. The public went to see his movies because they thought he was a real gangster. Guilt by association worked well for Raft. (And it did not stop him from testifying on behalf of one of Al Capone's brothers. Again, his actions provided copy for gossip columnists.) Raft didn't care what producers said or what was printed in gossip columns. He let the world know that he enjoyed the company of gangsters. He reminisced to a reporter about the gangsters he had known: "I knew them all. They were guys I looked up to. They were interesting company and when you talked to them, as I did, you learned a lot. Over dinner at a nightclub or restaurant, they were more fun and laughs than any businessman or studio head I ever met."[8]

After the courthouse photo generated an avalanche of publicity, Siegel commented to a reporter that he considered Raft the most authentic movie tough guy. Raft could not have been happier. That was the kind of praise that fed his ego.

Raft did not dim his star appeal by letting the world know that he regarded gangsters as his friends; rather, he undermined his career by turning down important movie roles, such as the leads in *Double Indemnity* and *The Maltese Falcon*. In the later years of his career, however, he ruefully bemoaned his errors of judgment and accepted supporting roles in the popular movies, *Some Like It Hot* and *Oceans 11*. Nevertheless, as he admitted a few years before his death, his telephone had stopped ringing, and nobody had any parts for him.

Throughout his life, Raft never spoke of the crimes Siegel had committed or had been suspected of committing. Some of the stars with whom Siegel had associated may have suspected him of everything from being a member of Murder Inc. to having had a hand in the killing of Greenberg. Yet they continued to attend his parties and tell reporters that they paid no attention to rumors. At best, Siegel was a romantic rogue; at worst, he was a cold-blooded killer. It didn't seem to matter in the world of make-believe, for

Siegel was a fantasy turned into a reality, more fascinating than any silver screen gangster.

But Siegel also knew not to reveal his true sociopathic self to those who were tickled to be in his company. So that movie stars and their producers and directors would not witness his rough, threatening ways of doing business, he used the services of Mickey Cohen, for whom charm was a nonfungible foreign currency. He was all business. And when it came to that business, there was no opportunity for small talk, no conventional facades. If he wanted your money, he barked: "Give me the fuckin' money or I'll shoot you right now." If there was any hesitation by the victim, Cohen clubbed the person with the butt of a pistol. The bloody victim, if not unconscious, handed over the money with the speed of a magician's hands.

Cohen, a small man, not more than five feet five, was fearless and pugnacious. He would just as soon shoot an opponent as negotiate with him. He often responded to resistance by either pistol-whipping an opponent or shooting him.

His brutish approach to his victims nearly cost him a long prison sentence. In a restaurant in Chicago, he clubbed a man with a sugar bowl, fracturing his skull and leaving the bloody corpse for the police. He pleaded self-defense, and it took an Outfit attorney to fix the case, paying off a corrupt judge. To avoid appearing corrupt in the media, the judge said that Cohen had to leave Chicago. And not for a few weeks or months, but for the rest of his life. Lansky and Luciano agreed with the heads of the Outfit that Cohen should go to LA and work for Siegel. It would be a perfect setup for Siegel, who could present clean hands to Hollywood society, while Cohen handled all the dirty work. Cohen was perfectly cut out for his role as Siegel's henchman: he was a former boxer (eight wins and eight losses) who carried the violence of the ring into his encounters with those it was his job to beat into submission. His presence could be menacing. Large men melted when confronted by Cohen's hard-edged glare, the snarl of his upper lip, and the sight of a pistol in his waistband. Given an assignment by Siegel, Cohen always remained laser focused on achieving results.

That he was headstrong and antiauthoritarian would be an understatement. Ever since his years as a teenage punk, he loved embarrassing cops, often referring to them as low-life scum. When he arrived in LA, where he had lived in the Boyle Heights neighborhood from ages eight to fifteen, he was eager to make as many scores as possible. Instead of immediately contacting Siegel upon his arrival as he had been instructed to do, he began putting together a gang of vicious heist men. First recruited to Cohen's ranks were the Sica brothers, Fred and Joe. The threesome started knocking over gambling joints, bookie joints, and brothels. Some days, they hit two or three locations. They were so busy that Cohen brought in other heist men from New York, New Jersey, Chicago, Cleveland, and Detroit. They were soon known as the most aggressive gang on the West Coast. By comparison, Dragna's Mafia men were as well-mannered as Boy Scouts.

Cohen and his men had no respect for limitations or rules. They were completely and sometimes foolishly indiscriminate in their targets. One day they made the mistake of hitting a mob-protected bookie joint. It was owned by Morris Orloff, who ran the biggest bookmaking operation in LA. The mob regarded Orloff as golden: he regularly produced an enormous cornucopia of cash. Cohen, either unaware of Orloff's importance or not caring, had decided to rob him. Pretending to be a messenger, Cohen knocked on the door of Orloff's office and told the man who opened a peephole that he had an important package for Mr. Orloff. Cohen was told to slip the package it through the peephole. Cohen laughed at the suggestion, saying the package was too big and he also needed Orloff's signature. The man said Orloff wasn't in but opened the door. Cohen pushed the door with such violent force that he knocked the man to the floor. He was a big man, a former cop, and Cohen stood over him with a revolver in one hand. He instructed the fallen doorman to lie prone with his nose sniffing the dirt on the floor or he would split his head like a ripe watermelon. Cohen then herded the three other men into a corner of the office and said that he would wait for Orloff. "Listen you dago bastard," Mickey yelled at the man, "mind your own business or I'll put a phone through your head. I'm staying for Morey Orloff if I gotta stay till tomorrow."[9]

One of the men then spoke up, saying, "Look kid, you gotta alla the money. . . . Whatta ya wannaa stay around here? A copper could come in."

After a few minutes, one of the men in the corner piped up, announcing that he was Morey Orloff. Cohen strode to the man, demanded his wallet, which was quickly handed over, and then took Orloff's watch and a ring. Cohen next took each of the other men's money and jewelry.

As he was about to leave, one of Orloff's gofers knocked on the door. Orloff sighed, his face falling into a deep frown. The gofer was carrying a bag full of money. Cohen grabbed it and looked inside, delighted to find $22,000. Mickey told Orloff he was a punk, then he and his gang took off with a much bigger score than they had anticipated.

Later that day, Cohen got a phone call from one of Siegel's go-to guys, Champ Segal. He told Cohen that Ben Siegel wanted to see him right away. Since none of Siegel's friends or associates ever used the name Bugsy, Champ didn't as well. Cohen inquired, "Ben who?" Champ was not amused by Cohen's pretense of ignorance. He simply ignored the question and told Cohen he better show up and, when speaking to Siegel, he better use the name Ben or Benny. He warned Cohen that he might not be long for the world if he didn't show Ben the proper respect.

Siegel, having emerged from a steam room at the Hollywood YMCA, was wrapped in a towel and relaxing on a lounge chair, waiting for the irascible Cohen. Cohen swaggered over to Siegel, who did not waste time on small talk or polite pleasantries. He sternly told Cohen that he was supposed to have contacted him as soon as he arrived in the city. Cohen said he forgot. Siegel then told Cohen that he wanted him to kick back the money he robbed from Orloff. Cohen's indignation exploded like a hand grenade. He shouted that he had risked his life to make that score and wouldn't kick back even to his own mother. He then told Siegel to fuck himself before striding out of the Y. Champ ran after Cohen, warning him that he just asked Siegel to kill him. Instead, Siegel arranged for Cohen to be arrested and jailed for several days. No charges were filed. After Cohen had time to reconsider his resolve not to repay the money he had stolen, he was released and taken to the office of Siegel's lawyer, Jerry Giesler. There, he was met by Johnny Rosselli, the Outfit's man on the West Coast. He laid it out for Cohen: you work for Siegel, and you better do whatever he tells you to do.

Siegel gave Cohen the job of taking over a big bookie operation run by Eddy Neales, who also owned the Clover Club. Cohen told Neales that he and Siegel wanted to buy his operation or maybe become his partners. But Neales refused to sell, and he certainly would never agree to accept Siegel as a partner. Cohen's response was to pistol-whip Neales, who soon thereafter went into hiding. After a few anxiety-filled days, Neales sent his partner Curly Robinson to negotiate some kind of deal with Cohen and Siegel. To show Neales that the time for negotiating had passed, Cohen and a few cohorts knocked over the Clover Club. They emptied the cash registers then relieved all the guests of their money and jewelry. The Hollywood star Betty Grable watched with dismay as Cohen snatched her diamond necklace then dropped it into a patch pocket of his sports jacket. She later laughingly said it didn't matter because it was insured. Cohen, over the next few days, hit five of Neales's bookie joints, destroying each one. Neales, Siegel learned, was being protected by the sheriff's department, so Siegel made a $125,000 donation to the department. Neales's protection was withdrawn as swiftly as a lizard's tongue. Robinson soon received a phone call from Neales instructing him to let Cohen know that he had capitulated. The war was over. Siegel had won.

Neales was the last LA bookmaker to resist Siegel's offers. The bookmakers of LA were now Siegel-owned franchises from which he collected his weekly tributes. The shark had not paused. He was still swiftly moving; his appetite for movie studio cash was the next temptation on his menu. As long as he retained Cohen's services, he never personally had to threaten studio bosses: Cohen did it for him. Cohen approached studio heads or their flunkies with his demands, all delivered in blunt terms, accompanied by a few temperamental expletives. If that didn't produce the desired effect, he would place a pistol on a reluctant executive's desk. And what did Cohen demand? Either regular payments of tens of thousands of dollars or there would be labor strikes against the studio, thus shutting down numerous productions and driving up costs. None of those who were threatened wanted to lose hundreds of thousands of dollars to cost overruns. They all fell in line and paid the cost of labor peace. (For more about Mickey Cohen, please see chapter 3.)

Though Cohen never hid his contempt for others and used his belligerence to intimidate victims, Siegel was more strategic: he knew that giving a rival a piece of his action was a small price to pay for defanging a rival. Recognizing that Dragna resented him and could pose a hidden threat, Siegel cut in the Mafia don for some extortion money. It didn't matter that Dragna had never extorted the movie studios. He primarily made his money from gambling, loan-sharking, and prostitution. Dragna, though still resentful, pretended to be grateful for the crumbs Siegel brushed onto his plate. After all, Dragna had been warned by Lucky Luciano and Meyer Lansky that Siegel was his boss, so he had no choice but to accept the new status quo, which he did with a politician's forced smile.

Johnny Rosselli also advised Dragna to be satisfied that Siegel hadn't taken over all of his operations.

Though Siegel focused his energies on obtaining power and money, he had an equally strong drive to seduce as many Hollywood stars who were easy targets for his seductive charm. One redheaded beauty who ignited his lust was Virginia Hill. He pursued her with the stamina and determination of a rutting buck going after a doe in heat. She was not as beautiful as Wendy Barrie or Marie McDonald, two of Siegel's lovers, but her sexual skills, talents, and devotion to pleasure were all that were needed to entice Siegel. When asked by a Senate investigations committee what about her attracted so many mobsters, she proclaimed: "I'm the best damn fuck in the world."[10]

Hill was born in Lipscomb, Alabama, the seventh of ten children, who received little if any guidance from her parents. At age fifteen, she quit school. The following year, she married George Randell, divorcing him a year later. She moved to Chicago, hoping to go into the pornography business; instead, she became a waitress then branched out into prostitution. She became a mistress of Outfit bookmaker Joe Epstein, though he was rumored to be homosexual. The two remained close until Hill's suicide in Europe. When Meyer Lansky asked Epstein why he maintained a relationship with Hill, he replied: "Once that girl is under your skin, it's like a cancer. It's incurable."[11]

In addition to Epstein, she became a lover of Joe Fischetti, a cousin of Al Capone and the man who sent Frank Sinatra to Cuba with an attaché case containing $1 million for Lucky Luciano. She allegedly demonstrated her oral-genital skills on Fischetti amid a crowd of guests at one of his Christmas parties. Fischetti's wife either didn't notice, pretended not to notice, or didn't care. Though Fischetti enjoyed Hill's sexual skills, he sent her to New York to keep an eye on Joe Adonis (formerly Joseph Doto, who changed his name because he thought he was gorgeous). Adonis and Hill, unsurprisingly, became lovers, then she met Siegel on one of his trips East. They spent a night together at the Waldorf Astoria: it was the beginning of their passionate romance. It was also the beginning of Adonis's deep animosity for the pair. No man so convinced of his own beauty and the magnetic power he had over women was going to forgive the guy who took away his lover.

Hill had enormous confidence in her sexual skills and Siegel became addicted. She also said that the best sex she ever had was with Siegel. Adonis responded by calling her a slut.

Sex wasn't the only bond that tied Siegel and Hill to one another. They both had a love of larceny and thrived in a world of money laundering, betting on fixed fights and horse races, and importing and selling narcotics. When not scamming the world, the two had a tumultuous affair, often accusing each other of being unfaithful. Their accusations often erupted into battles in which Siegel left Hill bruised and screaming at him. Their knockdown fights were followed by intense lovemaking that Hill told a friend was the best kind of sex.

The fights, accusations of infidelity, and jealous rages—such as when Hill belted another of Siegel's lovers in the lobby of the Flamingo—did not end their relationship. It was their love of scheming and scams that brought on their downfall: Siegel had skimmed millions of dollars from his mobster partners while building the Flamingo Hotel and Casino. And so he paid for his larceny with his life, shot in the head while reading the *Los Angeles Times* in the living room of Hill's rented house on North Linden Drive in Beverly Hills.

Following Siegel's murder, Hill lived out her remaining years in Europe, where she was visited by Meyer Lansky, who instructed her that Siegel's partners expected her to repay the money she and her lover had stolen. She supposedly paid to stay alive; however, a few years later she committed suicide by swallowing a handful of sleeping pills in Koppl, Austria, on March 24,

1966. She was forty-nine years old. There was speculation among several investigators that the mob may have done her in. They usually make an example of someone who steals from them, even if the money is repaid.

In addition to Hill, Siegel had another well-publicized affair, with Countess Dorothy di Frasso, an American heiress married to an Italian count. It was a marriage of money and title. She threw lavish Hollywood parties and had collected a salon of celebrities. She had just ended an affair with Gary Cooper when she met Siegel. She immediately fell for the suave and dangerous gangster. They soon became lovers (though Siegel often treated her contemptuously), and she introduced Siegel to all of her socially prominent friends. When Siegel learned that Dorothy's husband was a friend of Mussolini, he asked for an introduction. He thought he might be able to sell the dictator American weapons. She agreed to introduce him, and the two sailed for Italy.

As anti-Semitism was spreading like a plague in Europe in the 1930s, the countess decided that Siegel needed a non-Jewish nom de guerre, and so she altered Siegel's pedigree with the snap of her fingers. He became a British baronet named Sir Bart. When the pair arrived at her husband's villa, they discovered that the count had invited two Nazi houseguests: Joseph Goebbels and Hermann Göring. Siegel was furious. He referred to Goebbels as "that weaselly cripple" and Goring as an "overfed pig" whose belly would nicely accommodate a barrage of .45 slugs. He told the countess that he planned to bump off the two Nazis. The countess became alarmed and beseeched him not to take such foolish actions. If he did, she and her husband would wind up in a concentration camp, if not worse, and Siegel might not get out of Italy alive. Siegel relented and the two packed their bags and traveled to the south of France. There, the ersatz baronet and the countess partied with rich expatriates. Back in LA, Siegel didn't realize that his mob partners were planning his demise. But it would not take place in Vegas.

Casino owners wanted to project an image of their city as being free of crime and criminals. Those marked for death were always killed outside city limits and buried in the desert or, even better, they were killed in other states.

Siegel, who had avoided being killed all of the years he was a member of the Bugs and Meyer Gang and of Murder Inc., believed that he led a charmed life. He had killed many others, but no one had so much as wounded him. He thought he could charm his mob partners into believing that he would turn the Flamingo into a cash cow and pay them back many times over. But as the mob's $1 million investment rocketed to $6 million, and still more money was needed to complete the building of the Flamingo. Lansky, Luciano, Costello, and a vengeful Joe Adonis decided it was time for their indebted colleague to make a quick exit into an early grave.

Shot in the head by former partner Frankie Carbo, Siegel's rule ended. With Siegel dead, Dragna attempted to regain his former power, but he would have to fight with Cohen. And Cohen had every intention of taking over all of Siegel's operation.

The Hollywood studio bosses and the mob back East were all glad to be rid of Siegel. Though intent on filling the vacuum created by Siegel's murder, Cohen was full of indignation and a deep need for revenge. He ran into the lobby of the Hotel Roosevelt, where he believed Siegel's assassin was in hiding. He fired round after round from two .45 caliber guns into the ceiling of the lobby, causing guests and bellhops to flee like panicked rabbits. He then shouted for the assassin to meet him—one on one—in ten minutes. No one showed up, and Cohen eventually stormed out of the hotel, cursing less loudly than when he had arrived.

Following his bravado of gunfire in the hotel, Cohen proceeded to take over all of Siegel's operation, just as he had promised and just as Dragna had predicted. Dragna and Cohen fought numerous battles, killing members of each man's gang, but the two managed to avoid violent ends.

Raft, too, felt bereaved. On the night Siegel was assassinated, he had invited Raft for dinner. Raft begged off, telling Siegel he had other commitments and would call him the next day. When he learned that his closest friend had been murdered, Raft said that if he had he gone to Siegel's house that night, he might have been collateral damage. He ruefully reflected that banner headlines would have screamed "Mobster and Star Murdered!" Though he was lucky to have declined Siegel's invitation, he mourned the loss of his dearest friend.

The city of angels would attract less glamorous gangsters than Bugsy Siegel; ones who were more vicious and merciless than their legendary predecessor. Compared to what was coming, the Hollywood studios had gotten off lightly from Siegel and Cohen's shakedown racket. They would dread having to deal with the vile Willie Bioff. (See chapter 4.)

NOTES

1. Tim Adler, *Hollywood and the Mob* (London: Bloomsbury, 2007), 37–38.

2. Kitty Kelley, *His Way* (New York: Bantam, 1986), 111.

3. www.dailymail.co.uk/tvshowbiz/article-9451341/The-mobster-Hollywood-adored-1930s-gangster-Bugsy-Siegel-Tinseltowns-darling.html (accessed June 15, 2022).

4. www.dailymail.co.uk/tvshowbiz/article-9451341/The-mobster-Hollywood-adored-1930s-gangster-Bugsy-Siegel-Tinseltowns-darling.html (accessed June 15, 2022)

5. Stone Wallace, *George Raft: The Man Who Would Be Bogart* (Albany, GA: BearManor Media, 2008), 33.

6. Wallace, *George Raft*, 159.

7. Jeffrey Sussman, *Big Apple Gangsters: The Rise and Decline of the Mob in New York* (Lanham, MD: Rowman & Littlefield, 2020), 37.

8. Wallace, *George Raft*, 34.

9. John Buntin, *L.A. Noir* (New York: Harmony, 2009), 64.

10. www.youtube.com/watch?v=-Z4Rr6AloDs

11. https://themobmuseum.org/blog/virginia-hill-queen-of-the-mob-was-no-ones-pushover/

CHAPTER THREE

Mickey Cohen

Little Tough Guy

MICKEY COHEN MAY HAVE BEEN THE MOST SHOT-AT AND BOMBED gangster in the twentieth century. A bomb exploded beneath his bedroom. Another bomb failed to ignite. Bullets irregularly whizzed by his body, rarely wounding him. He was shot at in his driveway, in front of his haberdashery store, and outside restaurants and nightclubs. One time he was wounded in the shoulder. His friend and newspaper columnist Florabel Muir was shot in the ass while standing next to Cohen outside a restaurant on Sunset Boulevard. Jack Dragna, Mafia boss, wanted him dead, but Cohen frustrated him again and again. Dragna's trigger-happy henchmen formed a gang that couldn't shoot straight. Dragna, who had been humiliated by Bugsy Siegel and who lost many of his gambling operations to Seigel and Cohen, was intent on doing away with Cohen and reclaiming his fiefdom after Siegel's death. Cohen did not have the same protection from the National Crime Syndicate that Siegel had, so Dragna thought he could murder Cohen without bringing down the wrath of the East Coast mob. He was right, but Cohen was fortunate that Dragna was the boss of the country's most inept Mafia family, known among law enforcement and reporters as the Mickey Mouse Mafia.

Summoned to appear before the Kefauver Committee investigating organized crime in 1950, Cohen was queried by Senator Charles Tobey: "Is it not a fact that you live extravagantly . . . surrounded by violence?" Cohen indignantly responded: "Whaada ya mean, 'surrounded by violence?' People are shooting at *me*."[1] Indeed, they were. Nine attempts to extinguish his life had all failed. Friends laughingly commented that Mickey could walk through fire as if made of asbestos.

This man with a cat-of-nine-lives mystique was born on September 14, 1913, in the Brownsville section of Brooklyn, then a predominantly Jewish neighborhood of poor Eastern European and Russian immigrants. Meyer Harris Cohen (aka Mickey) was the youngest of six children. In September 1914, his father Max suddenly died. His mother, Fanny, barely literate, did not know how she would support her family. She was told that California was a good place to raise children. They would enjoy fresh air and sunshine, and she would have no difficulty finding work. The family journeyed west and settled in Boyle Heights, a mostly Jewish neighborhood. By age eight, Cohen was selling newspapers on a street corner. He fought with other boys to get the best corner, and he protected his turf with the ferocity of a hungry young lion.

His audacious criminal career had begun at age nine, when he and several preteen gang members held up the box office of one of the biggest movie theaters in Los Angeles. Cohen, who was only about five feet five as an adult, was so small at age nine that he hardly appeared menacing. Yet he wielded a baseball bat with such ferocity that he terrified the theater's female box office employee, who handed over all the money demanded by Cohen after he threatened to bash in her skull.

The tough guy was molded on those streets. He not only exhibited his ferocity as an effective means to intimidate his victims, but he also used it to uphold his idea of the brotherhood of humanity.

As he said years later, "If anyone called someone kike, spic, or wop in our neighborhood, we would beat his head in."[2]

By the time he was fifteen, Cohen decided that there was money to be made as a boxer. Boxing was one of the most popular sports in America not only for Jews, but for the poor unmelted ethnics who made up the tenement class of cities in the East, West, and Midwest. Unfortunately for Cohen, boxing was illegal in California, and Cohen was forced to fight three-round fights in small clubs. With limited ring opportunities in California, Cohen took his ambition to become a professional boxer to Cleveland, home of bootleg gangsters, Moe Dalitz, Sam Tucker, Morris Kleinman (a former boxer), and Louis Rothkopf, who would one day rule Las Vegas. Thinking that Irish fighters would be more popular than Jewish ones in the Midwest, Cohen began calling himself Irish Mickey Cohen, not seeming to realize that his surname immediately identified him as a Jew. But when he fought future featherweight champion Tommy Paul and was knocked out in the first round, he emerged with a new name: Gangster Mickey Cohen. It was prescient and fortuitous; however, the reason for the sobriquet remains unknown. He fought his last fight in Tijuana, Mexico, where he lost to another featherweight champion, Alberto "Baby" Arizmendi. With a record of eight wins and eight losses, a few scars, and a broken nose, Cohen hung up his gloves. It was now time to live up to his moniker, Gangster Mickey Cohen. He started heisting stores and extorting shopkeepers. One of his cohorts was killed during a holdup, and the cops—like bloodhounds—were looking for Cohen, whom they suspected of being the ringleader of the holdup gang.

Cohen consulted Rothkopf and Kleinman, who had been his mentors since his arrival in Cleveland. They suggested that Cohen get out of town, and they gave him introductions to top Outfit members in Chicago.

Cohen continued his criminal activities in the Windy City and was given permission from the Outfit to make book in the Loop. But Cohen's murderous temper was becoming a liability to the Outfit's operations. He had murdered a man by beating him on the head with a sugar bowl and killed several others in a card game. His actions were generating too many negative headlines, which was bad for the politicians whom the Outfit controlled. Capone's emissaries told Cohen he had overstayed his welcome. He should go back to LA and work for Siegel. The move was seconded by Luciano and Lansky. Cohen never held his forced departure against Capone. In fact, he maintained a lifelong admiration for the Big Man, also known as Snorky (which is slang for sharp dresser). So inspired was Cohen by Capone's wardrobe that he spent tens of thousands of dollars a year on bespoke suits, monogrammed shirts, and silk pajamas, silk ties, custom-made shoes, gold and diamond cufflinks, and other fashion accessories. Members of his LA gang marveled that they never saw Cohen in the same suit twice.

The well-dressed LA gangster was assigned the work of knocking over local gambling joints and brothels controlled by small-time local racketeers. Siegel would not get involved in such commonplace criminal activities and didn't need to. Cohen's targets learned quickly that a tough little gangster taking orders from Siegel was taking control. Those who didn't go along were quickly eliminated. Those who acquiesced were permitted to keep operating as long as they paid what was demanded of them. After Siegel was assassinated, Cohen, lacking Siegel's charm and finesse and control of labor unions, gave up collecting shakedown money from movie studios. Instead, he found easier targets of opportunity: movie stars whose indiscretions left them open for blackmail.

Cohen decided to fund the publication of *Hollywood Nite-Life*, whose ostensible publisher was Hank Sanicola, Frank Sinatra's tough-guy manager. Though Sanicola's name appeared on the masthead as publisher, it was there only to add a veneer of legitimacy to the publication. Cohen used *Nite-Life* as a vehicle for a successful blackmail racket. The advertising salesmen for *Nite-Life* threatened to print intimate details about the lives of movie stars, focusing on adultery, homosexuality, and drug addiction. However, before the publication went to press, one of the publication's salesmen (a euphemism for blackmailer) would call on a star about to be exposed and offer to cancel the article for a significant price plus the cost of a full-page ad. Even Sinatra became a target of *Nite-Life*: he was having an affair with Ava Gardner while still married to his first wife. If that information was revealed to the singer's fans, it could prove injurious to his career. The publication also had information that Sinatra had sexually assaulted a woman in Las Vegas. Sinatra prudently agreed to buy a full-page ad. Other targets for blackmail included Marilyn Monroe and Judy Garland. The publication had a list of Monroe's numerous lovers, some of whom were marquee names with wives and children. Garland was addicted to drugs, and she and her studio bosses were desperate to keep that information secret. The publication was able to gather information through secret phone taps and hidden cameras and informants. To lure and entrap unsuspecting stars, Cohen employed a stable of aspiring starlets who also worked as prostitutes as well as handsome aspiring actors, both straight and gay. Working on commission, they received payment only for the dirt they delivered. And they were as voracious and persistent as piranhas.

Nite-Life was regularly delivered to the desks of studio heads, producers, directors, and major stars. It was read avidly, often with a sense of relief, disbelief, anger, or schadenfreude. Readers' emotions varied, depending on who was being mocked as a hypocrite, fraud, thief, or adulterer. During its brief run, *Hollywood Nite-Life* made hundreds of thousands of dollars for Cohen.

The racket came to the attention of law enforcement when actor Robert Mitchum was arrested for possessing marijuana while in the company of a pair of beautiful prostitutes who worked for a Hollywood madam named Brenda Allen. Mitchum's manager, Paul L. Behrmann, told authorities about Cohen's extortion racket, but they were unable to get an indictment because Behrmann was considered an unreliable witness. Cohen, who was a friend of Mitchum, told the press that he had nothing to do with prostitution and drugs. At worst, he was a gambler.

Brenda Allen was another matter. She ran the biggest prostitution ring in LA. She was a former streetwalker whose beauty had kept her in demand and generated the funds she needed to become a successful madam. She had radiant red hair, a stunning figure, and movie-actress features—and the mind of a manager. Being a common prostitute had been a means to an end. Allen aspired to be chief operating officer of a business that employed the most beautiful call girls in California. She used her organizational skills to assemble a stable of 114 beautiful women. Clients were a who's who of wealthy businessmen, movie stars (such as Errol Flynn, Mickey Rooney, and Xavier Cugat), politicians, and corrupt cops who took partial payoffs in client services in exchange for providing protection and freedom from arrest.

The operation was simple and efficient. Each client would call Allen's unlisted number, 5-255. Once a client was identified, he was offered a magnificent heroine of a novel. He was told that she had long, luxurious hair that was either blonde, red, or dark brown, was five feet two or five feet three, and would be draped in a full-length mink coat over a clinging low-cut green, red, or black silk dress. The client was told he could pick up a copy of the "book" at 9:30 p.m. in front of a bookstore on Sunset Boulevard. The client would arrive at the designated time, and his date would emerge from a chauffeur-driven limo shortly thereafter like a salacious dream. The calls for girls never ceased, and clients referred other clients. Allen was earning more than $5,000 a week after splitting fees with her stable of call girls.

Her clever use of police payoffs, however, did not provide foolproof protection from the clutches of the law. A police phone tap had recorded her outgoing calls, one of which was about Cohen and corrupt cops. The bug had picked up a call between Allen and a vice cop named Sergeant Jackson, who not only provided her protection, but was also her lover. During the bugged conversation, Jackson bragged that he was shaking down some of Cohen's gambling dens.

Unfortunately for Allen, however, the bug led to her arrest, indictment, and conviction for pandering. She was sentenced to a year in jail. For Cohen, the publicity was just what he wanted: the police shakedown freed Cohen of Jackson's coercion. When interviewed by reporters, he laughed and said that Jackson was a fool.

The following year, Allen was taken from jail to appear before a grand jury investigating police corruption. She was conservatively and expensively dressed in a sleek gray suit. Her face was slightly obscured by large sunglasses and a translucent black veil. Her finely shaped lips were blood red. She admitted that she operated her call girl ring with the help of LA cops.

"Allen swore that she paid $150 a week per girl for police protection and proceeded to inform the panel: 'I paid for everything that I got, and I paid plenty. If they [the cops] got into this mess, it was their own business not mine. Now it's everybody for himself.'"[3]

Following her testimony, a number of cops were indicted, including Jackson and Police Chief C. B. Horrall. The exposure caused Horrall to resign; at trial, Jackson was acquitted. Though Jackson claimed he knew Allen only through his undercover work, it was reported that he had shot a holdup man who was necking with Allen in a parked car. The public was not only outraged by the reported level of police corruption, but also—following the trial—by the gruesome murders of several call girls who could have testified against the police.

The DA, nevertheless, was convinced that Allen operated in cahoots with Cohen, using prostitutes to obtain embarrassing information (usually films or photographs) about movie stars, businessmen, and some politicians. The DA asserted that Cohen would then have a member of his gang offer to sell the incriminating material to the blackmail subject, who would invariably pay the amount demanded. There were no negotiations. However, the DA's suppositions were not backed up by evidence, so no indictments followed.

Whereas the DA had one theory about Cohen's involvement in the Brenda Allen call girl business, LA Mayor Fletcher Bowron insisted that Cohen had set up the entire case to get the police to back off his various gambling operations. When asked by reporters if such an accusation was true, Cohen merely chuckled.

After several newspaper reports about the contents of the wiretapped recordings were reported, there was a public demand for an investigation of the entire police department. Cohen was now directing a media serenade as if he were an orchestra conductor. He was a hero on a pedestal. He had single-handedly exposed police corruption. Mayor Bowron heard the music and, as a result, decided to change his tune and play along with Cohen's orchestra. He announced to the press that Cohen was a civic-minded crusader and the citizens of LA owed him a debt of gratitude.

Taking advantage of his new role as a high-minded scourge of corruption, Cohen added encomiums to his perceived generosity and good-heartedness by riding to the rescue of Elsie Phillips. She had lost her house to an unscrupulous shopkeeper and radio repairman named Alfred Marsden Pearson, who operated the Sky Pilot Radio store. He was well known for overcharging his customers, for providing slipshod repairs, and even for attacking customers who complained. The police had arrested him five times, but Pearson remained unrepentant and unchanged in his dishonest activities.

He had repaired Elsie Phillips's radio and charged her $8.91, which Phillips claimed was considerably higher than the original estimate. She refused to pay. Pearson then sued her for $81 and won a judgment. Phillips was unable to pay that amount, so Pearson forced the sale of her house to satisfy the court's judgment. At a subsequent auction, he bought the house for $26.50, then charged her rent to stay in the house.

LA police Captain Harry M. Lorenson was incensed by the victimization of Phillips. He met with Cohen to find a solution to the problem. Cohen immediately proposed killing Pearson, but Lorenson ruled that out. Instead, he recommended that they organize neighborhood protests in front of Pearson's store. Among the picketing protestors would be seven members of Cohen's gang who would intimidate Pearson so that he turned over the deed of the house to Phillips. Cohen agreed. However, during the actual picketing, Cohen's men did more than wave their picketing signs and shake their fists at Pearson. They rushed toward the store as Pearson yelled for the protestors to disperse. Cohen's men pushed him inside. He fell to the floor, where Cohen's men punched and kicked him. (Several days later, a cartoon appeared in a local newspaper depicting Cohen and the seven dwarfs.)

Cohen's gang forced Pearson to sell the house to their boss, who then turned the deed over to Phillips and gave her a gift of cash. A photograph of Phillips hugging her benefactor appeared in local newspapers. William Randolph Hearst, who had been following the story, complimented his editor for a heartwarming story and praised Cohen. He stated: "This is a very kind and wonderful thing he did. I don't want you to refer to him as a hoodlum anymore. A man who does a thing like this isn't a hoodlum. You can call him a gambler, but I wish you'd see that he gets a fair break."[4]

Basking in his newfound role as a public benefactor, Cohen expanded his blackmail operations. He began making porno films using women who resembled famous movie stars. He then would sell the movies back to studio bosses who wanted to protect their investments in the popularity of their stars. In other cases, Cohen used hidden cameras to film well-known actresses in flagrante then proceeded to blackmail them. Having milked the stars of thousands of dollars, he would then extort their bosses, who paid huge sums to Cohen for destroying the films and negatives.

To help maintain his extortion racket, Cohen used the services of pimp and gigolo Johnny Stompanato. According to Stompanato's FBI file,

The Los Angeles Police Department has characterized Stompanato a notorious pimp in the Los Angeles area. He was regarded by the police as a procurer of girls for Mickey Cohen's out-of-town contracts. Stompanato was the subject of a Bureau White Slave Traffic Act case in 1956. Information developed that Stompanato was sending girls from Los Angeles to Las Vegas, Nevada. Prosecution was declined by United States Attorney.[5]

Stompanato was movie-star handsome with strong Mediterranean features and dark wavy hair. He always dressed in the latest fashions, wore gold chains around his neck, and sported a diamond pinky ring, all of it paid for by his various lovers. Unfortunately for his female lovers, Stompanato had a tendency to beat them up after they declared their love and devotion to him.

He had been profitably married several times to wealthy actress, but all his marriages were short-lived. When he wasn't seducing women to be blackmailed by Cohen, he made himself available to wealthy male homosexuals, whom he and Cohen would later threaten with exposure if they didn't pay them large sums of money, ranging from $50,000 to $100,000.

But it was female stars who were their primary targets. And Cohen regarded many of those stars as ignorant whores who deserved to have their reputations destroyed.

One of Stompanato's targets for seduction, as directed by Cohen, was Ava Gardner. She had a reputation for having a voracious sexual appetite and having sex with many partners. After being introduced to Stompanato, she was taken by his looks and his candid desire for sex, the wilder the better. The affair took off without time wasted on candlelit dinners and bouquets of roses. It was lust from beginning to end, gratification followed by more gratification.

Talk of Gardner and her new lover was gossip on the wind, though it was never noted in any newspaper columns. When Sinatra learned of the affair, he was furious. He was in love with Gardner, had left his wife Nancy for her. Rather than confronting Stompanato and telling him to find another lover, Sinatra called on Cohen. He told Cohen how upset he was, how much he loved Gardner, and asked him to talk to Stompanato and convince him to break off the relationship with Gardner. Cohen did so, and Stompanato broke off the relationship as easily as snapping a brittle twig in his hands. Cohen told other mobsters what had happened, that Sinatra would not confront Stompanato but had asked him to do so. Mobsters knew that Sinatra thought of himself as a tough guy, as one of them, but he was a mobster only in his imagination. That he hadn't dealt with Stompanato himself only served to further diminish his reputation with the mob. They had never thought Sinatra was a genuine tough guy, for—though he often started fights over trivial matters—he had his highly paid bodyguards step in to finish his fights. Asking Cohen to break up the relationship between Stompanato and Gardner was—to them—a sign of real weakness, and many mobsters began sneering, saying that Sinatra was not a real man. As Ted Schwarz wrote in *Hollywood Confidential*: "It was a terrible loss of face, yet Sinatra did not realize it."[6]

Cohen next directed Stompanato to beguile Lana Turner with his charm and sexual allure. Unlike his approach to Gardner, Stompanato sent Turner flowers and candy, took her out for romantic candlelit dinners. Soon they couldn't keep their bodies apart. Their relationship was as volatile as the one that had existed between Siegel and Virginia Hill: full of fights, apologies, frantic lovemaking, and promises to be more loving and kind. Forgiveness was followed by anger followed by sex. Lust without anger and anger without lust seemed impossible for the duo.

In 1958, Turner was in London filming *Another Time, Another Place* with Sean Connery. She begged Stompanato to join her, but he said he couldn't leave the gift shop he was running for Cohen and some mob investors. She implored him to come. He said he couldn't run out on his mob investors. She insisted and he finally relented. Following a few days of intense lovemaking, the two began fighting again. Stompanato accused Turner of having an affair with Connery and smacked her face. She threatened him. A day after their fight, Stompanato forced his way onto the movie set where Turner was being filmed in a scene with Connery. Stompanato pulled a pistol out of his waistband and threatened Turner and told Connery to back off. Connery instead grabbed and twisted Stompanato's wrist with one hand and landed a hard right with his other fist. Stompanato fell backward onto the floor. Turner called the police to have her lover evicted from the set. Two detectives from Scotland Yard told him he was not welcome in England. He was escorted to an airport then onto a plane. He was headed back to Los Angeles.

There, Stompanato helped Cohen sell black-and-white film clips of Turner having sex with him, though his face was blacked out. It proved to be a popular screening for some members of the Friars Club.

Not long afterward disaster struck. On April 4, 1958, Good Friday, Stompanato was stabbed to death in Turner's bedroom. Turner immediately called famed criminal defense attorney Jerry Giesler, the man who had successfully defended Siegel. Giesler took control of the situation and debriefed Turner and her daughter Cheryl Crane. When Cohen showed up at Turner's rented mansion, Giesler told Cohen to leave, otherwise the press might implicate him in the murder. Cohen agreed and quickly departed.

The press reported that Crane had entered her mother's bedroom as Stompanato was beating Turner. Stompanato turned and ran toward Crane but did not see a kitchen knife in her hand. The knife penetrated his stomach. After word of the murder had spread like a fast-moving storm, someone professionally burglarized Stompanato's apartment, taking away a trove of Turner's love letters, reels of film, and boxes of photos and negatives. Rumors spread that Cohen was behind the burglary.

Initially the press portrayed Turner as a loose, immoral Hollywood sexpot who killed a man who was about to reject her. The storyline changed, however, once Stompanato's background was made known to reporters. Studio publicists made it clear that Stompanato had been the menacing, abusive figure in the bedroom, not Turner. This hanger-on, this gigolo who lived off of women had attacked one of the great ladies of the silver screen after she told him that she wanted to end their relationship and insisted that Stompanato leave her home. Rejected, his rage consumed him, and as he beat Turner, her daughter ran into the room to protect her mother. Stompanato was successfully portrayed as a sleazy character who mistreated women and associated with gangsters. Cohen was infuriated by that portrayal of his pal; he set out to defend Stompanato's reputation. But first there would be a trial.

Indiscretions by celebrities can generate floods of gossip, and when a celebrity is accused of murder, that flood can turn into a tsunami of notoriety. Hundreds of newspaper and television reporters, wire service reporters, magazine writers, and photographers attended an April 12, 1958, inquest. The event was bigger than any Hollywood premier. Police had to hold back the media like cowboys containing a stampede of wild-eyed cattle. Testimony—each word of which was taken down by reporters who knew shorthand—went on for four hours. It was followed by a mere twenty-five minutes of deliberations. Turner gave a magnificent performance. Her tears came at just the right moments.

She used her handkerchief, like a strategically placed prop, to dab the corners of her eyes. Whenever she related particular horrors of the event, her voice cracked with emotion. Poor Cheryl. Unfortunate Johnny. Her voice dropped to a stage whisper. Only someone with a heart of stone could fail to laugh cynically at such a performance. No one was surprised by the result: it was clear case of justifiable homicide.

The *Los Angeles Times* reported the details and included information from an earlier *Times* story as well:

> *Stompanato had been stabbed in the abdomen with a butcher knife. Before the night was out, Turner's 14-year-old daughter confessed to delivering the fatal wounds. Cheryl Crane, whose father was restaurateur Stephen Crane, said she stabbed Stompanato to protect her mother from what she thought was Stompanato's homicidal rage. The killing led to what was surely the most titillating in LA's history of colorful coroner's inquests.*
>
> *Seven days later, Turner delivered what was described as the most important performance of her life, an hourlong recitation of the escalating argument that climaxed in the sudden and unexpected knife thrust that killed Stompanato.*
>
> *The first witness was Cohen, identified in news accounts as "the celebrated onetime mobster." Called to relate his identification of Stompanato as the deceased, Cohen was as obdurate as he had been nine years earlier at the inquest into the death of his alleged henchman Edward "Neddie" Herbert.*
>
> *"I refused to identify him as John Stompanato Jr. on the grounds that I may be accused of this murder,' Cohen testified before being dismissed.*
>
> *As detailed by* Times *newsman Jack Jones, Turner arrived in a gray coat and gray silk, tweed-type dress and worked her way to the sweltering Hall of Records hearing room through a mob of reporters, news camera crews and curious onlookers.*

Taking the stand, "she took one white glove off to expose silvered fingernails. She trembled, put her hands to her face from time to time and fought to control tears that threatened to overcome her," The Times *reported.*

While answering questions, "she stared down at her twisting hands or out over the heads of the spectators—as though mumbling the details of an incredible nightmare."

Turner characterized her boyfriend as hyper-possessive and prone to fits of violent rage. She described a running argument going back to their recent trip to London for a filming engagement. In their hotel, she said, Stompanato held a razor to her face and threatened to disfigure her. She recalled him saying he would "cut you just a little now to give you a taste of it." On the day of the fatal confrontation, she testified, she tried to prepare her daughter for a stormy night.

"I'm going to end it with him tonight, Baby. It's going to be a rough night. Are you prepared for it?"

When she told Stompanato it was over, "He grabbed me by the arms and started shaking me and cursing me very badly, and saying . . . that if he said jump, I would jump; if he said hop, I would hop, and I would have to do anything and everything he told me or he'd cut my face or cripple me. And if . . . when it went beyond that, he would kill me and my daughter and my mother."

Turner said she was unable to shield her daughter from the ugly scene.

"I broke away from his holding my . . . holding me . . . and I turned around to face the door, and my daughter was standing there, and I said: "Please, Cheryl, please don't listen to any of this. Please go back to your own room."

Cheryl returned to her room, but, Turner testified, she could still hear the raised voices as Turner told Stompanato: "Don't . . . ever touch me again. I am . . . I am absolutely finished. This is the end. And I want you to get out."

"I was walking toward the bedroom door and he was right behind me, and I opened it and my daughter came in. I swear it was so fast, I . . . I truthfully thought she had hit him in the stomach. The best I can remember, they came together and they parted. I still never saw a blade."

After hearing Turner's testimony, a 12-member coroner's jury quickly reached a unanimous verdict of justifiable homicide.

Turner, who had returned home, reportedly murmured, "Thank God" on learning the result. "She was put to bed immediately and given sedatives," The Times reported. But not all parties were satisfied with the decision. Outside the courtroom, a friend of Stompanato made a scene in the hearing room, saying he had wanted to testify. "It's a lie," the man said. "The girl was in love with him. There was jealousy between her and her mother. He was a gentleman. That's more than the rest of you Hollywood people are."

Another theory, proposed in a civil lawsuit filed on behalf of Stompanato's son, was that Turner had stabbed Stompanato and her daughter took the blame.

But [Turner's] epitaph inevitably still bears the stain of the editorial printed by The Times the day after the coroner's jury found Cheryl's fatal blow justified. The Times found Cheryl blameless, but took her mother to task as a hedonist whose narrative showed "the lack of almost any reference to moral sensitivity in the presence of a child."

"Cheryl isn't the juvenile delinquent," it said. "Lana is."[7]

Stompanato's family did not accept the official story; his family initiated a wrongful death suit, seeking $750,000 in damages. The action was brought against not only Turner, but also against her ex-husband and Cheryl's father, Steve Crane. In the suit, the Stompanatos claimed that Turner was responsible for the death of her lover and that she had gotten her daughter to accept blame in order to protect her career. The suit, as might have been expected, was settled out of court in May 1962. The Stompanatos were reported to have agreed to a $20,000 settlement.

Cohen was incensed that Turner's daughter took the rap for killing Turner's lover. He regarded Stompanato almost as a son. He believed that Turner had stabbed Stompanato but her lawyer convinced Turner's daughter, Cheryl Crane, to say that she had accidentally stabbed Stompanato, who was supposedly beating up her mother. Cohen wanted the world to know that Turner stabbed Stompanato multiple times while he slept in their bed and that his friend had not beaten Turner. (The sheets on Turner's bed were drenched in blood, but the floor on which Stompanato lay dead was absent blood. Cohen believed the body had been dragged to the spot where Crane claimed she accidentally stabbed Stomapanto.) Cohen told reporters that Stompanato never beat Turner. To prove his point, he released the Turner/Stompanato love letters to the press. He then provided a possible motive for Stompanato's murder. Cohen told the press that Stompanato was hired to buy films of stars having adulterous sex, sex with multiple partners, or sex with a partner of the same sex. Perhaps he was extorting his own lover, but that was certainly no cause for stabbing the guy multiple times, especially while he slept. Cohen noted that MGM hired Stompanato to buy a porno movie titled *Casting Couch* that featured a young Joan Crawford. Stompanato was also instructed to the buy the negatives. Large sums were spent to track down and buy copies of the movie. When Crawford left MGM, she had to repay that money. Tim Adler writes: "MGM's former head of security, Howard Strickling, told erstwhile colleague Samuel Marx that the studio had to buy up pornographic movies starring Crawford."[8]

Neither Turner nor her studio responded to Cohen's accusations. Studios were known to do whatever was necessary to protect their investments in their stars. And studio executives, especially their skillful publicists, had worked diligently and creatively to paint a picture of Turner as a victim, regularly hammering the point that Crane had heroically protected her mother.

Cohen ridiculed Turner's studio bosses. He would remain steadfast in the media spotlight as Stompanato's loyal defender. He bathed in the attention and was quick to offer his opinions not only about the murder, but also about two of his favorite subjects: Zionism and the plight of Jews. Reporters were eager to hear his colorful opinions on whatever subject he decided to declaim, for his words always made for compelling copy. You want to talk about Israel and the Jews? We're all ears. For years, Cohen had been one of Israel's most ardent and successful fundraisers, leaning on his mob cohorts to regularly empty their wallets to help the Jewish state.

In the late 1940s, Cohen's energetic efforts on behalf of the Israeli paramilitary organization, the Irgun, made him one of Israel's foremost fundraisers. Cohen would explain to reporters that the policy of the Irgun was based on the teachings of Ze'ev Jabotinsky. To wit: all Jews have the right to live in their ancestral homeland, and if it takes armed retaliation to keep the Arabs from attacking the Jews, then tough Jews with guns would make sure that the Jewish state survived.

Cohen, who was not religious, had become an active supporter of Israel after screenwriter Ben Hecht explained to Cohen the travails facing young Jews fighting for a homeland in Mandate Palestine. Cohen early on had decided to do all that he could to support the birth of Israel. He organized numerous fundraising dinners in cities where mobsters had headquarters. Jewish mobsters invited their Italian cohorts to the fundraising dinners, where they were expected to open their wallets and pledge thousands of dollars. In Los Angeles, Cohen held one of his biggest fundraisers at Slapsy Maxie's Cafe. The place was packed with mobsters of various ethnicities from all over the Southwest: California, Arizona, Nevada, and Texas. Each mobster was told to stand and announce how much he was giving. When Cohen thought the donation insufficient, he yelled, "Not enough!" And the mobster would cough up a larger sum. Cohen announced that he was pledging $25,000, which inspired or embarrassed attendees to come close to matching Cohen's pledge.

Jimmy "the Weasel" Fratianno wrote: "After that, forget about it. Everybody's pledging thousands. Even the bookmakers are pledging five and ten grand. They know Mickey's running the show and they're going to have pay. I see all this shit going on and I ain't going to pledge nothing. So Mickey kicks me and says 'Pledge fifteen thousand.'"[9]

Fratianno, who was later called a rat for testifying against his Mafia cohorts and seeking safety in the Witness Protection Program, resented Jews. He once said that the reason Jewish mobsters controlled Las Vegas was because they had intelligently invested their bootlegging profits in legitimate businesses, while the Italians buried their profits in their backyards. With excellent credit ratings, the Jews could legitimately borrow money from banks for building casinos, while the Italians—with no credit ratings—had to turn to other sources, such as the Teamsters Central States Pension Fund for their casino loans.

Cohen's ability to raise money for Israel was celebrated in that country. However, in the United States, many German Jews (who did not support the creation of a Jewish state) were appalled that a gangster had positioned himself as a savior of Jews. To the Israelis, the opinions of German Jews did not matter. The Israelis honored Cohen for his many services, and eleven years after the Slapsy Maxie event, Cohen received a silver box with the following engraving: "In Gratitude, to a Fellow Fighter for Hebrew Freedom, Mickey Cohen, From the Hebrew Committee of National Liberation."[10]

In a veiled response to his critics explaining his commitment to supporting Israel, Cohen commented that he was a Jew first and a mobster second.

Yet that didn't stop him from forming a close friendship with the famed evangelist, Reverend Billy Graham, and considering converting to Christianity. One of Cohen's men had found salvation in Christ at a Billy Graham crusade. Cohen was fascinated. He invited Graham to his home for hot chocolate and cookies. (He thought that would be more appropriate than whiskey and gefilte fish.) Each man was fascinated by the other: the short, heavy-set gangster and the tall, lean, blonde preacher. Graham saw Cohen not only as a possible convert, but as someone who could be celebrated in the media for turning his life around by turning to Christ. Cohen saw an opportunity to burnish his image in the media.

Cohen was quoted in *Time* magazine:

Los Angeles' onetime Racketeer Mickey Cohen, loose since 1955 after serving a stretch on an income tax rap, and now trying to go straight as a horticulturist operating an outfit called Michael's Greenhouses, Inc., had a Manhattan rendezvous with Evangelist Billy Graham. Preacher Graham, though deploring the publicity about their meeting, acknowledged that he had first gone to work on Mickey in 1949, now had high hopes that Cohen will repent in earnest. Said Cohen: "I am very high on the Christian way of life. Billy came up, and before we had food he said— What do you call it, that thing they say before food? Grace? Yeah, grace. Then we talked a lot about Christianity and stuff."[11]

Cohen went to claim that since there are Christian football and baseball players, why not a Christian gangster?

Graham invited Cohen to his New York revival meeting to take place at Madison Square Garden. His roundtrip airline tickets and all other expenses were paid for by W. C. Jones, an evangelical minister who was a board member of Graham's ministry. Cohen was put up at the Waldorf Astoria, where he was photographed in monogrammed silk pajamas as he enjoyed a tray of food sent up by room service. Cohen repeated to reporters he was very high on Christianity. "Billy has guided me in many things. He's my friend. . . . But it's hard for me to say if I'll be converted."[12]

An audience of 17,500 of the faithful filled Madison Square Garden and greeted Graham with thunderous applause and numerous hallelujahs. They expected to hear Graham announce that former gangster Mickey Cohen had turned his life over to Christ and would lead a good Christian life. Following Graham's enthusiastic introduction and another round of applause, Cohen strode onto the stage, smiled, and waved to the crowd. He made a half bow, turned, and exited behind a curtain. The audience didn't know what to make of it. Graham, though stunned, said nothing about it to those in attendance. However intense his disappointment may have been, he later told reporters that he had not given up hope that Cohen would convert. Graham said that Cohen's conversion, when it occurred, would help curtail crime in the United States and dissuade youngsters from taking the same wrong turns that Cohen had taken years earlier. Reporters asked Graham if he had paid for Cohen's appearance and possible conversion. They also said there were rumors that Cohen was disappointed in the amount of money Graham had offered him. Graham insisted that he did not pay Cohen and that he would never pay anyone to appear on a stage with him. Cohen told a reporter that the possibility of his conversion had nothing to do with money. He simply had no intention of converting. Though Graham was disappointed that Cohen backed away from announcing his conversion at Madison Square Garden, the two men remained friends, and Graham never gave up hope that Cohen would one day see the light and become a Christian.

Though Graham was willing to talk about Cohen's possible conversion, he would not talk about other aspects of Cohen's life, such as his involvement with strippers and porno actresses. Knowing as much as he did about Cohen, it would have been surprising if the straitlaced, puritanical Graham did not know about it. But Graham was discreet, and reporters did not raise the subject with him. One person whom Cohen never discussed with Graham was Candy Barr, Cohen's lover and the highest paid stripper in the United States.

When she was thirteen years old, Barr (née, Juanita Dale Slusher) ran away from her hardscrabble family in Edna, Texas, to Dallas. There, she married a safecracker, Billy Joe Debbs, but soon divorced him and turned to prostitution. As a prostitute with a desire to exhibit her talents, Barr was easily lured into starring in a porno movie. It was a twenty-minute, black-and-white movie titled *Smart Alec*, which years later earned her recognition as the first actress of porno. Her luscious figure, uninhibited sexual performance, platinum-dyed hair, and baby-doll face made her an instant star. Thousands of copies of the movie were sold, but Barr received no royalties. Though it had been a pay-to-play scenario, her performance opened doors to a lucrative career as a stripper. Any man who had seen *Smart Alec* was more than eager to watch Barr take off her clothes while a drummer, trumpeter, and saxophonist provided the burlesque soundtrack for her every bump and grind. She became the biggest draw at the Colony Club in Dallas, where raucous fans often had to be turned away, not because they were ill mannered, but because the club couldn't accommodate the torrent of horny men who came to yell, "Take it off! Take it all off!"

From Dallas, Barr moved to Hollywood, where club managers bid for her services. She signed a contract with the Largo Club for $2,000 a week plus tips. She quickly became the hottest attraction on the Sunset Strip. However, her career was about to go into the proverbial toilet, for she was facing a fifteen-year prison sentence for marijuana possession. Her manager, Joe DiCarlo, introduced her to Cohen, who was immediately smitten by the stripper with the perfect figure. Cohen thought she was gorgeous: he loved her long, lean legs, dyed platinum-blonde hair, and well-shaped breasts. To help her legal appeal, Cohen spent $15,000 hiring top appellate lawyers, including Melvin "King of Torts" Belli. Cohen and Barr became one of the most photographed couples in LA. In photos, Cohen often looked starstruck as he smiled at his lover. The two announced they were engaged to be married, though each was married to someone else. (Cohen's wife, LaVonne, was in the process of divorcing him and would soon marry Cohen's associate Samuel Farkas.) In addition to getting Barr engagements as a stripper at conventions and large private parties, Cohen got her a job as a consultant on the movie *Seven Thieves*, for which she taught Joan Collins how to strip. In the first of her two autobiographical books, *Past Imperfect*, Collins describes Barr as "a down-to-earth girl with an incredibly gorgeous body and an angelic face . . . [who had] taught me more about sensuality than I had learned in all my years under contract."[13]

Barr's popularity increased as she posed nude or seminude for numerous men's magazines. Gary Cartwright, in *Texas Monthly* magazine, wrote that the forty-one-year-old stripper, who posed nude for *Oui* magazine, was still as sexy as ever. He added that Barr had epitomized "the conflict between sex as joy and sex as danger. The body was perfect, but it was the innocence of the face that lured you on."[14]

Though Cohen loved having sex with Barr, he had no intention of marrying her. She was too wild and unpredictable to be introduced to some of Cohen's respectable Hollywood friends and business associates. He told a reporter: "There's a lot of girls I went with that I couldn't take to certain types of parties."[15] The lovers gave a final press conference during which they expressed love and admiration for one another but announced that they had decided not to marry due to their different lifestyles. Cohen told Barr that he hoped she would marry a man who would be good to her and that she would have children and enjoy the rest of her life. And if she ever needed money or anything else, all she had to do was contact him.

The FBI, always suspicious of Cohen, thought that he had been using Barr to blackmail wealthy businessmen. When some of those men were confronted by police and FBI agents, they refused to press charges or even to admit that they had paid for silence. Without sufficient evidence for an indictment, no charges were ever brought against the former lovers.

Cohen continued to regard Barr with almost brotherly affection long after their romance ended. None of his friends was surprised to learn that Cohen had called upon Peter Lawford to help raise money for Barr's appeal of her marijuana conviction. Since they were unable to raise much money, Cohen instructed Barr to hide out in Mexico. He told her to dye her hair brown and not to appear too sexy. He gave her false identity papers and enough money for her travel and living expenses. Cohen was soon pleased to learn that Barr was joined in Mexico by her Hollywood hairdresser, Jack Sahakian; he was even more pleased when the two married on November 25, 1959. Barr had thought that the law might lose interest in her while she was living a low-profile life in Mexico. It did not. The Supreme Court denied her appeal, and nine days after her marriage, she was back in the United States. No longer elusive, she was sent to the Goree State Farm for women near Huntsville, Texas. During her imprisonment, she was subpoenaed and brought back to LA to testify in Cohen's trial for tax evasion. Her testimony did not help Cohen, and she was sent back to prison, where she served three years of her fifteen-year sentence for marijuana possession. She was paroled on April 1, 1963.

Cohen was disappointed by Barr's testimony, but it did not deter him from his fixation on strippers. He had affairs with Tempest Storm and Beverly Hills. Being seen so often in the company of Hills in nightclubs and restaurants, Cohen was asked if he intended to marry her. Yes, he said. They would soon marry. But as with other women whom he dated, Cohen soon decided against marriage. He terminated the relationship on his normally friendly and generous terms, letting Hills keep the jewelry and furs he had given her. She always spoke kindly about Cohen.

Though Cohen would have loved letting his good times with strippers to roll on and on, the Department of Justice had a different future in mind for him. The DOJ set out on a mission to nail Cohen. As with many gangsters, his primary nemesis was Attorney General Robert Kennedy. Cohen's celebrity made him a perfect target for the prosecution. District attorneys, attorneys general, and US attorneys hate gangsters who parade their celebrity for public view as a challenge to the laws of the United States. Cohen's regular appearances on television, radio, and in magazines and newspapers were seen as a poke into the eye of law enforcement officials. His actions drew their vengeful wrath.

First came a summons to testify before the McClellan Committee investigating organized crime. Cohen did not attempt to evade the summons, but he wanted first-class accommodations as a guest of the US Senate. Instead, he was given a stipend of $8 per day to defray the cost of staying in a $100-a-night hotel room. Sitting before the committee, Cohen expected to be asked about his gambling activities. Instead, Robert Kennedy, counsel for the committee, immediately began portraying Cohen as a greedy consumer of luxury goods: expensive monogrammed silk pajamas, a bulletproof Cadillac, three hundred bespoke suits, sixty pairs of shoes, hundreds of silk ties, plus much more, and all on an annual income of less than $2,000. In response, Cohen's upper lip arched in a snarl, and he murmured to his lawyer that Kennedy was a snotty little kid whose daddy paid for everything.

Throughout Cohen's testimony, Kennedy acted as if he were getting the better of the mobster; the following day, he asked an angry Cohen: "What's the meaning in the underworld or the racket world when somebody's lights are to be put out?"

Cohen, with typical wise-guy humor, responded: "I don't know what you're talking about. I'm not an electrician."

The audience laughed. Kennedy, the object of Cohen's humor, looked embarrassed and then furious. His face flushed red, and he leapt from his seat and angrily strode toward Cohen. Fortunately for witness and interrogator, Kennedy was pulled back by Senator McClellan. Cohen, whose fists were clenched and ready for combat, looked disappointed that he had been denied the opportunity to trade blows with Kennedy.

He said, "I would have torn him apart [and] kicked his fuckin' head."[16]

Cohen had made an enemy of Kennedy, who was known for carrying grudges and seeking to nail those who had dared to arouse his anger. When someone—most spectacularly Jimmy Hoffa—attempted to humiliate and challenge Kennedy's authority, he pursued his challenger with the all the powers of his office. (So intensely single-minded was Kennedy's pursuit of Hoffa that many civil libertarians thought that Kennedy had gone beyond the limits of the law in order to win a conviction.) Kennedy was determined to nail Cohen.

When Kennedy graduated from counsel to the McClellan Committee to being the attorney general of the United States, he aimed his prosecutorial zeal at Cohen with the energy of an attack dog. Kennedy got the Treasury Department to go after Cohen for unpaid taxes. He instructed prosecutors for the US Attorney's Office to indict Cohen on thirteen counts of tax evasion and fraud. They charged Cohen for not having paid taxes on more than $400,000 of income. At trial, prosecutors called a series of witnesses, one of whom (as noted earlier) was Candy Barr, who had been subpoenaed to testify at Cohen's trial. She testified that Cohen had given her $15,000 to cover her lawyers' fees and bought her expensive jewelry, clothing, luggage, and an adorable poodle puppy. (Cohen loved dogs and was invariably accompanied by one when he was in a restaurant or nightclub. No maître d' ever had the temerity to tell him that pets were not allowed on the premises.) Altogether, agents estimated that Cohen had spent $60,000 on Barr.

More than 194 witnesses testified to Cohen's exorbitant spending; he claimed that his money all came from unsecured loans from friends, and he was never asked to repay those loans. He said the accusation that he earned his money from illegal gambling operations was untrue. On Friday, June 30, 1961, Cohen was convicted of eight counts of tax evasion and was fined $30,000 and sentenced to fifteen years in prison. Robert Kennedy proudly announced to reporters that "This was a major case and a very significant verdict."[17]

Once in prison, Cohen was surprised to be offered a deal by one of Kennedy's emissaries who told Cohen that if he agreed to testify against the bosses of the Outfit, his prison sentence would be reduced. Cohen told Kennedy's emissary to "go fuck yourself."[18] Mobsters noted that Cohen was a standup guy, meaning he would never testify against his friends.

Cohen was sent to one of the most notorious and primitive prisons in America: Alcatraz, where Al Capone had been sent following his conviction for tax evasion. Alcatraz was so medieval that an embarrassed government finally closed it then sent Cohen to a federal penitentiary in Atlanta, Georgia. Compared to Alcatraz, Cohen said it was paradise. And once again, Kennedy offered Cohen a deal, this time asking in person. And again, Cohen turned him down, refusing to testify against any other mobsters.

Ultimately, Atlanta wasn't the paradise Cohen thought it was. On August 14, 1963, Estes McDonald, a mentally ill inmate, snuck up on Cohen, who was engrossed in a television program. He clubbed Cohen's head again and again with a lead pipe. McDonald fractured Cohen's cranium, leaving a permanent indentation where the pipe had hit him. Cohen was transferred to a medical facility where he underwent surgery on his brain. He lost the use of one arm and partial use of one leg. He limped even while using a walker. He underwent months of physical therapy, which helped to restore some of his mobility. It was an amazing recovery for man who had been in a coma for six hours and whom doctors thought had only a fifty-fifty chance of survival.

On January 6, 1972, he was finally released from prison. His old friends welcomed him back. He visited numerous mobsters on their home turf, including Carlos Marcello in New Orleans.

Marcello had been another victim of Robert Kennedy's dogged pursuit. Kennedy had arranged for Marcello to be flown to a Guatemalan jungle and left there. An angry Marcello made his way back to New Orleans, where he vowed to get rid of Kennedy. According to Robert Blakely (chief counsel for the House Select Committee on Assassinations, who had been an attorney in the Organized Crime and Racketeering Section at Department of Justice, working under Attorney General Robert F. Kennedy), President Kennedy's murder was planned by Marcello, Santos Trafficante, and Jimmy Hoffa, all of whom believed that the only way to stop Robert Kennedy's pursuit of the mob was to kill his brother, President Kennedy.

Marcello had been glad to meet with Cohen. They had both appeared before the McClellan Committee and shared a hot hatred for its chief counsel. After leaving Marcello, Cohen appeared on numerous TV shows, letting the world know he was not only broke, but completely legitimate. He eventually would sell his memoirs, but before doing so, he continued borrowing money from wealthy friends. Sinatra, for example, gave him $25,000 to get back on his feet.

Suffering from what he thought was a stomach ulcer, Cohen checked into the UCLA Medical Center. There, surgeons performed exploratory surgery and discovered that Cohen had stomach cancer. The disease killed him on July 29, 1976. His funeral was attended by 150 mourners, one of whom was reported to have said that Mickey was the nicest killer anyone could meet. He was sixty-two years old.

Ben Hecht, screenwriter, novelist, memoirist, and friend of Cohen wrote:

A remarkable era of lethal violence bloomed for the Los Angeles underworld. In three years, Mickey was Bookie Czar of the West Coast. Under him was an army of strong-arm henchmen and millions of dollars were rolling in; most of them rolling out again for "the fix."

There was no organization behind Mickey. No syndicate Mahoffs guided or eased the way for him. Mickey did his own fixing. His pockets bulged with available $1,000 bills.

In the time of Mickey's Czardom, one of his cohorts (Nate S.) said to me proudly of himself, "I have been 35 years in organized crime—and never a black mark against me."

Mickey's reign, though briefer, was from the same point of view reasonably feckless. He paid off on the dot and to the nickel. He fixed fights and let his pals in on the take. He operated hideaway gambling rendezvous where the dice, wheels and cards were as on the level as any operator could afford to have them. On the side he beat up Nazi propagandists, staked bums to binges, never overlooked the birthday of a policeman's kid, paid medical bills for all wounded supporters and was good for a touch from anybody who smiled and said, "Hello, Mickey."

Despite these good deeds, innumerable gun battles blazed around the beneficent bookie Czar. A dozen or so of Mickey's closest friends were killed in these shootings and an equal number of the opposition bit the dust. Mickey himself escaped destruction on the average of once a month. His house and office quarters were blasted by bombs. During this time of give and take havoc, the police kept pinching Mickey on "suspicion of carrying concealed weapons." In one Sunset Boulevard engagement, Mickey was wounded in the shoulder and his hospital convalescence enabled Hollywood to concentrate on movie making.

Although most of the carnage took place on public highways, only one citizen bystander was hurt. A newspaper woman was nicked in the rear while interviewing Mr. Cohen as he was leaving a fashionable restaurant.[19]

Cohen should probably have the last word in defense of his murderous career as gangster. Though his top priorities remained extortion, gambling, loan-sharking, and drug dealing, he never stopped killing people who got in his way. As he said in a TV interview conducted by Mike Wallace, "I didn't kill no men that, in the first place, didn't deserve killing."[20]

NOTES

1. Carl Sifakis, *The Mafia Encyclopedia* (New York: Checkmark, 1999), 86.

2. Tere Tereba, *Mickey Cohen* (Toronto: ECW Press, 2012), 7.

3. Tereba, *Mickey Cohen*, 7.

4. Tereba, *Mickey Cohen*, 119.

5. Tereba, *Mickey Cohen*, 217.

6. Ted Schwarz, *Hollywood Confidential* (Lanham, MD: Taylor, 2007), 254.

7. www.latimes.com/local/california/la-me-stompanato-turner-201508 10-story.html (accessed July 20, 2022).

8. Tim Adler, *Hollywood and the Mob* (London: Bloomsbury, 2007), 66.

9. Brad Lewis, *Hollywood's Celebrity Gangster* (New York: Enigma, 2007), 79.

10. Lewis, *Hollywood's Celebrity Gangster*, 82.

11. www.time.com/time/magazine/article/0%2C9171%2C862547%2C00 .html (accessed July 21, 2022).

12. Tereba, *Mickey Cohen*, 198.

13. Joan Collins, *Past Imperfect* (New York: Simon and Schuster, 1984), 165.

14. https://freerepublic.com/focus/f-news/1551009/posts (accessed July 26, 2022).

15. Lewis, *Hollywood's Celebrity Gangster*, 248.

16. John Buntin, *L.A. Noir* (New York: Harmony, 2009), 251.

17. Buntin, *L.A. Noir*, 287.

18. Buntin, *L.A. Noir*, 287.

19. www.lamag.com/longform/mickey-cohen-memoirs-of-the-good -days/3/ (accessed July 27, 2022).

20. www.youtube.com/watch?v=eqc7LA_jFG0 (accessed March 7, 2022).

CHAPTER FOUR

Willie Bioff

Solid Gold Extortionist

THERE WERE FEW GANGSTERS AS GAUDY, SELF-IMPORTANT, AND greedy as Willie Bioff. The fact that his father threw him out of the house when Willie was a boy of eight probably had a lot to do with his criminal pursuits. An eight-year-old on the streets of Chicago is hardly equipped to take care of himself; that Willie did so is testimony to his survival instincts. On the streets of 1908 Chicago, Bioff was not just another young punk: he was an eager student of the criminal life. He quickly learned how to steal and fence merchandise. He was like the Artful Dodger on steroids; by the time he was a teenager, he was operating a successful protection racket with the help of some older boys. Among youthful thieves, he was admired for his brazenness and cunning. By his early teen years, he had started his own protection racket, demanding payoffs from shopkeepers, peddlers, and newsstand owners. By his twenties, he had added another venture to his portfolio of businesses. He had been operating a sideline as a pimp but decided there would be more money to be earned from owning a brothel.

Bioff had married a woman who shared his ambitions and lack of moral righteousness. The two opened a brothel and recruited young girls fresh off their parents' farms to work as prostitutes. The Bioffs made many promises to lure the former farm girls into prostitution. For example, the girls would not have to get up before dawn and work outdoors in all kinds of inclement weather. The Bioffs also promised the girls lots of money, short workdays, glamorous lives filled with parties and nightclubs and shows, and dates with wealthy men. The eager naive girls signed up for new lives, not realizing that they would have to service man after man, hour after hour. (One young girl, after four months as a prostitute, told Bioff that she would have preferred milking cows to men.) For their diligence, the girls would get to keep only a pittance of what the Bioffs collected. Growing angry about the lies they had been told and finding themselves treated like sexual automatons, many of the girls attempted to quit. They were met with imprisonment, beatings, and violent rapes. Nobody quit the Bioffs. Yet Willie, who considered himself a man of principle, neither raped nor seduced any of the girls. He instructed others to do it. The Bioffs managed to skate along without police harassment, for Willie had learned the art of the payoff. One day, however, an escaped prostitute made her way to an honest cop and complained that she had been forced into prostitution, raped, and beaten. An outraged cop arrested Willie, who was tried, convicted, and sentenced to six months in prison. Willie, as a result of police carelessness and perhaps a few payoffs, was able to walk out of prison as if his cell door had never slammed shut. Willie thought he had out outfoxed the law and was home free. It would not be until years later that he was forced to serve more than the five and half months remaining on his sentence.

Not one to look back, Bioff, an impatient and restlessly energetic man, had more important things to consider than an unserved jail sentence. Shakedown rackets had been the bread and butter for many small-time hoods, so Bioff joined his friend and future union partner, George Browne, to shake down small shopkeepers. As Bioff was Jewish and Browne Christian, they decided to divide their potential targets by religion. Bioff specialized in shaking down Jewish store owners, telling them he would protect them from anti-Semites who might break their windows, ruin their merchandise, or even burn down their businesses. As might be expected, if the store owners refused to pay, their businesses were indeed burnt to the ground. Browne, the more polished of the two, focused on shaking down gentile store owners. He played up his American roots and told gentile shopkeepers that hordes of immigrant Jews would try to take over their stores, but he would protect them.

Though the two had succeeded in their shakedown racket, they were not satisfied with the relatively small amounts they were able to squeeze from their victims. They decided to expand into a bigger, more profitable arena than poor shopkeepers. Browne was a business agent for a Chicago local of the stagehands union; he had failed to win enough votes to become a union officer. But that failure did not mean that he and Bioff couldn't use Browne's position as a business agent to shake down theater owners. The two scammers threatened theater owners with strikes if they didn't pay for labor peace. That neither Browne nor Bioff had the power or authority to call for strikes remained unknown by the theater owners. The few independent owners whom they threatened agreed to pay. It was better to pay than have rats running through their theaters or stink bombs tossed from balconies. And the payoffs to Browne and Bioff were significantly greater than what they got from the shopkeepers.

Based on their success, the two scammers decided that they now had the experience and smarts to threaten and pressure some of the wealthiest theater owners. To begin their new assault, they chose two of the biggest owners. Their target was the Balaban and Katz chain of theaters.

Barney Balaban and his brother-in-law, Sam Katz, were two extremely ambitious, hard-nosed businessmen. Katz would become the owner of MGM Studios, and Balaban would serve as president of Paramount Pictures from 1936 to 1964. As teenagers, they began their careers in show business by running nickelodeons; then in 1916, they moved on to producing silent movies. Balaban would not be an easy pushover for Bioff and Browne. Indeed, when the two extortionists demanded a sizeable payment for labor peace at their initial meeting with Balaban, Balaban threatened to throw them out of his office, if not out of the window. Bioff and Browne, taken aback by Balaban's hair-trigger temper, scampered out of his office like a pair of rabbits who just heard a shotgun being fired in their direction. Though Browne was hesitant to continue the attack, Bioff refused to be defeated. Bioff would initiate future assaults without the aid of Browne. He was as determined to extract money from Balaban and Katz as they were to be rid of him. He made another appointment with Balaban, this time offering to maintain labor peace for a fraction of what he would normally charge. Balaban told Bioff he was already paying $150 a week to the projectionists union and had no intention of making additional payments to the stagehands union. Bioff believed that Balaban's resistance was softening. He made another appointment and, rather than demanding a payment, he spoke about the financial benefits that could accrue to Balaban. Following that meeting, Balaban decided he would pay Bioff and Browne the same amount of money that he paid the projectionists union. The amount of money was negligible compared to the profits the two theater owners were raking in. The payments were a small price to pay for labor peace. Strikes could be far more costly than $150 a week. Bioff had the temerity to laugh at Balaban's offer and instead demanded $50,000. Balaban could not believe Bioff's audacity and again Balaban told him to get the hell out of his office. As he was leaving, Bioff tried to explain that the money was not for him and Browne, but would be given to stagehands whose salaries had been cut and to those who had been laid off. Balaban shouted at Bioff to leave.

Yet Bioff was undeterred; he was as determined as a beaver. He figured he could wear Balaban down, even if it took months to do so. At yet another meeting at which Balaban had reluctantly agreed to meet Bioff, he was told that the money Bioff was asking for would go not just to workers in need, but also to their families, helping them pay rent and put food on their tables. Balaban would be a hero to the common man, Bioff explained. Dripping crocodile tears, Bioff said he didn't want little children to go hungry and become homeless. He and Browne would even open a soup kitchen to feed the unemployed. It was pure fantasy. Bioff and Browne had no intention of parting with any money they could squeeze out of Balaban. Bioff then told Balaban that he understood how $50,000 might be too much money. He would be willing to accept $20,000, the minimum that was required to provide the necessary assistance to workers and their families. Balaban again shouted at Bioff to leave his office. Bioff believed that Balaban agreed to the meetings because he wanted something from him. He didn't know what, but he was determined to continue playing along until he found out. As Bioff was yelled at again to leave, he whistled and shook his head in exaggerated disbelief. Balaban looked at the departing shakedown artist and said nothing.

The next day, there was chaos at all the Balaban and Katz theaters: movies were shown backward, movies were shown upside down, crucial scenes were blacked out, only the endings of movies were shown. Audiences revolted and demanded their money back. The two scammers contacted Balaban and demanded to meet. Browne led off by saying that they were not unreasonable men. They didn't want to squeeze the two theater owners beyond what they could afford. Bioff then said he would hate for Balaban and Katz to close their theaters because of projection problems or other kinds of problems. Browne agreed, adding that they wanted to work with Balaban, not against him. Balaban finally agreed to pay the two $20,000.

Balaban, who insisted that a receipt from the two scammers exclude the amount of money paid, saw a means of profiting from the extortion. Balaban would fill out the receipt himself. He knew that Bioff and Browne were not about to enter the donation on their books, and he didn't want it to appear on his. Since the money would not be recorded on anyone's books, Balaban could declare it as a $100,000 charitable donation, a much larger tax deduction than the original $20,000. To guarantee that there would be no paper trail, Balaban paid the $20,000 in cash; his lawyer, Leo Spitz, delivered the money, taking $1,000 for himself. The lawyer told Bioff that the full amount was $19,000 because he had deducted a $1,000 carrying charge.

Bioff and Browne were nearly ecstatic about the scam they had pulled off. So excited were they that they behaved like a pair of drunken sailors on shore leave. They drank and gambled, losing several thousand dollars at a mob-run casino. At Club 100 in downtown Chicago, the pair continued blabbering to all who would listen about their great good fortune. The club was owned by the Outfit and run by Nick Circella, alias Nick Dean, who worked for Outfit boss Frank "the Enforcer" Nitti. Circella, who had known Bioff and Browne for years, was invited to join their celebration. Circella couldn't believe that these two fools were loudly bragging about a scam they had just pulled. A good criminal would have kept his mouth shut. Who knew who could have been listening? Two days after their celebratory night of drinking, gambling, and bragging, Bioff and Browne got a phone call. The caller extended an invitation for the two to visit the home of Frank Nitti. The gruff conveyor of the invitation ended the call with words that were interpreted as a threat: "Be there!"

Like a pair of recent college graduates going on their first job interview, Bioff and Browne dressed in their best suits then nervously headed off to Nitti's twenty-room mansion. The nervous pair arrived fifteen minutes early then anxiously waited for nearly half an hour in the vestibule for their meeting to begin. Whereas Bioff was excited about meeting with Nitti, Browne grew ever more nervous, often chewing on a thumbnail. What if Balaban already had a deal with Nitti, and they took money that was earmarked for the Outfit's tough boss? They could be killed. Bioff told him not to worry. If they had angered Nitti, they would already be dead. Nitti wouldn't waste his time calling for a meeting if all he wanted to do was kill the pair. Something good was about to happen, Bioff assured a doubtful Browne.

The waiting came to an end when a well-tailored slick young hood, his black hair greased straight back and smelling of an expensive cologne, entered the vestibule and told the men to follow him. He escorted Bioff and Browne into a large living room where Nitti, Paul "the Waiter" Ricca, Phil D'Andrea, Louis "Little New York" Campagna, and Charles "Cherry Nose" Gioe gave them hard looks. To Browne, they looked like a firing squad awaiting orders to shoot. Bioff merely smiled. Nobody said a word. Nitti's expression grew even more intensely angry than those of his cohorts. After a few minutes of silence, Nitti said he wanted to know where they got the money. He added that if they lied, they wouldn't live to see the sun rise.

Browne, who looked as if he were about to wet himself, lowered his head like a man waiting for the blade of a guillotine to slice through his neck. Bioff, however, was all energy and enthusiasm. He explained how he had planned the extortion, working on it day by day until he finally got what he wanted.

Nitti waved a dismissive hand at Bioff, indicating that Bioff should stop talking. Nitti didn't need to hear any more. From now on, he told the pair, the Outfit would take 50 percent of everything the pair extorted. He didn't mention that in time he would modify the arrangement so that the Outfit got 70 percent. Nitti wanted the huge amount of money the two could extort from the tens of thousands of theaters across the United States. And through Bioff and Browne, he would get his hooks into all of the owners.

Next, Nitti told Browne that he would arrange for him to become the figurehead president of the stagehands union, and

Bioff would be his personal assistant and representative. As president of the union, Browne would have the power and authority to call strikes. But the ultimate role of the two scammers would be to extort, collect, and deliver money to the Outfit. They would be two of the mob's most efficient extortionists and bagmen. Nitti said he didn't want to be bothered with the day-to-day details of running the union. If there were any problems, the president or his representative were to let Circella know about it. They were never to contact Nitti. He told them they would soon be on their way to Hollywood, where the movie studios would be worth millions of dollars to the Outfit.

Nitti next conferred with Lucky Luciano in New York. The two agreed that the East Coast and Chicago mobs would take control of the movie studios, using Bioff and Browne to carry out their orders. Bringing in the East Coast mobsters was necessary, since they controlled the stagehands and projectionist locals on the East Coast.

In June 1934, the union held its national election in Louisville, Kentucky. With the weight of the entire national syndicate behind him, George Browne was elected national president of the International Alliance of Theatrical Stage Employees (IATSE), the union that effectively controlled the entertainment business, and Willie Bioff was appointed Browne's "special representative" at a salary of $22,000. The Chicago mob's takeover of a giant American industry had begun.

After the convention, Frank Nitti called Bioff and Browne into his office and told them that now was the time for them to take their operation to Los Angeles, where they would be closer to the studio's offices and production centers. Browne and Bioff were warned not to skim any of the money collected for the Outfit. If they did so, they would be killed. Bioff and Browne were also instructed to work closely with Johnny Rosselli (see chapter 5), who was the Outfit's watchdog in Los Angeles. He had contacts with the studio bosses, was a friend of Harry Cohn, president of Columbia Pictures, and could be relied on to smooth any wrinkles in the extortion of the studios.

Before departing for California, Bioff was ordered to pay another visit to Balaban. At that meeting Bioff told Balaban that he was no longer operating alone; he now had bosses he reported to. They were hard men who would not take no for an answer. They demanded a 20 percent increase over what Balaban had already paid. If Balaban didn't go along with the demand, his entire chain of theaters would be struck. Balaban refused, and all of his theaters were struck. After a few weeks, the chain closed its theaters, and Browne paid a visit to Balaban. Acting as a good cop to Bioff's bad cop, Browne said he could end the strike based on a mutually acceptable agreement, which would include a small raise for the projectionists. The strike was settled.

That taken care of, Bioff settled in Los Angeles, eager to make millions for himself and the mob. While Browne spent most of his time locked behind his office doors drinking beer, Bioff was a busy salesman, selling labor peace, while refusing to cut prices.

One of Bioff's first pieces of business was dealing with Nicholas Schenck, chief executive of Loews and MGM. Accompanied by Browne, Bioff began the meeting by complaining about the hardships faced by overworked, underpaid union members. Suddenly, he began ranting about the greed of the studios. The surprised Schenck, caught off guard, was stunned by Bioff's sudden rage. Bioff, red faced and furious, yelled that the studio heads had two days to come up with $2 million or there would be massive strikes. Schenck couldn't believe what he had just heard and asked Bioff to repeat himself. Bioff, his demeanor calm again, told Schenck that he had two days to come up with the money. Bioff and Browne calmly walked out of Schenck's office.

The next day Bioff again met with Schenck, telling him that perhaps $2 million was too much for the studios to come up with on such short notice. He generously lowered his demand to $1 million. On the following day, Bioff again met with Schenck. This time, he said that he and Browne had talked it over, and they would accept $50,000 annually from each of the major studios (Metro, Warner Brothers, Paramount, Fox, United Artists, and Universal) and $25,000 annually from each of the smaller studios (Columbia and RKO). A relieved Schenck agreed. Bioff added that he wanted the money in cash, and it had to be paid within twenty-four hours in person by the studio heads. The next day, Schenck delivered the money to Bioff in his office and was told to wait while Browne counted it. Bioff told Schenck not to say a word, just to stand still while the money was being counted. Having grown up in poverty and having suffered at the hands of rich people, Bioff took his revenge by humiliating men he considered big shots. After the money was counted, Bioff told Schenck to leave.

In less than three months, Bioff had extorted $250,000 in cash from the movie moguls at Warner Brothers, 20th Century Fox, Paramount, Metro, Universal, United Artists, and RKO. While he was waiting for payment from Columbia, he would look at the stacks of money on his desk, smile, and puff on his cigar. It was imperative that the studios pay in cash so that there would be no paper trail. The cash arrived in suitcases, attaché cases, or valises. Fifty percent of the take was then sent via courier to the Outfit. When the cash arrived, Nitti would congratulate himself on his choice of Bioff to carry out the extortions of the Hollywood studios.

Bioff and Browne proved to be so successful not only because they could shut down the movie industry with a strike, but because they actually saved the studios millions of dollars. By paying off the two extortionists, the studios were able to keep employee wages low. In addition, the studios were given a free hand to fire employees who were regarded as troublemakers, which included workers who circulated petitions for higher wages, communists, those who complained to shop stewards, those who confronted managers about poor working conditions, and those who attempted to establish a union that would rival the IATSE.

As an adjunct to the studios, the union was able to impose a modern-day form of serfdom. For example, the union let the studios compel employees to work overtime with no additional compensation. By paying off Bioff and Browne, the studios were able to reduce production costs and increase profits. Bioff estimated that as a result of the studios' arrangements with IATSE, the studios were saving $15 million. As an added bonus for the studios, the IATSE demanded that so-called legitimate theaters, which did not screen movies but put on live plays, operas, ballets, and concerts, increase the amount of money paid to the union. To cover those costs, the theaters increased the price of tickets. By comparison, movie theater tickets were a bargain and attendance increased. Though Bioff regularly expressed his concern for the working men and women in the movie industry, he made such sweetheart deals with the studios that the members of the IATSE received minimal wage increases.

Flush with more cash than he ever dreamed possible, Willie Bioff "went Hollywood." He started to wear expensive clothes and carried three diamond-studded, solid gold, union business cards in his wallet. He was living like a king. If the union members had seen the way that Bioff lived, they might have risen up with pitchforks and torches and stormed his palatial home.

He had the money to build his Hollywood palace not only because he had siphoned off union funds, but also because he had pressured Joe Schenck to lend him $100,000. Bioff's dream home, named Rancho Laurie (in honor of his wife), sat on eighty acres of fertile land in Woodland Hills. His neighbors were the top movie stars of the 1930s and early 1940s. Knowing that paying cash for the property would have alerted the IRS to his shakedown rackets, he had asked Schenck for a Fox company check in the amount of $100,000. Schenk agreed. The payment was listed as a commission for the sale of film stock.

Bioff had spared no expense on his home: the edifice was like a medieval castle with gun turrets and armaments. The bathrooms and the kitchen contained every imaginable amenity. The living room and bedrooms could not have been more luxurious. Though he did not read books, Bioff had an elegant wood-paneled library built for himself that was stocked with rare, leatherbound first editions. The library was his sanctuary; he would park himself in a large leather club chair, puff on a cigar, and listen to music. At night, he and his wife would retire to their enormous bedroom decorated with Louis XV antiques and rare Chinese porcelains. About Chinese porcelains, Bioff would pontificate to guests at mind-numbing length, presenting himself as a rarefied art connoisseur. Their backyard contained an enormous pool where Bioff, taking in the sun, floated on an inflatable raft while sucking on his cigar. It was indeed a palace fit for the man who considered himself the king of Hollywood, albeit a king who owed his existence to the Outfit. For Bioff, the street kid from the slums of Chicago, it was all a heady dream come true. Though he thought of himself as the royal boss of Hollywood, the studio bosses all considered him a thug, and his manners, gruffness, and diction were indeed those of a street thug, the kid of the streets who learned to survive through crime.

As more and more money poured into the Outfit's coffers, Nitti grew increasingly confident that his choice of Bioff was the right one. He bragged about his perspicacity to top Outfit members. He said that he made the perfect choice for extorting the studio bosses. And indeed, he had. The stout Bioff, dressed in a conservative three-piece suit that was as tight as a sausage skin and clenching a cigar between his grinding teeth, would appear regularly in the offices of studio bosses. Waving away the smoke from his cigar, he would sometimes talk about union activities; other times, he would indicate that next year's studio contributions to various union funds would have to be increased to meet the financial needs of its members. When he encountered recalcitrance, he would boldly and belligerently threaten to call strikes. Such threats worked on studio bosses like a diagnosis of a terminal disease.

Most often he merely had to ask for what he wanted. To emphasize that he was serious, he would open his suit jacket to reveal a revolver in a shoulder holster. So impressed was Bioff by his success that he would brag to Browne and Rosselli that he was the most powerful man in the movie business.

Nitti instructed Bioff to increase his take from studios by going after the theaters that owned the studios. Bioff agreed that the take from theaters could be enormous. If theaters refused to pay what was demanded, Bioff could close an entire chain with strikes. Without theaters to screen its movies, the studios would have to shut down production. Tim Adler writes: "IATSE members ran nearly every movie theater in the country. Nitti added that, contrary to popular belief, New York–based theater chains controlled movie production—not the other way around. MGM, for example, was a subsidiary of the Loew's theater chain."[1]

In addition to demanding payoffs from theater owners for labor peace, Bioff came up with a new threat. To wit: he demanded that each theater employ two projectionists, not one, as was the case across the country. The theater owners refused. Soon there were stink bombs in the aisles of their theaters. Hundreds of rats ran rampant through orchestra, loge, and balcony sections. Women and children screamed. Ticket holders fled, demanding their money back. Theaters shut down as if felled by a pandemic. If the theaters remained closed, there would be no outlets for movies. Theaters and studios would lose millions of dollars. It did not take long for the owners to accede to Bioff's demands: two regular salaries for projectionists were ultimately cheaper than losing millions of dollars in ticket sales and suffering severe cost overruns for productions.

Bioff's racket was a boon to the Outfit. Nitti could not have been more pleased. So pleased, in fact, that his greed overwhelmed him, and Nitti demanded Bioff turn over 70 percent of his take to the Outfit, rather than the 50 percent originally stipulated. Bioff swallowed his own greed as if it were a bad case of acid reflux and squelched his anger about the inequitable split. He decided he would mitigate his losses by not paying taxes. He was setting himself up for an investigation by the IRS and the Department of Justice, which was provided further impetus by the untaxed $100,000 check that Joe Schenck had given him to build Rancho Laurie. Government investigators were sharpening the hooks they would need to reel in the biggest extortion shark in Tinseltown.

Nitti, whose greed was now a raging fire, demanded that Bioff increase the membership of IATSE. Nitti wanted it to be the most influential union in the movie industry, one that would produce many millions of dollars for the mob. Following orders, Bioff and Browne increased membership from two hundred to twelve thousand in just three years. Their tactics were less-than-gentlemanly persuasion. Those who had refused to join the union were threatened with death. Those who merely expressed their reservations about joining the union suffered broken jaws, arms, and legs. Brass knuckles, blackjacks, and baseball bats were used to change minds. Though the members were promised annual salary increases, what they got were annual increases in their dues. Salaries, however, incrementally increased but by such small amounts that members regularly complained to one another. They would never voice their complaints to union officials.

Though all the bosses of the major studios had fallen in line with Bioff's demands, the boss of a minor studio refused to go along. He was Harry Cohn, head of Columbia Pictures. He was a friend of many mobsters and had taken a $500,000 loan from Longy Zwillman, mob boss of New Jersey. Zwillman also owned a piece of Jean Harlow's contract. Harlow had been a mistress of Zwillman, and he had advanced her career with the loan to Cohn. Johnny Rosselli, the Outfit's man in Hollywood, had partnered with Cohn for several business deals.

Cohn figured that his relationship with the mob excused him from being targeted for extortion; Bioff, however, didn't see it that way. Instead, he told Cohn that because Columbia was a small studio, he only had to pay $25,000. Cohn refused, angrily telling Bioff he wouldn't pay him a dime. Bioff, furious at Cohn, said he would return and make sure that Cohn paid what was demanded of him—or else. As soon as Bioff left Cohn's office, Cohn phoned Rosselli, who told him not to worry and not to pay.

On November 8, 1937, Bioff called for a strike, which shut down the Columbia studio. Cohn called his pal Rosselli to tell him what Bioff had done. Rosselli was furious and confronted Bioff at his IATSE office. He told Bioff he was out of line; he had no right to go after a friend of the mob. Rosselli demanded the strike be called off immediately. Bioff silently stared at Rosselli with what he must have thought was his most intimidating look. He then placed a revolver on his desk and coolly told Rosselli he would not call off the strike. He said that Nitti would not approve of the loss of $25,000. Rosselli told Bioff to call Circella, which he did. With a blank look on his face, he listened to what Circella told him then hung up the phone. Bioff's expression underwent a radical transformation. He now looked like a lugubrious child whose cookies had been taken away.

The strike was called off. However, to make sure that Bioff would not attempt another shakedown of Cohn, he was paid a late-night visit by Rosselli and Jack Dragna. They told him to accompany them on a visit to Cohn's home. At that meeting, Bioff was told to apologize to Cohn and reiterate that the strike had been a mistake. There would be no further problems from the IATSE. In response to Bioff's reiterated apology and offer of a handshake, Cohn simply grunted, turned his back to Bioff, and walked out the room. Had Bioff been a dog, his tail would have been quivering against his stomach.

The failed Columbia strike, which had been a humiliation for Bioff, was now the impetus for a state investigation, which intensified from simmering to boiling. State investigators were intent on uncovering the racketeering activities by the IATSE. Not one to wait and be served with a summons, Bioff made a generous donation to the candidacy of the head of the investigation. The temperature of the investigation rapidly cooled to lukewarm.

Bioff soon regained his nasty aggressiveness and aimed his belligerence at all the studio bosses, getting them to agree that only his union would be recognized as the legitimate representative of all stagehands. Independent stagehands, therefore, had no choice but to join his union or face unemployment. To demonstrate to unaffiliated stagehands that Bioff wanted only the best for them, he offered them a 10 percent increase over their current salaries if they joined the IATSE. Of course, Bioff would then get a larger amount from the dues they paid his union. In addition, he took 2 percent of their salaries for a union strike fund. Of the $1.5 million that Bioff collected, he secretly kept a few hundred thousand dollars for himself and sent the balance to his overseers in the Outfit. Bioff next told the company that supplied film stock to the studios that it would have to pay him a 7 percent commission on all of its sales. The company begrudgingly agreed.

After the Columbia strike debacle, Bioff was determined not to be the target of negative press reports. Positive publicity would offset his reputation as a ruthless shakedown artist. With the help of Rosselli, he enjoyed many puff pieces in the Hollywood trade papers and in local newspapers. Rosselli was able to generate such positive press because he controlled the insurance coverage for various newspapers. He made sure that employee claims were either disallowed or diminished and that premiums remained modest. As a result of Rosselli's influence, Bioff was portrayed in the press as a true friend of working people, always negotiating deals to improve their lives.

Nevertheless, disaffected members of the IATSE continued to leak information to state investigators about the union's illegal activities. It was later alleged that one or two studio heads also leaked information. In addition to state investigators, the leakers contacted out-of-state reporters and columnists. One such columnist was Westbrook Pegler, who was pleased to receive dirt about Bioff and print stories that criminals were extorting studio bosses. Pegler compared all unions to Nazi institutions. He asserted that they were all corrupt. And when he was fed information about specific acts of corruption, the information was ravenously swallowed and spit out in his column. Pegler loved demeaning Bioff and shattering his phony reputation as a friend to working people. Pegler disliked Hollywood and disliked its Jewish studio bosses even more. His venomous columns were syndicated to newspapers around the country and read by six million people. He exposed Bioff's past as a pimp and whoremonger who had avoided serving his full jail sentence. For his efforts exposing Bioff, Pegler was awarded a Pulitzer Prize in 1941. Later in that decade, President Truman referred to Pegler as a guttersnipe. But it was not until 1965 that Pegler's animadversions became so offensive that no publisher was willing to publish his columns. Pegler had written: "Some white patriot of the Southern tier will spatter [Robert Kennedy's] spoonful of brains in public premises before the snow flies."[2] Three years after that column appeared, Robert Kennedy was shot and killed by an angry Palestinian named Sirhan Sirhan, not some angry white patriot.

Pegler's columns and the leaks revived the state government's investigation of Bioff. As if that was not enough to unnerve Bioff, an army of treasury agents began looking into his financial dealings. They soon uncovered information about secret payments to the union, untaxed payoffs, and money laundering.

In 1939, IRS agent Elmer Irey began investigating the possibility that Bioff had either paid insufficient taxes or had not paid taxes at all. Bioff thought it a good idea to get out of town. He and his wife departed on a cruise to Rio de Janeiro, which was paid for by studio boss Joe Schenck. "Flowers filled Bioff's stateroom on the S.S. Normandie. All the studio heads came to see him off, presumably hoping the boat would sink somewhere off Guyana."[3] Following their cruise, the Bioffs toured Europe, staying at the fanciest hotels in Paris, London, Rome, and other capitals. Upon their return to Los Angeles, Bioff was met with a surprise: the IRS indicted him for tax evasion. He was charged with avoiding taxes on $85,000 dollars of income for 1936 and 1937. As an additional slap to his ego and standing in the Hollywood community, Bioff was extradited to Chicago to serve the remainder of his 1922 pimping/pandering conviction. It had not come as a surprise, for Bioff's pimping conviction had been reported in news stories and Pegler's columns. Bioff served five and half months in Bridewell Prison and then, seemingly unchanged, he returned to Los Angeles.

The IRS had not yet pursued a prison sentence for Bioff, because it did not want him to serve time for tax evasion while serving time for his pimping conviction. The IRS went after Fox chairman Joe Schenck, intending to wrap Bioff into another indictment. The IRS did not believe that the $100,000 check that Schenck had given Bioff toward the purchase of Rancho Laurie was a loan. They rightly believed it was an effort to launder money. In June 1940, the IRS indicted Schenck for perjury and tax evasion. After a lengthy trial, Schenck was found guilty and sentenced to three years in prison. Schenck was also threatened with deportation at the end of his sentence. When questioned about the check he had written to Bioff, Schenck said it was a loan. Later on, he made the mistake of testifying to that under oath. When the government was able to prove that Schenck paid Bioff the money as a means to avoid taxes, he was indicted on several counts of tax evasion. Schenck was not the kind of guy who could handle a prison term with the ease of a professional criminal, who regarded prison as the risk one took for committing crimes. Schenck was eager to find a way out. He wanted to make a deal, and the IRS agreed to negotiate a reduced sentence if Schenck would testify against Bioff, Browne, and Circella. Schenck agreed to do so and subsequently revealed the extent of the shakedown racket engineered and carried out by Bioff, Browne, Rosselli, and Circella. He testified to a grand jury, providing a wealth of information about the scam to extort the studios. The grand jury eventually found Schenck guilty of tax evasion, and he was sentenced to five years at a federal prison, but Joe Schenck wasn't just anybody. He wasn't going to serve a long prison term. The government agreed with prosecutors to cut Schenck's sentence in half. But he, in fact, only served just under a year, having been granted a pardon by President Truman. Rumors swirled that Schenck had arranged for $500,000 to be sent to the Democratic Party. Following his release, Schenck went back to running his studios as though nothing had happened.

Based on Schenck's testimony, the federal grand jury issued subpoenas for all the major studio heads. There were still many pieces of evidence that prosecutors needed to get convictions. They leaned on Harry Warner to provide evidence about the extent of Bioff's extortion scams and to tell what he knew about the involvement of the New York and Chicago mobs. Warner did not let down the prosecutors: he provided vital information that was absent from Schenck's testimony. His evidence was enough to put numerous mobsters in prison. On May 23, 1941, Browne, Bioff, Paul Ricca, Frank Nitti, Nick Circella, Charlie Gioe, and Phil D'Andrea were indicted for extortion and tax evasion.

The Outfit's legal eagle, Sidney Korshak, paid a visit to Bioff. His message from the mob was direct: fall on your sword, do your time, and the Outfit will pay your legal expenses. Bioff and Browne rebuffed Korshak. They had no intention of doing jail time. Bioff believed that because he was not a member of the Outfit, never subscribed to omertà, and never felt fairly treated by Nitti and others, he was entitled to make a deal. He figured that in exchange for leniency, he could testify against the top leadership of the Outfit about its role in the massive Hollywood extortion scandal. He knew the potential value of his testimony could put away Nitti and Rosselli, among other mob bosses. However, he would postpone offering his testimony until after a trial. He figured he might win and reiterated that he was innocent of all charges.

The Outfit was furious that the two brazen extortionists declared their innocence. Such a declaration would lead to damaging testimony at their trial that would probably make the Outfit complicit if not worse in the crimes of Bioff and Browne. Their innocent pleas, however, fell on deaf ears. The jury found both men guilty. Bioff was sentenced to ten years, Browne to eight years. And Nick Circella, following mob orders, pled guilty and was sentenced to eight years. Once in prison, Circella had second thoughts about his sentence; the more he obsessed about it, the angrier he grew. He contacted prosecutors and said he was willing to give evidence that would send mob bosses to prison in exchange for a reduced sentence. Word of his decision got back to the Outfit. Circella had to be strongly warned to keep his mouth shut. Nitti called upon the services of Marshall Caifano, one of the most vicious and sadistic killers on the Outfit's payroll; he was assigned to send a message to Circella via his beautiful mistress, Estelle Carey. On February 3, 1943, Caifano knocked on Carey's apartment door. She opened it to the last chapter of her life.

[Her] death was slow, painful, and methodical. She resisted, but was no match for her assailant. Her beautiful face was slashed with a knife. She was stabbed with an ice pick. She was beaten with a blackjack, a broken whiskey bottle, and an electric iron. The violence took place in both the kitchen and the living room, the walls of both locations were smeared with her hair, dyed red in her latest attempt at a disguise, and her blood.

*Finally the violence over, she was tied to a chair. Then, a
flammable liquid was poured over her body and set on fire.
Death, when it came, was caused by burning.*[4]

Circella, horrified after hearing the details of Carey's torture
and death, said he was finished cooperating. To discourage Browne
from cooperating, his wife received numerous threatening phone
calls, which she reported to prosecutors who moved her and her
family out of the city and secreted them in a hotel. Browne was
sufficiently intimidated, so he revealed no information that would
lead to any more indictments. Bioff, however, was outraged by what
happened to Carey. The Outfit had, as far as he knew, never murdered the wife of one of their own, and certainly never indulged in
such torture. It was one thing to do that to a man, but to do it to
a woman, Bioff said, was repugnant. He called US Attorney Boris
Kostelanetz from a jailhouse phone, opening the conversation by
identifying himself then announcing that he was willing to talk.
He said, "We sit around in jail for those bastards, and they go killing our families. To hell with them!" Prosecutor Boris Kostelanetz
asked Bioff if he was now willing to reveal all that he knew about
the extortion of the Hollywood studios. Bioff responded, "What-
cha wanna know, Boris?"[5]

Bioff not only laid out the entire scheme for Kostelanetz—
times, dates, places, names, and amounts extorted—he also negotiated a good deal for himself. In exchange for his testimony, the
government agreed to let Bioff keep the money he had stolen over
the past decade and walk away from any charges that could have
been brought against him based on his revelations.

After three weeks, Bioff finished giving his testimony to the
grand jury, and indictments were handed down for Frank "the
Enforcer" Nitti, Louis "Little New York" Campagna, Paul "the
Waiter" Ricca, Phil D'Andrea, Francis Maritote, Charles "Cherry
Nose" Gioe, Ralph Pierce, Louis Kaufman, and "Handsome

Johnny" Rosselli. The trial received enormous publicity, but to the disappointment of reporters, none of the outfit members took the stand in his own defense. It didn't matter, for the case against them was overwhelming. On December 30, 1943, the jury foreman handed the clerk the verdicts. The judge read that each of the defendants was found guilty. The defendants each received a ten-year sentence in a federal prison and were fined $10,000. In addition, they would be liable for back taxes. The *Chicago Herald American* wrote that the outcome of the trial would mean the total demolition of the Chicago syndicate. (The paper's optimism would be short-lived, for like a mythical monster, the Outfit—once its head had been chopped off—grew another one.)

The defendants would neither forget nor forgive Bioff. Giving his damning testimony, Bioff had been compellingly vivid in his revelations. The defendants had stared at him with murderous rage in their eyes. Bioff had spared no one, including himself. "I am just a low, uncouth person. I'm a low type sort of man. People of my caliber don't do nice things."[6]

Frank Nitti became the sacrificial lamb to Bioff's betrayal of the Oufit; his cohorts blamed him for recruiting and trusting Bioff. Nitti knew that he might be killed and didn't want to spend years in prison. In the mob, apologies for major screwups do not win you a reprieve. If Nitti didn't want to be killed, he had to take a fall, to relieve his cohorts of being proven guilty. He couldn't do it. Instead, he began drinking day and night. After several drunken days, he grabbed a .32 revolver and walked along the railroad tracks of the Illinois Central Railroad on Chicago's South Side. He drunkenly stumbled and wavered, then put the gun to his head and pulled the trigger. The bullet missed his head but left a hole in his hat. He fired again and again missed his head. He fired a third time, this time not missing. With a bullet lodged in his brain, he collapsed alongside the tracks. Ricca would take over as head of the Outfit.

Those who were serving time based upon Bioff's testimony were determined that their servitude would be cut short. The mob had many tentacles for reaching the right people. One of them was Tom Pendergast, the corrupt political boss of Kansas City and the man who had promoted Harry Truman into the White House. Pendergast had worked with Kansas City mob attorney Paul Dillon, who—at Pendergast's urging—had managed Truman's senatorial campaign. Dillon also managed Truman's presidential campaign in St. Louis. Truman would always remain grateful to Dillon, who never needed an invitation to visit the White House. He would simply announce, "I'm Paul Dillon to see my friend the president." The Outfit was well aware of Dillon's role in springing a number of gangsters from prison in Missouri. It was even reported that Dillon had a price list for the release of each gangster. As a go-between for the Outfit and Dillon, there was no one better than Edward "Putty Nose" Brady. Dillon had prepared a price list for the release of "Little New York" Campagna, Phil D'Andrea, and Charles "Cherry Nose" Gioe. He handed it to Brady, who was instructed to deliver it to the threesome. Another helpful lawyer was Maury Hughes of Dallas, who was a friend of Attorney General Tom Clark, who chose the members of the parole board who would determine the fate of the imprisoned members of the Outfit.

On August 6, 1947, Dillon made an application for the parole of Ricca, Gioe, Campagna, and D'Andrea. The application was strongly opposed by prosecutor Boris Kostelanetz and by the federal judge who had imposed the mobsters' sentences. Kostelanetz had written to Clark that parole for such convicted criminals was unwarranted and defied the law and the judiciary. But on August 13, 1947, exactly one week after the application for parole had been placed, Ricca, Gioe, Campagna, and D'Andrea were released: parole had been granted. The parole board, comprising three men, had unanimously agreed that parole was appropriate in the case of the convicts. Their decision, reached without an examination of the convicts' criminal records, was done so quickly and secretly that the parole office in Chicago was not able to participate in the decision; in addition, its analysis of the case had not been requested by the board, which was a breach of protocol.

The public, including formerly abused union members and extorted studio bosses in Hollywood, were outraged over the parole, claiming that there had been a payoff. Fred E. Busbey, Republican congressman from Illinois, having received numerous letters and telegrams, wanted to know if it were true that the board members had received a payoff of $500,000. The board members refused to either deny or confirm the rumored payoff. To Busbey, that was comparable to criminals invoking the Fifth Amendment to avoid incriminating themselves. Having raised the issue, Busbey served to implant the likelihood of a bribe as a fait accompli in the public's mind.

The House Expenditures Committee recommended that the four parolees be trucked back to prison posthaste and that their paroles be rescinded. The committee noted that the parolees had been given treatment that was impossible to justify. It didn't state that Dillon and Hughes were associated with unseemly characters, but it did note that they were friends of President Truman and Attorney General Clark and that the two attorneys enjoyed privileged access to both men. Nevertheless, the committee was unable to uncover any evidence that a bribe had been paid. As a result, neither of the two lawyers, nor the president, nor the attorney general were to be considered for indictment. Even without evidence, the committee noted that a good Samaritan had spent a large sum of money to hire the two lawyers who represented the parolees. The committee did not speculate on the identity and motive of the good Samaritan, but reporters asked if such a person was connected to the Outfit. They also noted that a large amount of money would not have been spent unless there was certainty of the result.

After being released from an abbreviated prison term, Bioff moved to Phoenix, Arizona, and legally changed his name to William "Willie" Nelson. (Nelson was his wife's maiden name.) Gregarious, likable, and rich, Willie was a natural for community affairs and politics; as a donor to many political campaigns, he hobnobbed with numerous local politicians. In 1952, he developed a close friendship with Senator Barry Goldwater.

Goldwater, a brigadier general in the Air Force Reserve, flew Bioff and his wife to parties in Arizona and Nevada. And Bioff never failed to make significant contributions to Goldwater's political career. He also went into business with the senator's brother, Bobby. When Bioff wanted to gamble at a Vegas casino, Goldwater would fly him there. For a man with a price on his head, hanging out in a city in which the Outfit controlled at least four casinos was a risk that no cautious man would have taken. Bioff often visited his friend and Outfit associate Gus Greenbaum, who had managed the Flamingo and other casinos. Eventually word of Bioff's activities got back to the Outfit bosses, and his days were numbered in single digits. On November 4, 1955, Bioff kissed his wife goodbye, left his home, and walked to his pickup truck parked in the driveway. He climbed into the cab, inserted a key into the ignition, turned on the engine, and blew himself into hundreds of bloody pieces spread over three hundred feet. The thunderous blast blew out a few neighboring windows and soon brought siren-wailing police cars. Glass and metal shards were scattered on the street. The FBI believed that Ricca, one of the few surviving members of the gang against whom Bioff testified, arranged for the truck bomb. In addition, mob informants told the FBI that the infamous Marshall Caifano was suspected of having planted the dynamite.

Barry Goldwater showed up for the funeral and, when asked by reporters about his relationship with Bioff, responded that he had not known Bioff's real identity. Later, as reporters badgered him about his reasons for associating with a former convicted racketeer, Goldwater claimed that his relationship with Bioff/Nelson was an attempt by his staff to obtain inside information about how the mob infiltrates unions and uses their positions to steal money and blackmail corporate America. That answer, whether believed or not, put an end to reporters' questions.

The end of Willie Bioff's career was headline news across the country. The theatrical newspaper, *Variety*, which had covered the IATSE, headlined its November 9, 1955, obituary, "Willie Bioff's Last Shakedown: Hoodlum's Boobytrapped Demise Recalls Blackmail of Studios." The conclusion of the story was a straightforward sentence: "Thus ended the career of a Chicago racketeer who, with George Browne, extorted over $1,000,000 in shakedown money from the Hollywood film studios."[7]

An Associated Press headline in the *New York Times* read, "Blast in Truck Kills Willie Bioff, Once Hollywood Racket Leader."[8] The photo accompanying the story shows a grim, fat-faced Bioff peering angrily through a pair of wire-rimmed glasses. The following day, the *Times* ran a story claiming that the authorities were looking for clues about who killed Bioff. The story's subhead read: "Mafia Operations Are Studied in the Car Bombing Slaying of Former Racketeer." The story concluded by stating that fragments of the bomb were being sent to the FBI laboratory in Washington, DC, for analysis. The final sentence of the story noted that Bioff's body had been blown through the roof of his truck.[9]

Bioff died without leaving a will, and his wife asked to be named executor of his estate. After a lifetime of stealing, Willie's estate was valued at only $60,325 according to the *Times*. It was hard to believe. Following the deaths of numerous mobsters, stories regularly appear that they died leaving small estates. That included Meyer Lansky, who had claimed that his mob was more profitable than US Steel. Mobsters are known for hiding cash in offshore banks, Swiss banks, and even their own small banks on Caribbean islands. In addition, a mob tradition has been to invest secretly in legitimate businesses run by front men who would regularly find legitimate ways of paying their mob owners and their heirs. Ralph Salerno, former New York City organized crime detective, told the author that the hardest thing for the IRS to accomplish was uncovering the hidden wealth of mobsters, either deceased or alive. Invariably the IRS fails to find assets, yet the heirs of mobsters have lived off secreted wealth for generations. Since Bioff's deal with prosecutors included his right to keep his wealth and since he contributed hundreds of thousands of dollars to numerous Arizona politicians, the sum of $60,325 seems to be a chimera.

Bioff was dead, but his role would be carried on by another. Emerging from the shadows of the extortion scandal was Bioff's liaison with the Outfit, "Handsome Johnny" Rosselli. He was charming, ruthless, larcenous, well-spoken, beautifully attired, and always a gangster whose greed was concealed by his natural discretion. Whereas Bioff had been crude and coarse, Rosselli was smooth and diplomatic. He continued to extort the movie studios, but his implied threats came with a serpent's smile, a pat on the back, and a joke—never a gruff Bioffian threat of murder. Of course, everyone knew that as a mobster with the backing of the Outfit, Rosselli didn't have to resort to threats. His requests implied that he expected compliance, and if that was not forthcoming, others could make threats that could, indeed, result in murder. Bioff had drawn the map for Hollywood extortions, and Rosselli used it to guide his own actions.

NOTES

1. Tim Adler, *Hollywood and the Mob* (London: Bloomsbury, 2008), 58.

2. Thomas Frank and David Mulcahey, *Boob Jubilee: The Cultural Politics of the New Economy* (New York: W. W. Norton, 2003), 358.

3. Adler, *Hollywood and the Mob*, 96.

4. Ted Schwarz, *Hollywood Confidential* (Lanham, MD: Taylor, 2007), 230.

5. Lee Server, *Handsome Johnny* (New York: St. Martin's Press, 2018), 200.

6. Schwarz, *Hollywood Confidential*, 232.

7. https://archive.org/details/variety200-1955-11/page/n85/mode/1up ?view=theater (accessed March 4, 2022).

8. Associated Press, *New York Times*, November 5, 1955, 1.

9. United Press, *New York Times*, November 6, 1955, 85.

Joseph P. Kennedy's portrait photo for Columbia Trust Company bank, East Boston, January 1914. UNDERWOOD & UNDERWOOD IN THE JOHN F. KENNEDY PRESIDENTIAL LIBRARY AND MUSEUM, BOSTON

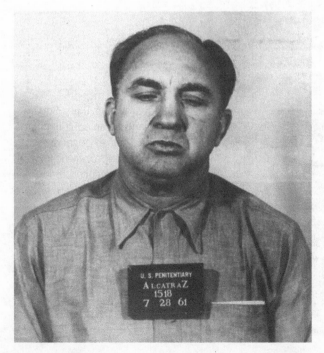

Mickey Cohen's 1961 Alcatraz mugshot.

Jean Harlow plays a close-up scene with a North Carolina senator. Reaching the Capitol today to attend the president's birthday ball, Jean Harlow, siren of the screen, paid her first visit to the United States Capitol. After greeting the senators, the blonde actress pulled Senator Robert Reynolds, Democrat from North Carolina, in for a close-up of her screen lovemaking. LIBRARY OF CONGRESS, PRINTS & PHOTOGRAPHS DIVISION, PHOTOGRAPH BY HARRIS & EWING, [LC-DIG-HEC-22087]

A marquee in Times Square advertising an adult film circa 1956. LIBRARY OF CONGRESS, PRINTS & PHOTOGRAPHS DIVISION, ANTHONY ANGEL COLLECTION, PHOTOGRAPH BY ANGELO RIZZUTO [LC-DIG-PPMSCA-69967]

Johnny Rosselli's mugshot.

Movie industry pledges cooperation with the government. Washington, DC, June 25. At a conference with President Roosevelt today, a group of motion picture company executives led by Will Hays emphasized the desire of the industry to cooperate with the government. In the front row, left to right: Barney Balaban, Paramount; Harry Cohn, Columbia Pictures; Nicholas M. Schenck, Loew's; Will Hays and Leo Spitz, RKO. In the back row, left to right: unidentified man; artists Sidney Kent, 20th Century Fox; N.J. Blumberg, Universal; and Albert Warner, Warner Bros. LIBRARY OF CONGRESS, PRINTS & PHOTOGRAPHS DIVISION, FSA/OWI COLLECTION, [LC-USE6-D-001599]

Shopping for cotton hose in a Hollywood store, Rita Hayworth finds that the shopgirl, too, is wearing hose much the same type that she plans to buy. Miss Hayworth is inspecting a diamond pattern lisle stocking, personally selected for her by Hollywood's famed designer, Howard Greer, to accompany her afternoon emsemble. LIBRARY OF CONGRESS, PRINTS & PHOTO-GRAPHS DIVISION, FSA/OWI COLLECTION, [LC-USE6-D-001599]

Harry Reems in a booking photo by the US Marshal Service in Memphis, Tennessee 1974.

Thelma Todd, 1933.

Thelma Todd in the 1931 film *Corsair*, which starred Chester Morris and Thelma Todd.

Chapter Five

Handsome Johnny Rosselli

Smooth as Silk

MANY GANGSTERS HAVE THEIR CRIMINAL ROOTS IN THEIR CHILD-hoods. Johnny Rosselli, born Fillipo Sacco in 1905 in Esteria, Italy, had his own unique introduction to crime. Following his father's immigration to Boston, little Fillipo was brought to the United States by his mother in 1911. His father unexpectedly died of a heart attack and his mother soon thereafter remarried. Fillipo's stepfather took a strong interest in educating the young boy. He taught his stepson the art of arson. The lessons would have a practical application, for the stepfather next ordered the boy to burn down the family home so that he could collect the insurance money. From there, it was one caper after another.

Rosselli chose his nom de guerre after reading about Cosimo Rosselli, the man who had completed the painting of the Sistine Chapel following the death of Michelangelo. But Handsome Johnny was no artist. Instead, he embarked on a criminal career, becoming a prolific thief, who in a few years graduated to membership in the Outfit. It began with a visit to Chicago in 1927, where he sought a more important role model than his stepfather. It was the infamous Al Capone, and young Rosselli was determined to work for the big man. Capone, sufficiently impressed with the ambitious young thief, invited him back to the Windy

City in 1928. Capone began mentoring Rosselli in the tactics and strategies of organized crime. Eventually the Outfit decided that Rosselli could do them the most good in Los Angeles. He was sent there to keep an eye on the Outfit's investments and to work for the local Mafia family run by Joseph Ardizonne, who would be replaced by Jack Dragna.

In short order, Rosselli became the right-hand man of gambler Tony Cornero, who operated a pair of gambling boats off the California coast. When Cornero took off for Canada to avoid arrest, Rosselli (with the Outfit's approval) took over the expatriate's gambling and brothel operations. The Outfit was pleased with the progress and the money he was sending back to Chicago. Meanwhile, Rosselli was becoming a man-about-town; his soft-spoken charm, handsome countenance, and stylish bespoke suits served him well. He was often seen squiring young, beautiful actresses to the best restaurants and nightclubs.

Though gambling and prostitution were typical mob operations, Rosselli—in an effort to hobnob with a better class of people than compulsive gamblers and johns—decided his future lay in the movie business. It would provide him a significant opportunity to increase his wealth and power. He needed someone to open doors for him, and that person was his longtime friend, Bryan Foy, the oldest son of vaudevillian Eddie Foy. Bryan had appeared with his brothers and father in an act known as "Eddie Foy and the Seven Little Foys." (A movie titled *The Seven Little Foys* was produced in 1955, starring Bob Hope as Eddie Foy and James Cagney as George M. Cohan).

Bryan Foy (aka Brynie Foy) was a prolific producer and director of what are known as B movies. In fact, he was known as the "Keeper of the B's": low budget movies often using unknown actors and having visual and sound effects and scenery that often challenged the credulity of moviegoers. He produced more than two hundred movies and directed more than forty. There were, however, two movies that he directed that were several cuts above his usual B-movie productions: *Guadalcanal Diary* and *PT-109*.

As a producer at Eagle-Lion Films, he was pleased to help Rosselli realize his ambitions. He immediately hired him for $65 a week and gave his pal the title of assistant producer. Since Foy was known for his mastery of low-budget gangster movies, he thought that Rosselli could provide insights and advice about the characteristics of gangsters: how they talked, walked, gestured, and used facial expressions to intimidate others. Whenever Foy was questioned about why he had hired an ex-convict and hoodlum, he would declare that Rosselli was a reformed gangster who had now found his true calling.

According to an Eagle-Lion actor named Paul Picerni, Foy and Rosselli "were funny together, they bounced off each other. Brynie was this fast-talking Irishman, kind of [a] high strung guy, slippery. Johnny was smooth, Italian, very soft spoken, handsome devil. Always smiling, easygoing but tough underneath. Brynie was not a tough guy. Maybe he wanted to be a tough guy."[1]

Lee Server, in his biography of Rosselli, writes:

Johnny the producer began looking for something to produce. Eagle-Lion's shaky circumstances meant only a certain kind of picture would be feasible. No stars, no costly adapted material. Nothing the big studios could do better. They had to depend on original stories. And sensation. A true story was best (and free), something "torn from the headlines" as it was put in the coming attractions.[2]

And the perfect story fell into his lap; on December 30, 1947, twelve convicted murderers and thieves broke out of the Colorado State Prison in Canon City, Colorado. Some were captured; some were killed. The story dominated the news throughout the West for several days. Foy jumped at the chance to turn it into one of his low-budget movies. He hired Crane Wilbur, a former silent screen actor, to write and direct the movie. The movie opened on July 3, 1948.

Canon City (as the movie was titled) was a "model of the new subset of 'authentic' crime movies, merging the dark melodrama (what illuminati in France were calling "film noir") with the trappings of documentary. Inspired by the famed March of Time *newsreels (and anticipating Italian neorealism) the films mixed actual stories and authentic backgrounds with actors and dramatic technique, movies such as* House on 92nd Street, Boomerang, The Naked City.[3]

Having achieved success with *Canon City*, Rosselli started looking for another project. He found it in articles about a series of burglaries and murders of cops committed by William Erwin Walker, who had stolen weapons, machinery, and electronics to build a ray gun that would destroy all known weapons and result in the end of warfare. At trial, he was found guilty and sentenced to death; later he was found insane and committed to a state hospital for the criminally insane.

The movie Rosselli produced was titled *He Walked by Night*. It was done in the same realistic style as *Canon City* and received rave reviews not only in the United States, but also in France and Italy. *Variety* wrote that it was a high-tension crime thriller. Audiences were drawn to theaters showing the movie, which earned $1,250,000 and cost only $360,000. Two successes in a row elevated Rosselli to the position of a successful producer. However, his criminal past suddenly arose like a vampire to suck the blood out of his success. Republicans in Congress had vehemently objected to the parole of Rosselli and his cohorts, who had been arrested for extorting the movie studios. A court revoked Rosselli's parole, and he was sent back to prison, where he was incarcerated for four months while his lawyers fought for his release.

No longer a reformed gangster, Roselli was the same old gangster he had always been, the guy who had extorted the studio bosses. Rosselli hoped that once he had completed his sentence, he would be able to return to Eagle-Lion and produce low-budget hit movies again. However, the company was in bad financial shape. Its two profitable movies had not been enough to turn red ink black. As Eagle-Lion sank deeper into debt, it was apparent to Foy that the company was on life support and about to expire.

Foy contacted Harry Warner, who was quick to retain the Keeper of the B's. But when Foy suggested that Rosselli be included in the deal as his assistant, Warner balked, barking "absolutely not." He had too many negative and costly experiences with Bioff, Browne, and Rosselli. Foy, always a loyal friend to Rosselli, was deeply disappointed. Years later, he said of Rosselli: "We never saw the gangster side of him. He was a great guy. Half the people in this town were his friends. No one who ever had a drink or dinner with Johnny ever picked up a check."[4]

Rosselli thought that Harry Cohn, president of Columbia Pictures, could provide him with gainful employment. He had been close to Cohn, a vulgar mean-spirited boss who regularly abused his employees, treating them as if they were indentured servants. He would curse them, mock their talents, and do all that he could to humiliate those whom he thought had become too and high and mighty. Others who reacted timidly or cowered in response to his abuse were told they were no better than insects and he should squash them. Budd Schulberg, writer of some of Hollywood's most critically acclaimed movies, such as *On the Waterfront* and *The Harder They Fall*, and son of producer B. P. Schulberg, said that Cohn was the most hated man in the movie business. He referred to Cohn as "White Fang." Yet Cohn loved Rosselli and the pair got along like partners in crime. Rosselli even arranged for New Jersey mob boss Longy Zwillman to invest $500,000 in Columbia Pictures. Though Cohn offered to sign a note for a loan, Zwillman insisted on receiving $500,000 worth of Columbia stock, which he might resell to Cohn, if it involved a substantial profit. As much as Cohn liked and admired Rosselli, the man whom Cohn most admired in the world was Benito Mussolini. Having visited Il Duce in 1933, Cohn returned to his office in LA and had it completely redecorated as a picture-perfect facsimile of Mussolini's office. He even kept a large framed photo of Mussolini on the wall adjacent to his desk.

Though the friendship of Cohn and Rosselli continued for years—with the two men enjoying prize fights, gambling casinos, brothels, and bars—the friendship lapsed while Rosselli was in prison for shaking down movie studios. Unlike Bioff, he served his term without turning on his bosses. He was released in 1947 and soon went to see his old friend at Columbia Pictures. Rosselli had done many favors for Cohn, so he expected Cohn to help him.

Cohn, delighted to see his old friend, embraced him and kissed him on one cheek. Rosselli reciprocated the signs of affection then explained to Cohn that he needed a job with a regular paycheck to satisfy the conditions of his parole. Rosselli said he would take anything that Cohn had available. If he didn't soon get gainful employment that came with a regular paycheck, he would forfeit his parole and be sent back to the joint.

Cohn suddenly looked as lugubrious as a frustrated bloodhound. His voice fell to funereal tones, and, he told Rosselli as if revealing an unpleasant secret, the board of directors would not permit him to hire someone with a criminal record. Cohn said that he was saddened to be so handcuffed, but he was constrained in this matter. Rosselli didn't believe Cohn and reminded him that he had protected him from Bioff's efforts to call a strike and extort money from Columbia. Cohn sadly nodded in agreement and offered to help set up Rosselli as an independent theatrical agent. Rosselli refused. He needed a regular job. Cohn sadly shrugged his shoulders and threw up his hands, indicating his helplessness. There was nothing he could do. Rosselli lost his usual cool and heatedly called Cohn an ungrateful son of a bitch and a bastard. He finally told Cohn to go "fuck yourself," then stormed out of the office. It was the end of their friendship.

One door that was not closed was one to which Jack Dragna had the key, and he welcomed Rosselli as the man who could help upgrade Dragna's degraded borgata, which was mockingly known as the Mickey Mouse Mafia. Rosselli would be enlisted to help Dragna take over the operations of Mickey Cohen, who had taken over Bugsy Siegel's operations after Siegel had been assassinated. Some of those operations had once been Dragna's, and he was determined to take control again.

One of the principals in this new war would be Rosselli's friend, Jimmy "the Weasel" Fratianno, who was operating a bookie joint in Santa Monica with Cohen's permission. Fratianno and Cohen had become friends, so it would be easy for Fratianno to spy on Cohen and report back to Dragna. Fratianno agreed not only because he admired Rosselli and wanted to be part of Dragna's Mafia family, but because Dragna offered him an opportunity to move up in the rackets. He later would be installed as cohead of the family, then once he had served his purpose, he would be humiliatingly demoted to soldier.

Cohen foolishly treated Fratianno as if he were a member of his gang. Cohen was known to give gang members and friends gifts, and one day he decided to give Fratianno and his family tickets for Irving Berlin's musical, *Annie Get Your Gun*. Cohen loved Berlin's music and could speak about it at interminable lengths. Fratianno was invited to pick up tickets for the musical at Cohen's haberdashery. Fratianno arrived at the store, knowing that Dragna's gunmen were waiting outside for him to leave. As soon as he and his family departed, the gunmen were to rush inside and kill Cohen and his henchman. Cohen, self-important and verbose, wouldn't stop talking about the merits of Berlin's musical. He sounded like a self-mesmerized autodidact who couldn't shut up. An exasperated and nervous Fratianno finally said he had to leave. Cohen handed over the tickets, and Fratianno and family departed. Before the gunmen could rush in, Cohen, who was an obsessive-compulsive germaphobe, strode into the men's room to wash his hands. He had shaken hands with Fratianno, a contagious act that set off his obsessive-compulsive need for cleanliness. Washing his hands just once was insufficient to quell his anxieties about germs, so he could spend up to a half hour washing and rewashing his hands, often until every available towel had been used. As he stood in front of the sink, repeatedly lathering and rinsing his hands under the hottest water he could tolerate, Dragna's gunmen burst into the store and riddled several of Cohen's men with an arsenal of bullets. Hearing the bursts of gunfire, Cohen quickly left the bathroom and made a rabbity exit out of the back door. He escaped with hot, wet hands and a dry mouth. The hot water continued to run, steaming up the bathroom mirror until a cop arrived and turned off the faucet.

A disappointed and angry Dragna was still determined to eliminate Cohen. One night, when Cohen was out on the town with a glitter of starlets and his hardheaded bodyguards, Dragna had members of his borgata sneak onto the grounds of Cohen's house and place twelve sticks of dynamite under the bedroom. After Cohen returned that night, he retired to his wife's bedroom on the opposite side of the house. Soon, a boom of a blast was heard hundreds of yards away as debris rocketed through the air and crashed onto neighbors' lawns and on the street. The damage to Cohen's house was significant, but it could have been worse if a huge steel safe in Cohen's bedroom hadn't deflected much of the blast, driving it downward into the ground. An aggrieved and stunned Cohen stood in his silk monogrammed pajamas on his front lawn. He could hardly believe what had happened, then yelled at police and firefighters, "the bastard'll never kill me." In his home, a frustrated Dragna growled like a feral animal, biting the knuckle of his right index finger as if he were going to chew it off his hand.

If Dragna couldn't kill Cohen, maybe he could drive him out of business by killing off his gang members. Several had been eliminated during and after the haberdashery shooting. Perhaps he could now get one to betray Cohen and kill him. Why he hadn't used Fratianno, who had already notched a few murders on his resume, to kill Cohen remains a mystery. Instead, Dragna sent Fratianno to convince Frank Niccoli, a member of Cohen's gang, to desert and join the Dragna family. Niccoli was generously paid for being Cohen's bodyguard and a collector of debts, payoffs, and tributes. It was unlikely that he would accept an offer to betray his boss and join the opposition. If Niccoli couldn't be convinced to leave Cohen's employ, then Fratianno was to kill him. Fratianno invited Niccoli to his home, where the two had drinks in the living room. Fratianno broached the subject of joining him as a member of Dragna's family. He would make more money; he would be more than a bodyguard and collector. He could be a loan shark. Niccoli said he would like to think about it, but Fratianno insisted he make up his mind immediately. Niccoli said he would stay with Cohen's gang. Joseph Dippolito and two other men emerged from the kitchen. They grabbed and held Niccoli, while Fratianno tied a rope around Niccoli's neck and strangled him. Once again frustrated and angry, Dragna wondered when Cohen might come gunning for him.

After that fiasco, Fratianno was arrested again. The government had plenty of crimes for which they could indict Fratianno, but that wasn't what scared him. He thought that Dragna had issued a contract on him for operating his own crew without permission and not sharing its take with Dragna. As with so many mobsters facing long prison terms and the possibility of being murdered, Fratianno decided to become an FBI informant. He testified against numerous mobsters and confessed to committing five murders. For his crimes, he was sentenced to five years in prison, placed in isolation, then released after twenty-one months. He immediately went into the Witness Protection Program.

Though Rosselli was up to his neck in crimes and scams, he still found time to live up to his reputation as a ladies' man. As a movie producer and gangster, he generated a frisson of danger and glamour and implicit career possibilities for aspiring starlets. So self-impressed was he by the ease of his seductions that he would test his partners' devotion to him by asking them to marry him. They all agreed, after which he would have nothing to do with them again.

One person with whom he followed up on a marriage proposal was Marajen Stevick. She was no wannabe movie star, but a high-living, fun-loving young woman who enjoyed a risky good time. Because her father was a rich newspaper publisher, she had plenty of his money to spend as frivolously as she wanted. She was a rich version of Truman Capote's creation, Holly Golightly. She was introduced to Rosselli by Billy Wilkerson, publisher of the *Hollywood Reporter* and the originator of the famous Las Vegas casino, the Flamingo. Rosselli had hoped that she would invest in one of his scams, but nothing came of it. All she wanted was a good time that consisted of lots of sex and drinking. And even without her money, Rosselli was eager to provide Stevick with what she needed. They convinced themselves that they should solidify their relationship by getting married. So one day Marajen rented a small plane, and the two lovers flew to Mexico. Once there, they wasted no time in getting hitched. Having enjoyed days of lustful fun, the couple decided to return to LA, but not before also deciding to annul their impulsive marriage. The two went their separate ways with neither animosity nor disappointment. Unfortunately for Stevick, her father was appalled by her wild behavior and arranged for his daughter to receive electro-shock treatments. She never heard from Rosselli.

Another woman to whom Rosselli proposed marriage was the beautiful blonde actress, June Lang. The two started dating, quickly fell in love, and decided to marry. They became a hot item for gossip columnists: the beautiful blonde and the tough-guy gangster. At nightclubs, restaurants, racetracks, and boxing matches, the two were photographed either arm in arm or kissing.

Prior to dating Rosselli, Lang's career had been steadily ascending, helped by her agent husband, Victor Orsatti. She appeared in a number of popular movies and proved so adaptable that she could play a variety of parts from low comedy to mawkish melodramas. She appeared with such stars as Laurel and Hardy, Shirley Temple, Fredric March, Lionel Barrymore, Cesar Romero, Betty Grable, Dinah Shore, and George Sanders. Many of those stars had been her husband's clients. The marriage of Orsatti and Lang lasted from May 29, 1937, to August 5, 1937, though the *Los Angeles Times* had headlined their marriage ceremony as the biggest of the year. What did it say about Hollywood marriages that one that lasted less than three months started off as the biggest wedding of the year?

On April 1, 1939, Lang and Rosselli married, and shortly thereafter her career started a downhill trajectory. Fox did not renew her contract, and she found only middling roles with smaller studios. Those roles soon dried up, and she found even less-promising roles at fly-by-night studios. The lowest ebb of her career came with small uncredited roles in minor movies.

Her marriage had hurt her career. The studio bosses, who wanted no part of Rosselli, now wanted no part of his wife. Following their honeymoon in Arizona and Las Vegas, the couple returned to LA. There, they grew increasingly distant, often arguing and then not talking to each other for days. (Rosselli figured he would soon be going alone to Las Vegas, where he would be an emissary and fixer for the Chicago Outfit.) Yet Lang wanted to start a family and buy a house in the valley with a big yard where their kids could play, but Rosselli was all about the hustle. He was frequently away from their luxury apartment in Beverly Hills. He often traveled to Chicago, where he met with his Outfit handlers. Though he was hustling as much as he could to earn big scores, few of his schemes bore fruit. Her career on the rocks, his schemes nothing but pipe dreams, the two became even more antagonistic toward one another. In January 1942, Lang filed for divorce, which was granted on the grounds of extreme cruelty, and was finalized on March 1, 1943.

Another beautiful blonde on Rosselli's menu was the seductive and ambitious Jeanne Carmen. Though they never married, Carmen and Rosselli not only had a torrid affair, they put together a golf hustle that fleeced rich suckers out of thousands of dollars. Their marks had refused to believe that a gorgeous pinup model could also be a superb golfer.

Carmen had run away from her home in Paragould, Arkansas, after deciding that she did not want to spend her life picking cotton. The year was 1943, and the thirteen-year-old wanted to find adventure. She arrived in New York and, due to her voluptuous figure and beautiful face, got a job as a burlesque stripper and straight woman to comedian Bert Lahr. Her sexy dance routines won loud plaudits from young soldiers waiting to be shipped overseas. Burlesque led to jobs posing seminude in girlie magazines. Her platinum blonde hair outlining a provocatively come-hither look and her voluptuous figure helped sell copies of *Titter*, *Beauty*, and *Wink* magazines. When not posing for what was then known as cheesecake photos, Carmen got a job modeling a variety of outfits at Jack Redmond's golf range. Redmond thought it a good idea for Carmen to learn the basics of golf, so one day he handed her a club and told her to hit the ball he had placed at her feet. With one quick swing, she accurately smacked the ball and sent it flying at a target painted on a canvas backdrop. He whistled in astonishment and asked her if she had ever played before. She had not. He asked her to repeat the shot, and she easily did so. That was it. Redmond realized he had an act that could go on the road. Up and down the East Coast, the two put on exhibitions of trick golf shots, including one in which Redmond lay on his back, a golf ball perched on a tee between his teeth. Carmen would hit the ball two hundred feet without touching Redmond's clenched teeth and pursed lips. After the first few times, Redmond no longer oozed a sigh of relief. The couple was making a $1,000 a day, and when not performing, they were driving hundreds of miles to fairs, carnivals, and theaters, where Carmen was booked to perform her tricks.

Prior to beginning her career as a trick-shot golfer, Carmen had married Sandy Scott, who accompanied the impresario and his performer on their tours. It proved less than an ideal arrangement, for Redmond and Scott competed for Carmen's affections. They each told her that they loved her, and Carmen enjoyed coquettishly fanning the flames of their erotic intentions. The two men often argued with one another, and sometimes their arguments were explosive. One night while driving south, Redmond and Scott got into such a ferocious argument that Redmond pulled his car to the side of the road and demanded that the couple get out. He threw their luggage onto the road and drove off. After sitting on their suitcases for more than an hour, a car approached and stopped in front of them. It was Rosselli, dressed in a bespoke white suit. He asked Carmen if she needed a ride. When Scott started to answer, Rosselli said that he wasn't talking to him. At Rosselli's invitation, the couple piled into his car and continued heading south. Soon, Scott demanded they stop so he could relieve himself at a gas station. During Scott's absence, Rosselli asked Carmen if she wanted to continue the trip without her husband. Carmen said "sure," and the two took off. They drove to Las Vegas and registered at Moe Dalitz's Desert Inn. The DI had a magnificent eighteen-hole PGA golf course. Day after day, the statuesque blonde in high heels and short, low-cut, tight-fitting dresses would be introduced to high rollers away from the gambling tables. Rosselli would challenge them to golf matches with Carmen. Taking one look at her, most of her victims regarded her as a showgirl trying to prove herself. They accepted the challenge, bet large sums, and lost. When someone refused to pay, Rosselli would call upon a couple mob associates, who would threaten the recalcitrant losers, sometimes by forcing them onto the roof a hotel then hanging them over the side. No one escaped without paying.

> *The two worked the scam for about a year, until one day when Carmen slipped. She'd had a drink while waiting for Rosselli to set up the mark, and, a bit tipsy, started playing too well too soon. The man knew he had been set up. "He was carrying on, complaining," Carmen says, "and Johnny said, 'Look, pay up, you lost the bet. Pay up and let's call it a day.' But this guy refused." Rosselli told Carmen to go to her room; he'd call her later. "He then roughs this guy up. He calls me and tells me to get to the roof of the Sands Hotel. I get up there and open the door to see Johnny toss this guy over the side. Oh, my God. I'm in shock. I'm crying. So Johnny says, 'Come over here and look.' I didn't notice that the guy had a rope tied around his ankle. I go over and see this guy dangling down there. . . . He pulls the guy up and . . . Johnny's got his money and cuts the guy loose."⁵*

The Carmen/Rosselli relationship and scam had an unexpected conclusion. Frank Sinatra was performing at the Sands, and Carmen asked to meet the singer. Rosselli introduced the two. Sinatra stood in front of Carmen, who was wearing a short, tight-fitting dress, and his eyes caressingly moved over her body. His eyes then flashed with desire, and he placed one hand on her shoulder. He told her she was wasting her time as a golf hustler and should accompany him back to Los Angeles. She agreed and would begin an affair that lasted off and on for several years.

In Hollywood, Sinatra launched Carmen on a movie career that included appearances in numerous forgettable B movies and westerns. She even had a small role in a Three Stooges movie. However, she developed a cult following that culminated in a TV biography in 1998, titled *Jeanne Carmen: Queen of the B Movies*, which aired on the *E! True Hollywood Story* series. The show stated that Carmen maintained a

dangerously close friendship with Marilyn Monroe and the Kennedys and that after the death of Monroe, Carmen was told to leave town by Johnny Rosselli who was working for Chicago mob boss Sam Giancana. Believing her life was in danger, she fled to Scottsdale, Arizona, where she lived incognito for more than a decade. Carmen abandoned her platinum-blonde locks, had three children, and lived a quiet life, never mentioning her prior life in Hollywood.[6]

Always on the lookout for profitable scams, Rosselli found another ideal set up at the famous Friars Club in Los Angeles. In 1962, he applied for membership and was sponsored by Sinatra, Dean Martin, and one of the club's founding members, George Jessel. The club would be an ideal sanctuary for Rosselli, especially since no other clubs in LA would accept a notorious mobster as a member. The club would also serve as Rosselli's office: he could make and receive phone calls, send notes to colleagues, and hold meetings in one of the club's private rooms.

One of Roselli's close friends at the club was millionaire entrepreneur Maurice Friedman, whom Rosselli had met in Vegas, where Friedman had been president of the New Frontier Hotel and Casino. He was a short, aggressive man who always had feelers out for new opportunities; whether the deals were illegal or legal made no difference to him. He was only interested in a good score. As a compulsive card player, he hated losing and was always on the lookout for an opponent he could fleece. At the club, he found a perfect opponent in shoe magnate Harry Karl, husband of Debbie Reynolds. The two men engaged in card games that lasted hours, each man getting more belligerent as the time passed. Large sums were won and lost. Neither man graciously accepted a loss. They were like two boxers who continued throwing punches after the bell sounded the end of a round.

One day, the back-and-forth pattern became one-sided. For no reason that Karl could discern, Friedman started to enjoy an unprecedent winning streak, raking in tens of thousands of dollars. But Karl would not quit. Like many compulsive gamblers, he believed that one more deal of the cards would change his luck. Yet he continued to lose hand after hand. Rosselli smelled a scam and cornered Friedman, demanding to know how Friedman was pulling off so many wins. Rosselli wanted to be cut in. Friedman explained that he had hired a man named George Seach, who was a convicted burglar and electronics expert. In the crawl space above the card room, Seach had set up a peephole so that each player's cards could be seen. The information was fed electronically to Friedman and one of his partners, each of whom wore a receiving device concealed under his shirt. Rosselli liked what he heard and cut himself in for 20 percent of the take. And the take was sizeable, for Friedman and his accomplice swindled $400,000 from Phil Silvers, Zeppo Marx, and Tony Martin.

Such high-flying scams, if carried on long enough, often crash. The FBI, working with informants, learned of the scam, and on July 20, 1967, six agents raided the club. As the Christmas holiday season was about to start, Rosselli and five others who had been arrested were indicted in the Friars cheating scandal. As if that wasn't bad enough, Rosselli was also being indicted as an illegal alien. That case could not only land him in prison, but upon his release, he could be deported to Italy. Following a twenty-two-week investigation, a twenty-five-count indictment was brought against six men, including Maurice Friedman and Rosselli. The indictment noted that from the summer of 1962 to the summer of 1966, Rosselli, Friedman, and others rigged high-stakes gin rummy games at the Friars Club that generated $400,000 of income for defendants. Six defendants were ultimately convicted of conspiracy to violate interstate travel and use of interstate facilities in aid of racketeering and interstate transportation of fraudulently taken securities. As a result, the Friars Club formed an ethics committee and removed some members, while others were asked to resign, which they did. Rosselli was sentenced to five years in prison and fined $50,000. He served three years and was then paroled. The government decided not to pursue an immigration case against Rosselli, perhaps because he had found a way to ingratiate himself with the Department of Justice and the CIA.

He was recruited to participate in CIA plots, along with Mafia bosses Sam Giancana and Santo Trafficante, to assassinate Fidel Castro. The plots were known as Operation Mongoose. It is extraordinary that plots hatched by experienced Mafia killers all failed to succeed. Any number of James Bond–like plans succeed in the world of fiction, but in real life the mob failed to poison Castro, and its efforts to induce the Cuban dictator to light up an explosive cigar was more Marx brothers than James Bond. Of course, the most notorious failure was the Bay of Pigs attack, in which a brigade of armed recruits, known as Brigada Asalto 2506, landed in the Bay of Pigs to bring down the Castro government. During the attack, the brigade was under a heavy counterattack and pleaded for air and naval support, which the Kennedy admin-istration refused to provide. According to the CIA:

Without direct air support—no artillery and no weapons—and completely outnumbered by Castro's forces, members of the Brigade either surrendered or returned to the turquoise water from which they had come. Two American destroyers attempted to move into the Bay of Pigs to evacuate these members, but gunfire from Cuban forces made that impossible. In the following days, US entities continued to monitor the waters surrounding the bay in search of survivors, with only a handful being rescued. A few members of the Brigade managed to escape and went into hiding, but soon surrendered due to a lack of food and water. When all was said and done, more than seventy-five percent of Brigade 2506 ended up in Cuban prisons.[7]

Eventually members of the US Senate decided to investigate the role of the CIA in its attempts to assassinate Castro. Rosselli was called to testify before the US Senate Select Committee on Intelligence on June 24 and September 22, 1975. Another person called to testify about the failed operations and possibly on the assassination of President Kennedy was Sam Giancana. Shortly before Rosselli was to testify, Giancana was in the basement of his home frying sausages and peppers for a late-night snack. He was scheduled to testify a few days hence, but he was shot seven times in the head and neck with a .22 caliber pistol. Giancana's murder unnerved Rosselli, who fled the West Coast and moved in with his sister in Plantation, Florida.

Even before the murder of Giancana, Rosselli was being considered for a possible mob hit. It began shortly after Rosselli had been subpoenaed to appear before a grand jury investigating mob ownership of the Frontier Hotel and Casino. Upholding Mafia ethics, Rosselli initially refused to answer any questions on constitutional grounds. But the jury gave him immunity, thus obviating his right to remain silent. Now he was faced with a gut-wrenching choice: if he refused to answer questions, he could be sent to prison;

if he agreed to answer, he could face the wrath of the Mafia. If he were to be sent to prison, he figured he would be killed to keep him quiet. In addition, he was suffering emphysema and thought he would not get sufficient care in prison and therefore probably die there. Since he was promised that his testimony would be kept secret, he figured he could convince his bosses in Chicago that he had not said anything that would result in anyone being indicted. His information led federal investigators to Maurice Friedman, the developer of the Frontier, who testified that Anthony Giordano, the Mafia boss of St. Louis, and Anthony Zerilli and Michael Polizzi, Mafia captains in Detroit, held hidden interests in the casino. As a result, all three were indicted, convicted, and sent to prison. They, of course, suspected that Rosselli had made a deal to protect himself, and the price he paid to uphold his end of the deal was to rat out his friends.

Rosselli's bosses were furious that he had even appeared before a grand jury without first consulting them. They assumed that Rosselli had always intended to make a deal to protect himself. Rosselli, nevertheless, continued to see himself as a bon vivant who led a charmed life. He also believed that he was so valuable an asset to the government that it would protect him. He commented to a reporter, "I looked pretty good up there. In fact, they said I looked like a lawyer."[8]

By 1975, Rosselli had been living on borrowed time. On June 24 and September 22 of that year, Rosselli testified before the US Senate Select Committee on Intelligence (SSCIA), led by Idaho Senator Frank Church, about the CIA plan to kill Castro in Operation Mongoose. He also would have to testify about the assassination of President Kennedy. The original Senate Select Committee chaired by Senator Frank Church had recommended to a new Senate Select Committee to investigate the plots to kill Castro as well as the assassination of the president. Rosselli was considered an important witness who could reveal vital information.

On April 23, 1976, Rosselli was subpoenaed to testify about a conspiracy to kill President Kennedy. Although the information that Rosselli revealed was tantalizing, it was incomplete, and the committee decided to recall him. Three months after his original testimony, the committee attempted to do so. However, they learned that Rosselli had been missing since July 28. On August 3, Senator Howard Baker requested that the FBI launch an investigation into Rosselli's disappearance.

The Mafia was no longer hesitant about its need to silence Rosselli. His time had come. The Mafia believed that Rosselli had betrayed them and was about to reveal information that would send several bosses to prison. It was time to kill him.

On July 28, Rosselli met Florida Mafia boss Santo Trafficante for dinner at the Landings Restaurant in Fort Lauderdale. After a friendly dinner, both men toasted one another then bid one another a good evening. Rosselli got into his car and drove to a marina, parked the car, and boarded a cabin cruiser that was operated by one of his mob friends from Chicago. (Later, after the boat returned to the marina, a man was seen leaping from the boat to the dock, striding to Rosselli's car, and driving off. The car was found at Miami International Airport.) A Mafia informer said that Rosselli, while sipping a glass of iced vodka, was grabbed from behind by his Chicago mob pal, who held one hand over Rosselli's mouth and pinched his nose with the other hand. Rosselli was quickly incapacitated, unable to breathe. His emphysema had made asphyxiation an easy death sentence. Rosselli's heart stopped beating, and he collapsed onto the deck. His killers hauled an oil drum from below deck. Holes had been drilled into it so it would fill with water. However, they couldn't fit Rosselli into the drum. After undressing him, they sawed off his arms and legs. His appendages and torso were stuffed into the drum, which was tied with rope and weighed down with an anchor. The killers tossed the drum overboard and watched it sink. The anchor, which had not been tightly tied, broke away from the drum. In addition to not securely tying the anchor, the killers had not punctured Rosselli's gut with numerous holes to let gases escape. Those gases increased in volume until Rosselli's stomach was as tumescent as a balloon about to burst, but instead of bursting, it floated the oil drum to the water's surface. The drum was then carried by the current to a nearby sandbar, where three fishermen came across it and called police.

Rosselli had known too much and had been too eager to talk. He had to be killed. He had foolishly spoken with friends about the Kennedy assassination, stating that he had known who the killer would be and where, when, and how the killing would take place weeks before the assassination. Some dismissed his claims as typical gangster bravado and bullshit. Others thought he told the truth, thereby putting his life in jeopardy.

Was Rosselli privy to information about plans to kill President Kennedy? Was he a participant in the assassination? Bill Bonanno, son of Joseph Bonanno, boss of one of New York's five Mafia families, claimed in his 1999 memoir, *Bound by Honor: A Mafioso's Story*, that he had discussed the assassination of Kennedy with Rosselli, who implicated himself as a hitman in the Kennedy assassination. According to Bonanno, Roselli fired at Kennedy from a storm drain on Elm Street.

In 2010, *Playboy* magazine published an article by Hillel Levin in which two men, Robert "Tosh" Plumlee and James Files, an inmate at the Illinois Department of Corrections, implicated Rosselli in the assassination.

Charles Rappleye and Ed Becker write in their biography of Rosselli:

> But a close examination of the record places Rosselli in the nexus of the tangled web of events leading to Kennedy's assassination. The strongest indication that John Rosselli had a hand in the pre-assassination planning is a report of a direct

contact between Rosselli and Jack Ruby in early October 1963. There were two meetings, both taking place in small motels near Miami, and both observed by the FBI. One of the federal investigators probing Rosselli's murder thirteen years later came across an FBI report of the meetings and relayed its contents, on a confidential basis, to Washington, DC, reporter William Scott Malone. As an accomplished investigator himself, Malone said in an interview he was confident of the integrity of his source, and said the FBI had determined the actual site of the Miami meetings.[9]

Investigative reporter and columnist Jack Newfield reported that three witnesses support mob lawyer Ragano's statement that Carlos Marcello arranged the assassination. An FBI informant in 1976 said Trafficante told him Kennedy was "not going to make it to the election. He was going to be hit." The informant later recanted; in 1978, he was murdered. In 1976, mobster Johnny Rosselli said Sam Giancana told him he plotted the assassination with Trafficante and Marcello; Rosselli was also murdered. The House assassinations committee sought to interview Giancana about the allegations; before Giancana could testify, he was shot dead by unknown assailants. Newfield believes Trafficante and Marcello eventually will be shown to be the missing pieces to the "30-year jigsaw puzzle" about the assassination. So does Robert Blakey, a former member of the organized crime section and the counsel to the House assassinations committee. At the time of the committee's report, Blakey concluded, "The mob did it. It's an historical fact."[10]

NOTES

1. Lee Server, *Handsome Johnny* (New York: St. Martin's, 2018), 235.
2. Server, *Handsome Johnny*, 237.
3. Server, *Handsome Johnny*, 238.

4. www.nytimes.com/1977/02/25/archives/mafia-said-to-have-slain-ros selli-because-of-his-senate-testimony.html (accessed September 15, 2022).

5. www.americanheritage.com/articles/magazine/ah/2005/4/2005_4_58 .shtml (accessed September 13, 2022).

6. *E! True Hollywood Story*, "Jeanne Carmen: Queen of the B-Movies," directed by Bill Pruitt, aired October 4, 1998, on E!

7. www.cia.gov/stories/story/the-bay-of-pigs-invasion/#the-recruits (accessed March 4, 2022).

8. www.nytimes.com/1977/02/25/archives/mafia-said-to-have-slain-ros selli-because-of-his-senate-testimony.html (accessed September 15, 2022).

9. Charles Rappleye and Ed Becker, *All American Mafioso* (New York: Doubleday, 1991), 245.

10. www.washingtonpost.com/archive/opinions/1993/03/14/what-the -mob-knew-about-jfks-murder/9803e911-f52f-4944-88f1-c26863e35867.

CHAPTER SIX

Harry Cohn

White Fang

HARRY COHN CAME FROM A POOR FAMILY, BUT UNLIKE OTHER poor New York Jews in the early 1900s, Cohn's family lived on the Upper East Side of Manhattan and did not speak Yiddish at home. They spoke German.

Cohn began his career as a young song plugger for a company partially owned by Irving Berlin. Young Cohn's job was to visit singers at vaudeville theaters and encourage them to sing his bosses' songs in their acts. Eventually he hit upon a means more convincing than his normal sales pitch: he increased his success by providing short silent films, from two to three minutes in length, to accompany the songs. The moving images were meant to correspond to the lyrics of the songs. It worked, and Cohn had now stumbled upon a new career. Movies would become his métier.

He was finished with song plugging and asked his brother, Jack, to help him get a job with Independent Moving Pictures (IMP). Jack easily convinced his boss that Harry would be a valuable asset to the company. And so began the partnership of the Cohn brothers, a partnership that, over the years, would evolve into competition: the brothers becoming vituperative and combative, each attempting to outdo the other in belligerence. However, in the early days of their partnership, they successfully produced a movie titled

Traffic in Souls that established them as talented innovators. When IMP soon merged with Universal Film Manufacturing Company, Harry saw an opportunity to further advance his ambitions. He became secretary to the company's president Carl Laemmle, a legendary producer of more than four hundred movies, including such classics as *The Hunchback of Notre Dame*, *The Phantom of the Opera*, *Frankenstein*, and *Dracula*. In March 1915, Laemmle opened the largest movie production facility in California, Universal Studios Hollywood, on 230 acres in the San Fernando Valley. Harry Cohn could not have found a better launching pad for his own meteoric career as one of Hollywood's top producers.

He learned every aspect of movie production at Universal then decided to set out on his own. He invited his brother to leave the company, and the two—along with Joe Brandt—formed CBC Film Sales Corporation. But because their productions were of such low quality, CBC was derisively known in the industry as the "Corned Beef and Cabbage Company." Harry, who was never known to have a self-deprecating sense of humor, found such a sobriquet demeaning and insulting. Furthermore, how could the company become a well-respected entity in the movie industry if its name conjured images of a St. Patrick's Day feast? Harry quickly had Joe, a lawyer, file papers to change the company's name to Columbia Pictures.

The quality of Columbia's productions increased. Its movies were still low-budget genre productions that appealed to large audiences, but at least the movies were no longer the subject of caustic jokes and critical ridicule. Each of the partners was dedicated to making the company successful: Harry handled all productions out of his office in California; Jack handled financing in New York, and Joe handled legal work and marketing in New York. The competitive streaks of Jack and Harry, however, grew more pronounced, and often their interactions grew volatile. Each tried to prove he was smarter, more talented, and more resourceful than the other. Each tried to outdo the other, and their competitiveness may have been an impetus for the company's growing success. While Harry and Jack fought like an unhappily married couple headed for divorce, Harry's animosity for Joe boiled as hot as volcanic lava. The two had long nasty fights that ended in threats and accusations. Harry finally decided he had enough; Joe had to go. Harry told him to sell his shares in the company. Joe agreed to sell his share of the company for $500,000, a sum that Harry could not come up with. However, Harry had resources that could provide the money. He had long been friends with Johnny Rosselli, to whom he explained his problem. The handsome young gangster was well acquainted with Abner "Longy" Zwillman, a powerful mob boss known as the Al Capone of New Jersey.

Zwillman gave Cohn the money in exchange for $500,000 worth of Columbia stock. Zwillman's purchase set the stage for other mob deals: "the film industry moguls saw that Harry Cohn had gotten his money without a hassle. It was a sign that members of organized crime, always cash flush in their minds, would be willing to do straight business deals in Hollywood and perhaps even finance individual pictures. It also made Longy an instant man of importance and acceptance among the moguls."[1]

In addition to providing money to Cohn to buy out Brandt, Zwillman gave funds to Cohn to make Jean Harlow into the premier leading lady of Columbia Pictures. Since Zwillman took immense pride in having Harlow as his lover, he wanted her to be the cinema's most celebrated sex symbol. Why should he be enamored of anyone less sexy? As a result, Harlow starred in two movies, *Platinum Blonde* and *Three Wise Girls*. Zwillman cleaned up handsomely from his investments: the two movies were highly profitable box office hits. To coincide with the release of each of the movies, Zwillman organized publicity tours for Harlow and arranged press conferences where studio flacks posed as reporters and asked her prepared questions. To answer those questions with snappy wisecracks, Zwillman paid a couple of screenwriters to make the blonde bombshell sound nearly as witty as Dorothy Parker. Harlow remained ever grateful to her lover and gave him a gold locket that contained strands of her pubic hairs. Though Zwillman regarded Harlow as his trophy star, he also spoke degradingly of her as a sexual opportunist who would sleep her way to the top. Years after Zwillman had satiated his lust for Harlow, he married a woman of high social standing who had nothing to do with Hollywood and its casting couches, Mary de Groot Mendels Steinbach, whose grandfather founded the American Stock Exchange.

It wasn't only the studio bosses who knew about the connections of Zwillman and Rosselli to Cohn, but it was also well known among reporters and gossip columnists who regularly reported about the movie business. More names were soon added to the list of mob associates; since Rosselli was sponsored by the Outfit in Chicago, the bosses of the Outfit were also noted. In addition, East Coast mobsters, such as Frank Costello (prime minister of the underworld), invested in the movie industry. Years after Zwillman gave money to Cohn, Jerry Lewis commented: "They [the mob] had a lot of money in Columbia—namely Harry Cohn—and I knew it."[2]

And it wasn't just Hollywood studio bosses who accepted mob money to finance their movies. Many stars also owed their careers to mobsters, especially those who began as singers and comedians in mob-owned nightclubs. They included Frank Sinatra, Dean Martin, Al Martino, Sammy Davis Jr., and numerous others.

Cohn, who regarded the movie business as a racket, had no qualms about dealing with mobsters. In fact, he admired the power and influence of gangsters. However, none of the gangsters who invested in Hollywood productions could compare to Benito Mussolini, a dictator whom Cohn deeply admired as a tough hero who got things done. In 1933, Columbia released a documentary touting Mussolini's accomplishments as dictator of Italy. The movie cost $10,000 and grossed $1,000,000. Cohn was delighted about the magnificent return on his investment, and Mussolini was so impressed by the movie that he decided to award Cohn a special decoration. Cohn travelled to Italy for the presentation and returned to Hollywood with a signed photograph of Il Duce. The photo held a place of honor in Cohn's office, hanging on a wall adjacent to his desk where visitors couldn't miss it. (The photo remained in place until the outset of World War II.) In addition to the photo, Cohn had his office rebuilt and designed to look like the dictator's. And, indeed, it was an office befitting a man who saw himself as a Hollywood dictator who controlled the lives of thousands of employees from stagehands, technicians, and publicists to stars, directors, writers, and producers. Bob Thomas, in *King Cohn*, writes:

> *The outer office was occupied by a receptionist who admitted visitors to the inner office, where the head secretary and an assistant or two were located. It was here that visitors waited for admittance to the Cohn chamber. The length of the wait was judiciously calculated by Cohn. A writer, director, producer, or actor in disfavor might be detained for two or three hours. One who was being wooed by Cohn to sign with Cohn was admitted immediately.*
>
> *In keeping with the Mussolini tradition, the Cohn office was massive and elongated, with a desk at the far end. The visitor marched down the thick carpet to the huge semicircular desk, slightly raised above floor level. Cohn remained in the shadows while the visitor was clearly lighted.*[3]

Among those who were called into Cohn's office and subjected to his power-hungry ego were young women eager to become movie stars. Some were naive and easily manipulated, some were hardheaded and ready to submit to whatever was necessary to reach their goals. With the power to make and break budding careers, Cohn would seduce them as if they were already primed to satisfy his lustful desires. No one left his office not knowing the price of stardom.

In his office, he had shelves of cheap and expensive perfume, and he would decide who would be sophisticated enough to appreciate the more expensive ones. He also kept a drawer filled with costume jewelry: sparkling necklaces, bracelets, and pendants. Given before or after a sexual encounter depended on Cohn's level of appreciation and mood. There were two dressing rooms attached to his office, each furnished with a comfortable couch, large enough to accommodate two bodies. Known for chattering gossip, Hollywood starlets spread the word that Cohn was a sexual predator. It was long before the Me Too movement, and no one ever brought charges of rape or sexual harassment against Cohn. However, in an effort to monitor what actors and directors said about him, he had microphones installed on every soundstage and in offices so that he could eavesdrop. He also had loudspeakers installed on soundstages so that he could interrupt a production and make demands. He wasn't so much Big Brother as he was King Cohn—the boss of all those who cowered before him. No wonder screenwriter and novelist Bud Schulberg referred to him as "White Fang." Though many actresses emerged disillusioned from their encounters with Cohn, they continued to rely on him for their success.

[Each one had arrived] in Hollywood with a suitcase and a pretty face. Get discovered by an agent or, better yet, a movie exec. Next step: stardom. This seemingly simple formula was the dream of many aspiring Hollywood starlets—and the myth of Hollywood's Golden Age. For a significant number of movie stars, a career in pictures started instead with sexual exploitation on the "casting couch" of Harry Cohn, one of Hollywood's most powerful—and brutal—men.

As the head of Columbia Pictures from 1919 to 1958, Cohn expected sex in exchange for a chance at stardom. And as one of the most influential figures in Tinseltown, he usually got it. He was one of the men responsible for instituting the system of Hollywood's "casting couch," which demanded women trade sexual favors with powerful executives for a chance at a movie role. Although the casting couch cliché predates the Columbia head's career in Hollywood, Cohn helped entrench the system in the movie industry during four decades in film.

Part of his success rested on his ruthlessness, and from the start Cohn used that aggression to exert control over female stars. Not only did he force them to change their names and their appearances, but he regularly forced them to trade sex for employment, then scrutinized and even spied on them.

In the words of E. J. Fleming, whose book The Fixers *focuses on how Hollywood studios controlled their stars' images, Cohn "was said to have verbally or physically raped every woman that ever worked for his studio."[4]*

Nevertheless, a few claimed that they bravely had resisted his advances, though their protestations often fell on deaf ears, for—on the advice of their publicists—many were simply trying to convince their fans and sympathetic reporters that they had scruples and would not advance their careers at the cost of their virtue. Joan Crawford was one who claimed to have told Cohn to keep it in his pants; however, she was revealed to have appeared in early porno movies and had slept her way to stardom. Two of her notorious porno movies are *Velvet Lips* and *The Casting Couch*. The *Daily Mail* reported: "In 'The Casting Couch,' Crawford is reportedly seen performing a sex act on a producer before jumping on his couch nude and engaging in another sex act."[5]

MGM paid $100,000 to buy *The Casting Couch* and keep it away from the public. Throughout her life, Crawford claimed that there was no basis to the rumors that she had appeared in porno movies. "[She] denied ever appearing in an indecent film in her 1962 memoir, but her first husband Douglas Fairbanks Jr. claims she told him about the pictures."[6]

> In Joan Crawford: Hollywood Martyr, *author David Bret notes that Crawford's F.B.I. file stated "that as much as $100,000 may have been handed over to this unknown black-mailer at around this time—and that MGM had made a previous payoff, almost certainly to the same man, who some believed to have been Joan's brother, Hal.*[7]

> A document in Crawford's FBI file refers to a "story from a high police authority" that shortly after her arrest in Detroit for prostitution in the early 1920s, a pornographic film of Crawford was doing the rounds of stag parties. . . . In January 1974 MGM's former head of security, Howard Strickling, told erstwhile colleague Samuel Marx that the studio had to buy up pornographic movies starring Crawford.[8]

Another female star who proclaimed her resistance to Cohn's sexual advances was Rita Hayworth. However, because her declarations were made with such frequency, many doubted their veracity. It did seem as if "the lady doth protest too much." In addition to generating an image of a strong woman maintaining her moral integrity, Hayworth's protestations may have possibly reflected her strong Catholic background and devotion to her faith; yet numerous photos of her and Cohn, arm in arm, out on the town at parties, on cruises, at racetracks, and dancing exist. And Cohn certainly was not known for his platonic friendships with women. He would not have spent so much time with a woman who refused him.

Even while on vacation with his wife, Cohn felt the need for a quickie, a fling, or an affair. Neal Gabler in his book, *An Empire of Their Own*, writes:

On one vacation [Cohn] took his wife to Honolulu, where he ran into a girl he had known and liked back in Los Angeles. She was traveling with a banker named Al Hart, who was a friend of Cohn's, so Cohn suggested the couple join him and his wife, and he and the girl spent the rest of the vacation together. On Saturday afternoons in the fall, Mrs. Cohn would pack a picnic basket for her husband and send him off to watch football. Then he would pick up his latest girl and take her [Jonie] to Taps's apartment, where they could devour the lunch and presumably each other.[9] (Taps was a music publisher from New York who acted as a beard for Cohn.)

The most sexually alluring of Cohn's Columbia stars may have been Kim Novak, who Cohn molded—much like Pygmalion's Galatea—to be one of the screen's most subtly tempting sirens. The cynical Cohn referred to her as "that fat Polack," though never to her face. He nevertheless ordered his publicity department to distinguish her from Marilyn Monroe and other blonde bombshells. She would be more subtle than Monroe, Jayne Mansfield, Diana Dors, and Mamie Van Doren; there would be no giggly extroverted sexuality in her personality. Novak would be bathed in the color lavender, a pastel color that suited her. She would be softly sexy, not a big, brassy blonde. She dressed in lavender, drove a lavender-colored car, slept in a lavender-colored nightgown, and even spoke on a lavender-colored telephone. Whereas Monroe was basically comedic in such movies as *Gentlemen Prefer Blondes, How to Marry a Millionaire, The Seven Year Itch,* and *Bus Stop,* and Mansfield something of a cartoon version of Monroe in such movies as *The Girl Can't Help It, Promises! Promises! Will Success Spoil Rock Hunter?* and *Too Hot to Handle*, Novak had an understated come-hither look and sleepy bedroom eyes that were a subtle invitation to the sexual pleasures she could provide.

Cohn felt betrayed by Novak, who was becoming a source of torment for him. In 1957, Novak met Sammy Davis Jr. at a party thrown by Tony Curtis and Janet Leigh. Davis was known for being attracted to sexy white blondes (e.g., from May Britt to Marilyn Chambers). Novak aroused his desire just by entering the room; she was the woman who millions of male moviegoers imagined making love to. Davis was immediately fixated on her, and she was drawn by Davis's extraordinary talents as a singer, dancer, actor, and musician. He was dynamic, unique, and amazing. What Novak didn't know was that Davis was in debt to the mob. To say he was a spendthrift would be an understatement. He received generous salaries for his nightclub gigs but spent his money almost as fast as he earned it. He was frequently borrowing money from the owners of the nightclubs where he performed, and those clubs were all owned by mobsters. And the vigorish on those loans kept multiplying like cancer cells, so Davis could never retire his loans. In addition, the more he owed, the more he borrowed. In effect, he became a mob-owned property. For Davis, a romance with Novak was an escape from anxiety; for Novak, it was an escape from Cohn's stranglehold on her. He had told her what to say, what to wear, who to date, what restaurants to eat in. By dating Davis, she was telling Cohn to go fuck himself; she wouldn't let him completely possess her. Davis, meanwhile, generated an extraordinary amount of publicity for himself, some of it good, some of it negative. In 1950s America, interracial dating was considered scandalous, and in numerous states, interracial marriage was against the law. By publicly dating, Davis and Novak had become larger-than-life poster children against racism. Their romance was a means for both entertainers to thumb their noses at bigots.

Cohn and the Columbia board of directors, however, were not interested in fighting racism. They wanted their movies to make money in every state of the union. If Davis and Novak continued dating, Novak's movies would be banned in the South. Such a loss of money was anathema to Columbia. Something had to be done to end the romance.

But Davis and Novak were like criminals on the lam, escaping from the Columbia octopus. Arthur Silber, a friend of Davis, was often conscripted to drive the couple to a secret hideaway in Malibu. In the car, Davis would lie on the back seat, while Novak rode up front, a scarf concealing her features.

"It was like we were in the FBI or something," Silber says in an interview. "I would drop him off in front of her house in Beverly Hills and we would set up a time or a day for me to pick him up." Davis also had a private phone line installed at the Sands Hotel in Las Vegas where he worked so he could talk to Novak without the hotel switchboard listening in. When Cohn found out, he became enraged that his star—whom he regarded as property he'd invested in—was dating a black man."[10]

Cohn didn't stop at being enraged: he decided to get his mobster friends to kill Davis unless the entertainer ended his romance with Novak and married a black woman. Cohn sent his pal Mickey Cohen to warn Davis what was in store for him if he didn't acquiesce to Cohn's demands. And Cohn wanted it done within the next forty-eight hours.

Not relying solely on the persuasiveness of Cohen, two additional emissaries were sent to visit Davis. Tim Adler writes: "Meanwhile, two gangsters accosted Davis. One of them said, 'You're now a one-eyed nigger Jew. You ever see this blonde again, you're going to be a blind, nigger Jew. You're getting married this weekend—go figure out who you're marrying.'"[11]

Davis, as might be expected, was consumed by fear and anxiety. He thought that Sam Giancana, the boss of the Chicago Outfit for whom Davis had done favors, would be able to get the murder contract rescinded. Davis phoned Giancana at his home in Chicago. He begged Giancana to do something. The mobster sympathized with Davis and warned him not to return to Los Angeles unless he did as he had been warned and married a black woman. He said he could protect Davis in Vegas and in Chicago but not in LA. Davis put down the phone and pulled out his address book. He went through a list of names, then settled on Loray White, a twenty-three-year-old black singer who performed at the Silver Slipper.

She and Davis had gone out a few times in the past. Now Davis offered her a lump sum (between $10,000 and $25,000) to marry him and act as his wife. She agreed. In pictures of their Las Vegas wedding, White and Davis drink out of an oversized martini glass beside a tiered cake with the word "Happiness" written on it. But Silber, who drove the couple to their wedding suite, recalls that Davis drank heavily all evening and became so distraught in the car that he tried to strangle White. Silber restrained Davis and carried him to his room.[12]

The marriage existed on paper and within a few months, newspapers ran gossip items that Davis and White were getting divorced. Each profited from the short-lived marriage: Davis saved his life, and White was bathed in much publicity. Though Davis had given up Novak, he would soon be tying the nuptial knot with another blonde beauty.

One day, a couple of years later, Sammy and Silber were having lunch at 20th Century Fox when a woman walked in. She was tall and lovely with shiny blonde hair and a husky voice. Davis promptly introduced himself.

Her name was May (pronounced "My") Britt, a 26-year-old Swedish actress who was filming a remake of The Blue

Angel. *She and Davis started seeing each other. Soon he proposed marriage and she accepted. An outsider to American racial politics, Britt didn't see why race should keep her away from the person she loved. On June 6, 1960, while in England, Davis announced their engagement to the press.*

"The public went mad," Burt Boyar, a close friend who co-wrote Davis's autobiography, says in an interview. "When they got engaged, all hell broke loose. The studio immediately canceled Britt's contract. They assumed that she was no use in the box office married to a black man." He also campaigned for John F. Kennedy during his 1960 presidential campaign, performing in 20 cities, usually alongside the rest of the Rat Pack. But at the Democratic National Convention in Mississippi, he was booed while singing the national anthem—an incident that left him near tears.

After he won the election, Kennedy snubbed Davis on two occasions. Davis had been invited to Kennedy's inauguration gala and was so proud to be going that he had a special suit made. Britt bought a Balenciaga dress. But three days before the inauguration, Kennedy's secretary called to say that the president was uninviting them. The move was political—the president-elect had won the election by a slim margin and he didn't want to alienate Southern congressmen by presenting them with Davis's controversial marriage. Davis was deeply hurt and embarrassed by the snub.

Then in 1963, Davis and Britt were invited to a White House reception for African-American leaders. Raymond said in an email that when Kennedy saw them there he hissed at his aides to "Get them out of here" and herded the couple away from photographers.

Davis and Britt divorced in 1968. The marriage lasted eight years and resulted in three children.[13]

That Cohn behaved like a gangster regarding the Davis-Novak romance is indisputable. It is one reason why he became a model for Jack Woltz, the tough, uncompromising studio boss in *The Godfather*. He is portrayed as adamantly refusing to give a much-sought-after part to Johnny Fontaine, a character based on Frank Sinatra, who needed to play the part of Maggio in *From Here to Eternity* in order to resuscitate his nearly moribund career.

Though *The Godfather* is considered a great cinematic achievement, it's necessary to note that no one threatened Cohn to give Sinatra the part of Maggio. Cohn was connected to mobsters in Chicago and New York; he was family, and no one would be sent to threaten him. Words were spoken; favors were asked. But threats to his well-being were never part of the scenario. The scene where a horse's decapitated head placed on Woltz's bed is not only a fiction, it is a preposterous fiction. What person would not have awoken with a heavy horse's head bleeding onto his bed? In addition, Cohn didn't own racehorses. Mario Puzo, the author of *The Godfather*, said the book is a fairy tale for adults, or just a family soap opera. Puzo even created the concept of a Mafia godfather when the word godfather had never been used to refer to a Mafia boss. Lucky Luciano, who was the most powerful boss in the country during the 1930s, never had his ring kissed. That was reserved for popes. As one elderly gangster told me, *The Godfather* is a great comedy. There are more unintentionally funny scenes than in any other gangster movie. It's one Mafia cliché piled on another cliché. It makes for great drama but has little basis in reality.

Sinatra begged everyone connected with Cohn to get him the part of Maggio. Sinatra's wife, Ava Gardner, convinced Cohn's wife, Joan, to speak with her husband and convince him that Sinatra was perfect for the part but Cohn refused. He wanted Eli Wallach, but the actor was committed to playing a role on Broadway in a Tennessee Williams play.

It was not until Frank Costello got involved that Sinatra's chances of being cast in *From Here to Eternity* became better than even. The mob had done many favors for Cohn, and he had done favors for them. No one was going to end a mutually profitable relationship to help a singer whose career was nearing death's door. But there were some favors that needed to be repaid. Though the mob wound up helping Sinatra, they treated Cohn as a business partner, not an obstacle. Sinatra's comeback would not have happened if not for Willie Moretti, the New Jersey Mafia boss who had helped launch Sinatra's career back in Hoboken.

According to mobster insiders, Moretti told Sinatra to phone Moretti's cousin Frank Costello at the Copacabana nightclub, which Costello secretly owned. Sinatra and Costello had met several times, but they were not friends. Costello knew the role that Moretti had played engineering the birth of Sinatra's career and later threatening bandleader Tommy Dorsey to release Sinatra from his big band contract. Costello told Sinatra he would see what could be done then sent a pair of his associates to visit Cohn. They explained that Costello wanted him to grant a favor and hire Sinatra. Cohn thereupon agreed to give Sinatra a screen test for the part, and if it was successful, Sinatra would be hired for $1,000 a week. His full pay for the movie would be $8,000.

Sinatra was always touchy about how he got the part, and when the BBC reported that Costello arranged for Sinatra to get the part, Sinatra successfully sued. The movie not only revived Sinatra's career, it sent it into the stratosphere; he went on to win the Oscar for Best Supporting Actor for his role, and his future salaries were on the same level as the most popular movie stars. He bathed in the reviews, which praised his performance as nothing short of magnificent. Ava Gardner, however, said of her husband, "When he was down and out, he was so sweet. But now that he's gotten successful again, he's become his old arrogant self. We were happy when he was on the skids."[14] He may have been arrogant, but he helped to support Gardner during the last years of her life and paid for her medical care. There was Sinatra the violent, aggressive bully, and Sinatra the thoughtful, generous friend. He was a Janus-faced celebrity whose friendly moods could erupt in anger at seemingly minor provocations.

Not only had Sinatra been angry at the BBC for reporting that Costello had gotten him the role of Maggio in *From Here to Eternity*, but he was even angrier at Mario Puzo for his depiction of a Sinatra-like character who got his part in a career-changing movie through Mafia intimidation. Sinatra said: "I read off Puzo one night in Chasen's. What phony stuff! Somebody going to the mob to get a role in a movie. Puzo turned out to be a bum. He prostituted his own business making up such a phony story. I screen tested for Cohn and he hired me for the role in [*From Here to Eternity*]. Period."[15]

According to an article in *Billboard* by Ryan Parker, Sinatra said if Puzo wasn't so much older than he, he would beat the hell out of the author. Puzo was not frightened of being beaten; instead, he was upset by Sinatra's misunderstanding of the difference between northern and southern Italians. "What hurt was that here was a northern Italian threatening me, a southern Italian with physical violence.... This was roughly equivalent to Einstein pulling a knife on Al Capone. It just wasn't done. Northern Italians never mess with southern Italians except to get them put in jail or get them deported to some island."[16] Before Puzo could depart the restaurant, Sinatra called Puzo a pimp. In 1972, Puzo wrote, "The worst thing he called me was a pimp, which rather flattered me since I've never been able to get girlfriends to squeeze blackheads out of my back, much less hustle for me."[17]

During the filming of *The Godfather*, Sinatra tried to have the part of Johnny Fontaine, played by Al Martino, cut down. Sinatra called his friend Sam Giancana, boss of the Outfit, to lean on the director and have him cut Martino's part to a fraction of what it was. Giancana told Sinatra not to try and interfere with the production, for Martino had his own mob connections. Martino not only owed his career to mob boss Russell Bufalino, but he owed his part in the movie to Bufalino. The role of Johnny Fontaine was originally offered to Vic Damone. Martino asked Bufalino for his help. Damone dropped out of the movie shortly thereafter, not wanting to provoke the mob's anger. He also claimed that the payment for the role was too small. Dick Kleiner writes that "the suspicion was that Damone had gotten the word from the Mafia to bow out because they had officially sanctioned Martino previously."[18]

For Cohn and Columbia Pictures, *From Here to Eternity* was a triumph. The movie won eight Academy awards, including Best Picture, Best Director (Fred Zinnemann), Best Supporting Actor (Sinatra), and Best Supporting Actress (Donna Reed). Cohn could not have been happier; he was the toast of Hollywood; no one mentioned his mob connections, his sexual predations, or the Davis-Novak affair. He could do no wrong.

And as bad as he was, Cohn managed to produce more than two hundred movies, forty-five of which won Academy Awards, and many others are considered classics. Among the more well-known movies are *Lady from Shanghai*, *Lost Horizon*, *Twentieth Century*, *It Happened One Night*, *Lady for a Day*, *Platinum Blonde*, *Mr. Smith Goes to Washington*, *Ladies of Leisure*, *All the King's Men*, *The Big Heat*, and *On the Waterfront*.

When he died in 1958, he may have been the most hated man in Hollywood, but he was also highly respected. His accomplishments were promethean. Two thousand people attended his funeral. Seeing the large number of mourners who showed up for his funeral, Red Skelton commented: "Give the people what they want, and they'll turn out for it!" When a member of the Jewish Temple asked the rabbi to say "one good thing" about the deceased, he paused and said "He's dead."[19]

Stories about Cohn the tyrannical producer proliferated after his death, including the following anecdote: "Last night I saw the lousiest picture I've seen in years," said Cohn. After mentioning the title, one producer reported that he had seen it with an audience and they had loved it. He suggested that maybe Cohn would have had a different reaction if he had seen it with an audience. Cohn replied, "That doesn't make any difference. When I'm alone in a projection room, I have a foolproof device for judging whether a picture is good or bad. If my fanny squirms, it's bad. If my fanny doesn't squirm, it's good. It's as simple as that." There was a momentary silence, which was broken by Herman J. Mankiewicz. "Imagine," he said to the others present. "The whole world wired to Harry Cohn's ass!"[20]

Cohn also is noted for stating that "I don't have ulcers; I give them"; "I am the king here. Whoever eats my bread, sings my song"; and "The movie business is a racket."

In an interview, Cohn said the following:

> *Let me give you some facts of life. Every Friday, the front door of this studio opens and I spit a movie out onto Gower Street. . . . If that door opens and I spit and nothing comes out, it means a lot of people are out of work—drivers, distributors, exhibitors, projectionists, ushers, and a lot of other pricks. . . . I want one good picture a year, and I won't let an exhibitor have it unless he takes the bread-and-butter product, the Boston Blackies, the Blondies, the low-budget westerns and the rest of the junk we make.*[21]

Cohn is interred in the Hollywood Forever Cemetery, section 8, lot 86, between the lake and the entrance to the Cathedral Mausoleum. "I picked out a great plot," he said. "It's right by the water, and I can see the studio [Columbia Pictures] from here." Cohn's aboveground tomb has a cross entwined with a Star of David. He was not religiously observant and there is no evidence he converted from Judaism to Christianity, but he had an attraction to Catholicism. Both his wives were Catholics, and he allowed his second wife, Joan Perry, to raise their children in the Catholic Church. The inscriptions on his crypt were ordered by Perry.[22]

NOTES

1. Ted Schwarz, *Hollywood Confidential* (Lanham, MD: Taylor, 2007), 184–85.

2. Gus Russo, *Supermob* (New York: Bloomsbury, 2008), 154.

3. Bob Thomas, *King Cohn* (Beverly Hills, CA: New Millennium, 2000), 100–101.

4. www.history.com/news/this-tinseltown-tyrant-used-sexual-exploitation-to-build-a-hollywood-empire (accessed October 17, 2022).

5. www.dailymail.co.uk/news/article-4397748/Joan-Crawford-porn-films-brother-threatened-leak.htmlMail (accessed October 17, 2022).

6. www.dailymail.co.uk/news/article-4397748/Joan-Crawford-porn-films-brother-threatened-leak.html (accessed October 17, 2022).

7. www.vanityfair.com/hollywood/2017/04/feud-joan-crawford-fact-check-stag-film-brother?redirectURL=https://www.vanityfair.com/hollywood/2017/04/feud-joan-crawford-fact-check-stag-film-brother (accessed October 17, 2022).

8. Tim Adler, *Hollywood and the Mob* (London: Bloomsbury, 2007), 66.

9. Neal Gabler, *An Empire of Their Own* (New York: Crown, 1988), 247.

10. www.smithsonianmag.com/arts-culture/hollywood-loved-sammy-davis-jr-until-he-dated-white-movie-star-180964395/ (accessed October 17, 2022).

11. Adler, *Hollywood and the Mob*, 132.

12. www.smithsonianmag.com/arts-culture/hollywood-loved-sammy-davis-jr-until-he-dated-white-movie-star-180964395/ (accessed October 17, 2022).

13. www.smithsonianmag.com/arts-culture/hollywood-loved-sammy-davis-jr-until-he-dated-white-movie-star-180964395/ (accessed October 17, 2022).

14. Adler, *Hollywood and the Mob*, 127.

15. Kitty Kelley, *His Way* (New York: Bantam, 1986), 392–93.

16. www.billboard.com/music/music-news/frank-sinatra-100-birthday
-berated-mario-puzo-godfather-johnny-fontane-al-martino-6805707/#!
(accessed October 17, 2022).

17. www.billboard.com/music/music-news/frank-sinatra-100-birthday
-berated-mario-puzo-godfather-johnny-fontane-al-martino-6805707/#!
(accessed October 17, 2022).

18. www.vanityfair.com/news/2009/03/godfather200903 (accessed October 17, 2022).

19. www.imdb.com/name/nm0169902/bio?ref_=nm_dyk_trv_sm#trivia
(accessed October 17, 2022).

20. www.imdb.com/name/nm0169902/bio?ref_=nm_dyk_trv_sm#trivia
(accessed October 17, 2022).

21. www.imdb.com/name/nm0169902/bio?ref_=nm_dyk_trv_sm#trivia
(accessed October 17, 2022).

22. www.imdb.com/name/nm0169902/bio?ref_=nm_dyk_trv_sm#trivia
(accessed October 17, 2022).

CHAPTER SEVEN

Thelma Todd

The Death of the Ice Cream Blonde

SHE WAS BEAUTIFUL, CHARMING, SMART, AND SO DELICIOUS SHE was called the Ice Cream Blonde. She was Thelma Todd, an actress who could do comedy as well as melodrama. Her future seemed bright until she was found dead, slumped over on the front seat of her car.

Thelma Alice Todd was born in Lawrence, Massachusetts, on July 29, 1906. Her mother Alice was determined that Thelma would become a movie star. Mrs. Todd also hoped that her daughter would make her rich.

Young Thelma had ambitions that were not as grand as her mother's: she was determined to become a teacher. Mrs. Todd would not stand for it: Thelma must enter beauty contests and take acting classes. Her future was to be a rich movie star, beloved by millions of fans. To ensure that her daughter had a winning figure, Alice put Thelma on a diet of chicken and salads for several weeks. Alice knew she had acted wisely, for Thelma won the Miss Massachusetts beauty contest. It was a door opener. Thelma's photos (no doubt with Alice's fingerprints on them) landed on the desks of movie scouts and agents. One of them thought Thelma was a cut above the typical aspiring movie stars. He signed her to a contract with Paramount Studios. It was a standard beginner's contract, big on clauses, low on salary. She was enrolled in the Paramount School for Junior Stars, not all of whom would graduate to dominant positions on the silver screen. Some became character actors; others returned home.

Because Thelma had a tendency to overeat, thus gaining too much weight, she was warned by producer Hal Roach that if she wanted to become a star, she must maintain an attractive figure. He placed a clause in her contract that if she became fat, she would be cast aside. The solution was amphetamines. The drug became part of her daily regimen. She combined it with a love of alcohol. As if that were not sufficiently self-destructive, on July 18, 1932, she eloped to Prescott, Arizona, with a minor gangster and talent agent named Pasquale "Pat" DiCicco, who was rumored to be Lucky Luciano's man in Hollywood. Minutes after the wedding ceremony, Thelma wired her mother news of the marriage. Like a good publicist, Alice made phone call after phone call to newspaper editors, gossip columnists, and wire services with the nuptial news. Reports of the marriage of Thelma, who became known as Hot Toddy, and Pat DiCicco went national.

Thelma was not just a wife for DiCicco, she was also an agency client. He used her to lure other clients to his budding agency, but he only succeeded in developing a stable of minor actors. When DiCicco wasn't making deals for his wife, he was beating her for various perceived infractions of his code of ethics. She initially had been drawn to DiCicco by his air of danger and the implicit threat of violence lurking behind his snakelike smile. But the thrill of danger was soon replaced by her fear of his menacing and brutal behavior. That the couple had an unstable marriage would be an understatement, for it often erupted into angry drunken brawls. During one such brawl, Thelma broke DiCicco's nose, and he punched her so hard in the gut that she required immediate surgery.

Ted Schwarz writes in *Hollywood Confidential*, "The marriage was emotionally over almost from the time they eloped. . . . Todd would not get the wedding annulled, but she began drinking more heavily and taking more diet pills."[1]

They finally divorced in March 1934; in 1941, DiCicco married seventeen-year-old heiress and socialite Gloria Vanderbilt. That marriage shattered on the rocks of his cruelty. It is one of the subjects of Vanderbilt's novelistic memoir, *Black Knight, White Knight*. Vanderbilt claimed in court documents that DiCicco often beat her while calling her "Fatso Roo." (He seems to have had a violent antipathy to his wives gaining weight.) Vanderbilt also claimed that DiCicco had slammed her head against a wall. The next day, she would look at her face in a mirror and curse him for her two black eyes. The miserable marriage lasted for four years.

The gossip surrounding the Todd-DiCicco marriage paled in comparison to the scandalous rumors that flew like bats on a moonlit night that Thelma began an affair with Lucky Luciano. And since gangsters often obtain their ends through murder, Luciano was rumored as a possible suspect in Thelma's death. Yet there is no evidence that Luciano ever visited Los Angeles or that he even knew Thelma. True, he had emissaries, such as Bugsy Siegel and Mickey Cohen in town, but Luciano operated principally in New York with occasional visits to Florida and Hot Springs, Arkansas. Since the mob was known to control gambling and Thelma owned a restaurant (see below) that would have been suitable for a casino, rumormongers asserted that Luciano had Thelma killed so that his cohorts could take over her restaurant and convert it into a high-class gambling casino. However, there were plenty of gambling operations in Los Angeles, so Thelma's restaurant would have been unnecessary. Furthermore, gangsters such as Tony Cornero were operating highly profitable luxurious gambling casinos on cruise ships just off the coast.

Though neither Luciano nor Cornero had anything to do with Thelma, rumors sprouted like wild mushrooms that she had always been attracted to dangerous men, that she was extremely insecure and needed such men as life preservers, that she was a masochist, a woman who had an insatiable sexual appetite, a woman who would submit to any man of power who would then control and humiliate her. Such rumors were the building blocks for constructing an image of Thelma as a victim of Hollywood greed.

No Hollywood martyr, Thelma was a smart, tough woman who took control of her destiny by using her talents and superior negotiating skills to become a major Hollywood star. Her thespian abilities as a comedienne and dramatic actress meant that she was in demand by numerous producers and directors. Her comedic talents proved ideal in comedies with Laurel and Hardy and in two Marx Brothers classics: *Monkey Business* and *Horse Feathers*. Having proven herself a top-flight comedienne, she set out to prove that she was as talented in straight dramas as she was in comedies. Her acting abilities shone in *Corsair* (in which she appeared as Alison Loyd to distinguish herself from her comedic roles). She also was in the 1931 version of *The Maltese Falcon*, starring Ricardo Cortez (né Jacob Krantz). Alice Todd proudly declared that her daughter succeeded in anything she did.

Roland West, her director in *Corsair*, had been irresistibly drawn to Thelma's beauty and brains. The two briefly became lovers. It didn't matter to either of them that West was married to actress Jewel Carmen, who didn't mind her husband having an affair. West and Carmen would soon divorce, but his infidelity was not the cause. They simply wanted to go their separate ways, but that did not stop the duo from partnering with Thelma when they created the restaurant Thelma Todd's Sidewalk Café.

The restaurant was to be Thelma's annuity that would support her following the demise of her movie career. Though she appeared in more than fifty movies, she understood that her career would fade as she grew older. Young beautiful women, then as now, dominate the world of movies. They rarely advance to playing older women. Thelma said that she didn't mind developing wrinkles and gaining weight as long as she was intelligent enough to make a living for herself. The restaurant was to be her source of comfort and financial well-being.

Since Roland West's career as a director was slipping away, he thought that owning a restaurant would serve his needs, as well. He always wanted to own a restaurant, and Thelma Todd's name was a perfect magnet for drawing the crème de la crème of Hollywood. Carmen agreed to fund the opening of the restaurant for a one-third share of its ownership. All that Thelma had to do was lend her name. Thelma Todd's Sidewalk Café opened to much fanfare in August 1934 at 17575 Pacific Coast Highway in Pacific Palisades. Her swanky restaurant occupied the entire ground floor. On the second floor were separate apartments for Thelma, West, and Carmen. The remainder of that floor was occupied by a private club, Joya, for Hollywood celebrities who did not want to mingle with crowds of fans. On the third floor was a hexagonal-shaped structure that included a dance floor and bandstand. The structure housing the Sidewalk Café is a magnificent, sprawling, fifteen-thousand-square-feet edifice built in a Spanish Colonial Revival style with Moorish influences. It can be seen for a little more than a minute in the 1958 movie *Murder by Contract* starring Vince Edwards. (Incidentally, Martin Scorsese said that movie influenced him more than any other.)

Michelle Morgan writes,

Thelma would work all day at the studio and then head to the [café] just in time to give the preparation her undivided attention.

When she worked so hard in the evening that she couldn't bring herself to make the trek home, she stayed at the apartment above the café. These rooms also provided her with enough privacy to renew the romance between herself and West, and while his room was separated from Thelma's with a wooden sliding door, it is easy to assume that is was rarely closed.[2]

Though always crowded with celebrities as well as politicians and gangsters, the restaurant was losing money. West confronted the restaurant's accountant, Charles Smith, for an explanation as to why an apparently successful restaurant could be losing money. West soon learned that the mob had moved in shortly after the restaurant opened. As in many cities, the mob took control of the delivery of food, beverages, linens, and anything else the restaurant required. The restaurant even had to hire bartenders who were members of a union controlled by the mob. And of course the mob charged outrageously high rates for all the supplies that it delivered. When West complained, he was told he had no choice if he wanted to keep the restaurant open. If he didn't want the goods that were delivered, he could refuse delivery; however, he would still have to pay as if the goods had been delivered. West believed that DiCicco, as an instrument of mobsters, was responsible for the shakedown. When West asked Thelma to make up the shortfall, she wanted to know why she should be responsible, since she was only supposed to be fronting the restaurant. In addition, she demanded to know why the restaurant was losing money, since it was packed with customers every night. West told her to speak with DiCicco.

When she asked DiCicco about the shakedown of her restaurant, he responded that he could end it if she permitted him to open a gambling casino on the third floor. She adamantly refused, telling him there were plenty of other more suitable locations in Los Angeles and he could lease a ship to convert into casino, as other mobsters had. DiCicco, after that encounter with Thelma, may have begun circulating rumors that Luciano wanted the third floor of the café for a gambling casino. When Luciano supposedly demanded that Thelma agree to this arrangement, she ignited his anger by responding "over my dead body." The mob's predictable response was "that can be arranged." Although this scenario would be an engaging scene in movie, in reality, it never happened. It didn't matter to rumormongers that no one could verify such accounts; the rumors spread and finally found a home in Kenneth Anger's book, *Hollywood Babylon*, an engaging chronicle of sordid stories about Hollywood scandals. Anger wrote:

Thelma's lawyer demanded a second inquest which he said would bolster his theory she had been murdered by hit-men working for Lucky Luciano. Luciano was then making inroads into illicit California gambling establishments. He had approached Thelma with an offer to take over the upper story of her café for the installation of a secret and crooked casino which she was supposed to populate with fashionable customers from among her famous friends. The lawyer was convinced that in turning down Luciano's offer, Thelma had signed her death warrant.[3]

But why would Luciano—or any gangster—want the Sidewalk Café as a gambling casino when so many other locations would have been more suitable? Aha!—the rumormongers knew the answer; they decided that Luciano needed Thelma Todd's name to attract Hollywood bigshots—high rollers who would lose hundreds of thousands of dollars and pay off their IOUs with shares in their studios. Once Luciano had gained sufficient shares, he could extort the studio bosses. The theory gained momentum the more it was repeated. Those rumors then dilated to include tales of Luciano supplying Thelma with drugs and forcing her to drink herself into helplessness. That she was able to resist his demands to permit a gambling casino to open in the Sidewalk Café would, of course, be impossible if she were incapacitated by drink and drugs, but that inconsistency was unremarked on. The next chapter in tabloid-style rumors concluded that Thelma's refusal to accede to Luciano's demands left the gangster no choice but to murder her.

Thelma was no fading flower. So, for example, when she received threatening letters, she reported them to the LA district attorney, Buron Fitts. Not waiting for a response from the

DA's office, Thelma continued to live her life as if there were no threats, all of which—incidentally—came from cranks. On December 14, 1935, Thelma attended a party at the Trocadero that was hosted by comedian Stanley Lupino and his daughter, Ida, an A-list actress and director. Much to her surprise, Thelma encountered her ex-husband DiCicco there. He had arranged for a chair to be reserved beside hers. He arrived with a date. Thelma was nonplussed by the encounter, and the two exchanged heated words. DiCicco left the restaurant shortly thereafter, and Thelma went on to have a good time, socializing with friends. Following an evening of laughter, dancing, and general good cheer, Thelma decided she had had enough of partying and contacted her regular driver, Ernest O. Peters, to drive her home. It was a cold night on December 15 about 3:00 in the morning. Thelma curled up in the back seat of the car, wrapped in her fur coat. Peters drove her to the apartment and left. Thelma attempted to unlock the door of her apartment, but it was bolted from the inside. She ascended a hill to the garage where her car, an elegant two-toned convertible Lincoln Phaeton, was parked, climbed in, and turned the ignition key. Thelma, perhaps wanting to get warm, sat in the driver's seat as the car's radiator warmed the car. Unfortunately, she had closed the garage door and breathed in the carbon monoxide fumes. She fell into a deep sleep, a picture of dissipation in a mauve and silver party dress, a luxurious mink stole, a body highlighted with bling and baubles. She made a beautiful corpse.

On the morning of December 16, Thelma's maid, Mae Whitehead, was unable to find her employer. She called her name in the apartment then ascended to the garage. She opened the garage door, entered, and discovered Thelma's dead body slumped over the front seat of the Lincoln. The garage, suffused with carbon monoxide, caused a shocked Whitehead to repeatedly cough and gasp and flee into the fresh air. Deeply distressed, she phoned the police.

Later that day, West told police that he had bolted the apartment door. His reasons for doing so, which changed frequently, were as hard to pin down as a wet lemon pit and finally vanished like a mirage on a hot summer highway. The police were not sure whether he should be considered a suspect in a negligent homicide. Although he was ultimately cleared, his reputation was besmirched: he was generally regarded as a jerk.

The death of a movie star requires the denouement of a coroner's inquest, and the coroner's conclusion was awaited with morbid anticipation and curiosity. The autopsy surgeon A. P. Wagner testified that there were no signs of violence, but there was a superficial contusion on Thelma's lower lip, which may have occurred when, comatose, her head fell forward and hit the steering wheel. At the time of death, she was deeply inebriated and died of carbon monoxide poisoning. There was a 75 to 80 percent saturation of it in her blood. Wagner's conclusions were mocked by conspiracy theorists who began spreading tales of a Mafia hit ordered by Luciano, Cornero, or DiCicco, all because Thelma wouldn't allow a gambling casino on the top floor of her Sidewalk Café. Of course, no one presented a shred of evidence to prove such allegations. The logical explanation for the accidental death of a popular movie star was impossible for fans to accept. Just as many fans, two decades later, claimed that James Dean had not died in a car crash but was living out his life, disfigured, in a sanatorium. And that Marilyn Monroe died at the hands of the Kennedys. And that poor Elvis never died at all, for he was often sighted among the living as if he were an elusive UFO.

A grand jury also found that the sole cause of death was carbon monoxide poisoning and that Thelma was so inebriated that she fell into a deep slumber. It further decided, based on testimony, that West had stupidly locked her out of her apartment. Again, few people believed the grand jury's conclusion. As noted earlier, even Roland Button, Thelma's lawyer, believed that his client had been murdered by gangsters. Although he presented no evidence, his faith only helped to feed the deluded minds of conspiracists. The police, the DA, and the coroner, however, all remained convinced that Thelma Todd's death was an unfortunate accident. Remaining adamant in their beliefs, the conspiracists were regularly primed and aided by unscrupulous tabloid reporters who knew a good story would keep people talking and buying papers. Ever since 1935, the question of who killed Thelma Todd has refused to die. Was her killer DiCicco? Was it Luciano? Was it West? Or was it Alice Todd?

The only reasonable question, according to forensic pathologists, is whether Thelma's death was the result of an accidental suicide or an intentional one. Had she been fully conscious, she would have reacted violently to the ingestion of carbon monoxide. Her car generated such a large quantity of carbon monoxide that Thelma would not have been able to breathe. She would have coughed uncontrollably, and her eyes would have stung before she finally died. But because she was so inebriated, she became comatose. In such a condition, she would have quickly succumbed to the poisoned air. Marshall Croddy and Patrick Jenning write:

> *None of these factors absolutely precludes suicide of an "acute" suicide, but they raise stakes for demonstrating it. On balance, there is more evidence against this kind of suicide than for it.*
>
> *If Todd's death resulted from a depressed state, a more likely explanation for her demise rests with the "chronic" model for suicide. According to famed suicidolgist Karl Menninger, chronic suicides are those who exhibit ongoing, self-destructive behavior that is likely to end in accidental death as it is in any suicidal act. Researchers have demonstrated that many accidents, especially those involving motor vehicles, drowning and drug overdoses, can be interpreted as resulting from unconscious self-destructive drives.*
>
> *Thus Todd's death may have been partly suicidal.*[4]

Though careless behavior resulting in an accidental suicide is certainly a possibility, there's no denying that Thelma had a great deal going for her, including a new movie contract with Hal Roach, the Sidewalk Café, and many new movie roles on the horizon. She was intelligent, pragmatic, and ebullient. She was the toast of the town, not some tattered tart facing a future filled with failure. Suicide, whether intentional or accidental, seems highly unlikely.

The circumstantial evidence for murder has a list of characters, all of whom fail as killers.

First there is Pat DiCicco, who had had a violent relationship with Thelma. The heated words they exchanged at the Trocadero may have triggered his temper, and his violence may have escalated to a murderous rage. The reason for those heated words? Some conspiracists claim that DiCicco had wanted to remarry Thelma, but she rejected him, and that rejection sent him spiraling into a whirlpool of desperation and anger. He therefore sought revenge by killing her. After all, he was a gangster associate; he had the means and motive. The theory elaborates how DiCicco pulled off the murder: Peters dropped Thelma off at her apartment, where DiCicco was secretly waiting for her, hiding in the shadows. He crept up behind her, knocked her unconscious, and dragged her into the garage, whereupon he flung her onto the front seat of her car, turned on the ignition, made sure the engine was running, left the garage, and closed the door behind him. No one saw any of this. It was pure fantasy, suitable for film noir or the worst tabloid newspapers.

Others made Thelma's mother, Alice, out to be a devious, greedy, murderous Medea. Her supposed motive was to inherit her daughter's wealth, and as the only heir, she did. However, during her life, Thelma denied her mother nothing. She loved her and was committed to taking care of her. That Alice wanted to build a mansion and needed money to do so was another rumor that lit up dim minds. Yes, Alice had been a stage mother who pushed her daughter into a show business career, but rather than resenting her, Thelma happily thrived, luxuriating in all the benefits of her successful screen career. That Alice initially thought that her daughter had been murdered then changed her mind, telling the police and reporters that Thelma died accidentally only caused conspiracists to suggest that someone had threatened Alice. Alice said that the murderous scenarios were the work of unethical reporters who were charged with increasing the circulation of their newspapers. They were vultures who should not be believed.

Next in the lineup of possible murderers was Roland West and his alleged mob associates. Actress ZaSu Pitts, Thelma's good friend and costar, believed that Roland West may have arranged for Thelma to be murdered because he was being pressured by mobsters to allow gambling in the Sidewalk Café. He may have wanted the café all to himself and preferred lucrative gangster partners than a famous actress who refused to pour money into the café and to turn the third floor of the café into a gambling casino. Again, there is no evidence to back up such a theory. One sardonic reporter wondered if perhaps a jealous ZaSu Pitts murdered her friend.

ZaSu was not the only one close to Thelma who believed that the actress had been murdered. Years after she found her dead employer on the front seat of her Lincoln, Mae Whitehead told her granddaughter that she too believed that Thelma had been murdered by mobsters. She may have relied on the story of the waiter who had served Thelma at the Trocadero the night before she was murdered, who said that he had been threatened to keep his mouth shut or he would be kidnapped and murdered. When asked about it, police captain Blaine Seed said the waiter "knows nothing about the case and has nothing to conceal."[5] Even the grand jury foreman, George Rochester, perhaps influenced by rumors and articles suggesting that Thelma was murdered, came to believe the murder theory. However, he never mentioned any grand jury testimony or evidence that would have supported such a theory.

And what of the elusive and mysterious Lucky Luciano, who drops in and out of these conspiracies like a contagious virus? As noted earlier, he is first connected to the murder by Thelma's lawyer as reported in Kenneth Anger's 1975 book, *Hollywood Babylon*. Having researched the life of Luciano for my book *Big Apple Gangsters: The Rise and Decline of the Mob in New York*, I never found any reference to Luciano visiting Los Angeles. He and Meyer Lansky sent Bugsy Siegel there to take control of a racing wire. When the two mob leaders wanted Harry "Big Greenie" Greenberg assassinated, they told Siegel to return to New York for instructions about how to arrange the murder. Luciano never ventured farther west than Hot Springs, Arkansas. Furthermore, numerous memoirs by Hollywood celebrities never placed Luciano in Los Angeles. In fact, after he was arrested for pandering and prostitution, Luciano told reporters that the seat of his operations was in New York, though he had gambling interests in Chicago, Miami, and Saratoga, New York. His presence in New York would have been a sufficient alibi to prevent him from being tried and convicted of murdering Thelma.

Another reason to doubt a mob hit on Thelma is that the mob never used such subtle means as carbon monoxide poisoning to disguise a murder. When the mob killed someone, it was gruesome and public, the point being to scare anyone from challenging the mob's authority and operations. The only thing remaining undetected in the murder conspiracies was the killer himself. If there is no evidence to support theories of murder or suicide, then the only alternative is an accidental death. But what would Hollywood be without one more sensational myth?

In the end, a grand jury impaneled to investigate the case could reach no conclusion. It split between those who thought her death suspicious and those who thought it accidental, as the coroner first suggested.

The Sidewalk Café lived on for a while. Roland West continued to run the supper club after Thelma died. He was regarded as a lout for locking her out of her apartment. Those who once dined at the restaurant hoping to meet the illustrious Thelma Todd had no interest in meeting Roland West, a name that was generally unknown to the public. And those celebrities who had patronized the restaurant when Thelma was alive found other places for their dinners and parties. West realized that the café had lost its star appeal, and he eventually renamed it. No longer a successful director and a failure as a restaurateur, West lived on in poor circumstances. He was offered few jobs, and those he got paid just enough to live on. In the 1950s, he suffered a stroke, followed by a nervous breakdown, which made him unemployable. A friend told reporters that just before West died, he made a deathbed confession that he knew more about Thelma's death than he had told the grand jury. He died at age sixty-seven in 1952, a broken man and has-been. The last movie he directed was *Corsair*, starring Thelma Todd.

Dead all these years, Thelma Todd lives on as a sensational mythic figure, the subject of numerous books and even a movie. She has been cast as a martyr to Hollywood's greed and the movie industry's intolerance of women aging beyond their youthful beauty. Women cast aside and replaced by younger, more beautiful stars is the way of the world in Hollywood, without the involvement of murderers and the mob. Though the mob can be blamed for many things—including the extortion of Hollywood studios, owning major stars who remained forever in debt to their mobster handlers, and laundering money into the production of movies from which they profited handsomely—the mob cannot be blamed for the accidental death of a beloved movie star whose death profited no one.

NOTES

1. Ted Schwarz, *Hollywood Confidential* (Lanham, MD: Taylor, 2007), 147.

2. Michelle Morgan, *The Ice Cream Blonde* (Chicago: Chicago Review Press, 2016), 136.

3. Kenneth Anger, *Hollywood Babylon* (San Francisco: Straight Arrow, 1975), 204.

4. Marshall Croddy and Patrick Jenning, *Testimony of Death* (Redondo Beach, CA: Bay City Press, 2012), 246–47.

5. Morgan, *The Ice Cream Blonde*, 212.

Chapter Eight

Sidney Korshak

The Outfit's Fixer in Hollywood

HE WAS TALL, SLIM, ELEGANT, AND COMMANDING. HE COULD BE peremptory and imperious or engagingly charming. He kept his own counsel, never revealing a secret, often using his powers discreetly to get what his clients wanted or needed. He had affairs with Jill St. John and Stella Stevens. With a phone call, he could advance their careers or hinder the careers of others. Presidents, senators, governors, corporate CEOs, and chairmen always took his phone calls. He was often a guest in the Reagan White House. No one ignored his requests. He was said to be the basis of the character Tom Hagen in *The Godfather*. He was Sidney Roy Korshak, whom the FBI said was the most powerful lawyer in America. Though representing the Chicago Outfit, he was never arrested, never indicted. For the Outfit bosses in Chicago, Korshak walked on water. For others, he walked between land mines, never tempting fate, never the target of gangsters.

He was born in 1907, the son of Lithuanian Jews. He played basketball in high school and won a boxing championship at the University of Wisconsin. As both a high school and college student, he was admired for his toughness, never letting others push him around.

As a young Chicago graduate of DePaul University Law School, Korshak was introduced to the mob by Jake "Greasy Thumb" Guzik, who served as the mob's CFO and consigliere to Al Capone. Guzik mentored Korshak, while the ambitious young lawyer often chauffeured Al Capone to meetings with politicians. Having received Capone's stamp of approval, Korshak began representing Outfit members in court. Though Korshak displayed excellent legal skills, he became a savvy and circumspect briber of judges. He was a fast learner who quickly read the character of judges and thus succeeded as a reliable fixer of cases. He was known as such a subtle and secretive corruptor that law enforcement never laid a hand on him. As a master of manipulation, he developed close relationships with judges and politicians. Mayors, governors, senators, and congressional representatives all were recipients of his beneficence. The mob paid him handsomely and covered all his expenses, including his rent for a large suite at the Seneca Hotel in Chicago. Then, in 1935, the Outfit instructed him to go to Hollywood as the mob's man in Tinseltown. Korshak didn't have to be told to be discreet. His mind was like a locked safe and only he knew the combination. As he once said to movie producer Robert Evans, the key to staying alive is to keep your mouth shut. In their Bel Air mansion, Korshak's wife, Bee, wrote down phone messages for him when he was away. There were messages from George Washington, Thomas Jefferson, John Adams, and other historical luminaries. When Bee asked her husband the callers' true identities, her husband explained that they are who they say they are. Then added: "Any more questions?" Bee never asked again.

It did not take long for Korshak's skills as a fixer to be recognized by the movers and shakers of Hollywood. He was a master who could fix everything except the weather. His clients became a who's who of Hollywood stars, producers, and directors. He was also the Teamsters' man in California.

He quickly became known as a legal magician. His audience of clients never saw his shadowy tricks, but they all benefitted from his representation. Here was an outstanding lawyer who never bothered to get licensed in California. Though he called himself a lawyer, he was a manipulator of the legal system. With a phone call, he could bring a company to its knees by calling for a strike, or he could restore its operations with another phone call. With such power, why bother taking the California bar exam? Even if he had, he never would have gotten disbarred: he was too powerful to submit to rules and regulations.

During a busy day, he might buy the decisions of judges then host them at parties that night. He not only bribed with money, but also with the most beautiful prostitutes in the city. He could arrange for the offspring of the rich and powerful to be accepted at elite colleges and universities. He could arrange loans from banks and provide favors to and from politicians. He could round up enough celebrities and money to get those politicians elected and reelected. His favors were so great that no recipients wanted him harmed.

Although Korshak represented the mob, he was never considered a member of the mob. In California, he never appeared as official counsel for a member of the Outfit. Instead, he recommended lawyers to mobsters and provided discreet advice from a distance. So that he could represent legitimate businesses, it was essential to his success that he not be a member of the Outfit. And his list of Fortune 500 clients was impressive. His position was not only beneficial to him, but also to the mob. The heads of the Outfit wanted him to be seen as uncorruptible as a saint but as savvy as Machiavelli's prince.

In Chicago, Korshak had become close to Jimmy Hoffa, head of the Teamsters Union. Hoffa was in Korshak's debt for helping him become head of the union. Hoffa would do anything that Korshak asked him to do. Shortly after arriving in LA, Korshak began representing the Teamsters Union, whose trucking members carried loads of material in and out of the movie studios. A strike by the union could cost the studios millions of dollars. Korshak negotiated mutually agreeable contracts between opposing parties and billed extravagant sums to each. No one objected to his fees. A portion of those fees, after Korshak paid taxes, was given to business agents for the Teamsters as well as to the Outfit.

In a recorded F.B.I. conversation, Johnny Rosselli tells Jimmy "the Weasel" Fratianno, "One thing you got to keep in mind with Korshak. He's made millions for Chicago and he's got plenty of clout in L.A. and Vegas. He's really burrowed in. He's real big with the movie colony, lives in a big mansion in Bel Air, knows most of the big stars. He calls himself a labor relations expert but he's really a fixer. A union cooks up a strike and Sidney arbitrates it. Instead of a payoff under the table, he gets a real big fee, pays taxes on it, and cuts it up. All nice and clean."[1]

Korshak not only stayed out of the grip of law enforcement by never leaving a paper trail of his activities, but also by his wily resourcefulness. For example, when Senator Estes Kefauver subpoenaed Korshak to appear before a Senate committee investigating organized crime, Korshak put into motion a scenario that caused Kefauver to suddenly forget that Korshak existed. Korshak had arranged for a beautiful high-class prostitute to be with Kefauver in his room at the Drake Hotel. Unfortunately for the randy senator, a hidden camera had been placed in the room, its lens aimed at the bed. When Kefauver was shown the photos of his sexual acrobatics and told the photos would be made public and thus ruin his chances for running for president, Kefauver left town and Korshak's subpoena was shredded.

In Hollywood, Korshak was never seen in the company of mobsters. In fact, the Outfit instructed all LA mobsters never to call Korshak. If they needed a lawyer, they were to call Chicago and a lawyer recommended by Korshak would be assigned to them. Korshak wanted to be known as a fixer, not a litigator, and certainly not as some common defense lawyer. He positioned himself so that he could honestly state that he did not represent any gangsters, a statement that cleared him to work for legitimate corporations. He was a fixer, an adviser, a mentor, a sage statesman of the world. He advised clients on tactics and strategies, often while walking through elegant Beverly Hills neighborhoods. He may have been the originator of what became known as "the walk-and-talk conference," so prized by mobsters to avoid being taped. Korshak was so circumspect and protective of his image that he never gave interviews and refused even to be photographed. Yet at parties or in restaurants, he was always the center of attention, for he was considered the most powerful man in the room, the sun around which all the planets orbited. At one party, a gauche fan had the temerity to raise his camera and snap Korshak in conversation with the head of a studio. The room fell silent, and one of Korshak's emissaries asked the man for the film in his camera. The chagrined photographer apologized and emptied his camera, handing over a roll of exposed film. Party chatter resumed.

Connie Bruck, in her book *When Hollywood Had a King*, relates a story of Korshak's power: One day, he went to the Hollywood Park Racetrack. Its owner, Marjorie Everett, did not like Korshak because she considered him a gangster. Though he attempted to charm her, she had him thrown out of the racetrack. The next day, the Teamsters Union called a strike and closed the track. Everett wasted no time apologizing profusely to Korshak, and the strike was called off.[2] Everett told him he would always be welcomed back.

Perhaps one of the greatest beneficiaries of Korshak's power and influence was Paramount producer Robert Evans. Born in 1930 and originally named Robert Shapera, Evans grew up working for his brother Charles, who had founded the fashion company Evan Picone. Robert's career in the fashion industry was short-lived. Because he had such a deep, resonant voice, he was often employed as an actor in radio comedies and dramas. Then in 1956 while staying at the Beverly Hills Hotel, sleek and slender and tanned in a skin-tight bathing suit and sunning himself by the pool, he was being admired by movie star, Norma Shearer. She subsequently arranged for Evans to play her husband, Irving Thalberg in the movie *A Man of a Thousand Faces*. Soon thereafter, Darryl Zanuck, one of Hollywood's most powerful producers, hired Evans for the role of Pedro Romero in the movie version of Ernest Hemingway's *The Sun Also Rises*. Hemingway, who did not like Jews, protested Zanuck's choice of Evans. In his book, Hemingway created the character of Robert Cohn, a Jewish boxer who fights scientifically rather than passionately. Hemingway intensely disliked the scientific style of boxing exemplified by the Jewish boxer Benny Leonard. He thought it typified Jewish intellectualism; he wanted his boxers to be tigers. Critic Barry Gross wrote that "Hemingway never lets the reader forget that Cohn is a Jew, not an unattractive character who happens to be a Jew but a character who is unattractive because he is a Jew."[3] Hemingway certainly was unhappy to have a Jew playing the part of a heroic bullfighter who faced the chance of being gored every time he engaged an angry, tormented bull. (And Hemingway's good friend, Ava Gardner, who played the part of Lady Brett Ashley in the movie, also objected to Evans playing the role of the matador.) Nevertheless, Zanuck (who was known for his toughness) prevailed, and Evans played the role of a slick, sexy bullfighter whose skintight pants fascinated Lady Brett. (Skintight pants were becoming an Evans trademark.) He then appeared in a few other movies, but after his role in *The Best of Everything*, he realized that his talents would be better suited to producing movies rather than in acting. His first project as a producer was the 1968 movie *The Detective*, starring Frank Sinatra. His instincts were correct: the movie was a financial success.

It was Korshak who first thought that Evans's intelligence, creativity, farsightedness, and negotiating skills could make him a successful producer. The two had met in the 1950s in Palm Springs. Korshak was immediately taken by the charming, wisecracking young actor, who reminded him of Bugsy Siegel. Evans came to idolize Korshak, regarding him as a substitute father whose sage advice Evans regarded as close to holy scripture. Korshak, in turn, seemed to regard Evans as an adopted son. The mentor-protégé relationship quickly developed and continued for years to come. Back in LA, a day didn't pass when the two didn't speak with one another. Korshak initiated his plan to help Evans become a producer by touting him to Charles Bluhdorn, the president of Paramount's parent company Gulf + Western. It worked, and years later Evans insisted that Korshak had gotten him the job that paved the way for his career as a producer. Evans also hinted that the Outfit may have provided extra incentive.

When Evans was appointed head of production at Paramount, *Life* magazine wrote a scathing article that seemed motivated by a jealous tantrum:

> *Robert Evans is an outrage. He had no more right to be where he is than a burglar. He has no credentials, none of the requirements for membership. Robert Evans has never produced a film, doesn't know about movies, and so why should he be a boss at Paramount with control over 25 pictures a year, costing $100 million, influencing the cultural intake of millions of Americans? He is entirely too good-looking, too rich, too young, too lucky and too damned charming. The playboy peacock of Paramount. Who the hell does he think he is? If there's anything Hollywood wants out of Robert Evans, it's to see him fail.[4]*

Fail, however, he did not. In fact, his productions were all highly profitable, glittering successes; millions of people thronged to see his movies. Included in his long list of big-money hits are *Chinatown, Marathon Man, Urban Cowboy, Barefoot in the Park, The Odd Couple, Rosemary's Baby, Love Story, True Grit, Plaza Suite, Serpico, A New Leaf, Harold and Maude*, and most admired of all, *The Godfather* and *The Godfather Part II*.

When it came to the casting of *The Godfather*, no one was more helpful to Evans in securing Al Pacino for the part of Michael Corleone than Korshak. Pacino's agent had turned down Pacino's participation in *The Godfather* because the actor had other commitments. Evans, of course, knew who sat inconspicuously on the throne of power. Korshak called Jim Aubrey, head of MGM, and told him that Evans needed Pacino for the lead in *The Godfather*. Korshak was rebuffed by Aubrey, so he called Kirk Kerkorian, whose company owned MGM. Kerkorian was building a hotel in Las Vegas. The last thing he needed was a strike of construction workers and truck drivers that could bring construction to a halt. If he didn't want to lose millions of dollars to a strike, it would be wise of him to make sure that MGM released Pacino. Kerkorian said he would speak to Aubrey. Shortly thereafter, Korshak and Aubrey spoke. "After a 20-minute negotiation with Korshak, Aubrey called Evans, exploded with a series of expletives, and declared, 'I'll get you for this. . . . The midget's [Pacino's] yours." When Evans later asked Korshak what he had said to Kerkorian that swayed him to release Pacino, Korshak replied, 'I asked him if he wanted to finish building his hotel."[5]

If Korshak had not gotten MGM to release Pacino for *The Godfather*, it has been speculated that the movie would not have achieved the enormous success it has enjoyed. Francis Ford Coppola, the film's director, and its star, Marlon Brando, said that Pacino was essential to the movie. One cannot envision another actor being able to so inhabit the part of Michael Corleone as did Al Pacino. Evans went on to describe Korshak as his consigliere not only for the behind-the-scenes role he played in *The Godfather*, but for all his mountain-moving deeds. The choice of the word "consigliere" is significant and caused many in the movie industry to speculate if the character played by Robert Duvall was based on Korshak, though it should be pointed out that Korshak never needed to resort to the decapitation of a horse to achieve his goals. Mario Puzo, who wrote the novel on which the movie is based, claimed he never heard of Korshak. However, the makers of the movie certainly knew of his importance.

Korshak's power in service to Evans further revealed itself after Evans and his wife, Ali MacGraw, ended their marriage. Mac-Graw had been having an affair with Steve McQueen and the two eventually married. She and Evans had a son named Joshua, and McQueen wanted to adopt the boy and change his last name from Evans to McQueen.

Prior to the marriage of McQueen and MacGraw, Evans learned about their affair and told Korshak he wanted McQueen killed. McQueen heard about the threat and was frightened. He knew Korshak, for years earlier they had met at a party. Korshak had accidentally spilled his drink on McQueen, who became enraged and raised a fist to punch Korshak. Korshak held up a finger of warning and said: "Wait. You may be a big star, but if you lay one finger on me, I will have your fucking eyes ripped out."[6] Knowing Korshak's power and his relationship with Evans, a nervous, frightened McQueen, fearing for his life, later sought out Korshak and begged for his help. Korshak told him not to worry; he wouldn't be killed. McQueen thanked him and left.

McQueen, as smart as he may have been, did not learn from his encounters with Korshak nor did he intelligently evaluate Korshak's relationship with Evans. McQueen had the foolish boldness to phone Evans and tell him he wanted to adopt his son and change his last name. McQueen went on to say that he was having his lawyer draw up the appropriate papers. Evans's response was angry and direct: "Good. Take your best shot motherfucker. One of us pal, only one of us is going to come out in one piece."[7]

Evans called Korshak, who instructed him to hire a particular lawyer, who compiled a dossier on McQueen. McQueen and his attorney read the file, dropped their jaws, then dropped their case. "Not only was McQueen prevented from renaming the child, he was forced to eat more crow when he agreed to only refer to Joshua's father as Mister Evans."[8] No doubt the lesson of Korshak's power and his relationship with Evans finally penetrated McQueen's bloated ego.

Robert Evans was quoted in the *New York Times* obituary of his mentor: "Mr. Korshak could work wonders with a single phone call, especially [if] labor problems were an issue. 'Let's just say that a nod from Korshak . . . and the Teamsters change management. A nod from Korshak and the Santa Anita [racetrack] closes. A nod from Korshak and Vegas shuts down. A nod from Koshak, and the Dodgers can suddenly play night baseball.'"[9]

Though Evans occupied a warm place in Korshak's heart, the most powerful lawyer in Tinseltown helped others when called upon. So, for example, when Alan King, the comedian and actor, couldn't get a room in an expensive European hotel, he slid onto the stool in the hotel's phone booth and dialed Korshak. After a few polite queries, King explained to Korshak his problem and was told to hold on. A few minutes later, the desk clerk knocked on the glass door of the phone booth and told King his room was ready. King profusely thanked Korshak.

Korshak's power was so manifest that when he arrived at the Riviera Hotel in Las Vegas in 1961, his presence resulted in Jimmy Hoffa being moved from the presidential suite so that Korshak could occupy it. Hoffa did not utter a word of complaint: he was happy to oblige. At another time, Korshak was to meet with Jules Stein, head of MCA, in Stein's office. When Korshak arrived, Stein said that Korshak deserved to sit at his desk. Stein, as if a visitor in his own office, sat opposite Korshak. When their meeting concluded, Korshak asked Stein if he wouldn't mind leaving the office for a short period of time. Korshak needed the office for a private meeting with Meyer Lansky. Stein obliged and patiently waited outside, kibbitzing with his secretary. When the meeting was over, Korshak invited Stein back into the office.

Hollywood's elite so valued Korshak's power that they treated him as if he could move mountains, part seas, and bring down bolts of lightning on those who got in his way. One of his admirers was Warren Beatty, who called Korshak for help in finding a hotel room so that he could attend the 1968 Democratic Convention in Chicago. Try as he had, Beatty could not find an available hotel room in the entire city. He phoned Korshak and asked for his help. Korshak inquired where he wanted to stay, and Beatty said he favored the Ambassador East (the hotel featured in the movie *North by Northwest*). Korshak asked if he wanted a room or a suite. Beatty said a room would be fine. Korshak said he would call Beatty as soon as he could arrange something. Three minutes later, he called Beatty and told him that he could have his choice of three suites, each of which had been reserved in his name.

Being Hollywood's supreme power broker and a wizard at achieving what others thought impossible, Korshak was called upon to do more than arrange for hotel rooms. He reportedly used his creative skills to hide the investments of the Outfit in Columbia Pictures. Following the death of Columbia Pictures president Harry Cohn in 1958, Joan Cohn, his widow, married millionaire shoe manufacturer Harry Karl in 1959. The wedding took place in Korshak's Chicago apartment. Three weeks after the wedding, Joan Cohn filed for divorce. The FBI concluded that the marriage may have been a sham

for the financial convenience of people behind [Korshak]. The speculation was that Harry Cohn was fronting for Chicago investors in Columbia Pictures and when he died his estate went into probate and the marriage of Karl and Cohn was contrived as a method through which the real investors in Columbia Pictures could regain title to their property without disclosing themselves in public records.[10]

Evans was right: Korshak with a phone had more power than a mobster with a gun. He was not only the most powerful lawyer in America; he was the quarterback consigliere for the Outfit. No wonder Bill Roemer, celebrated FBI agent and organized crime investigator, said the mob had no more important person than Korshak for reaching into legitimate business, labor unions, Hollywood, and Las Vegas. And he seemed to be all over the map: he kept an apartment at 2970 Lake Shore Drive in Chicago, an office at 134 North LaSalle Street in Chicago, and maintained apartments in Las Vegas, another at the Essex House hotel in New York City, and a suite at the Beverly Hills Hotel. As if all that were not enough to keep his suitcases packed, Korshak also owned a home in Paris and a villa in Palm Springs. However, his Bel Air residence was his dream home; its multimillion-dollar art collection of impressionist, postimpressionist, and expressionist paintings was enough to tickle the palms of greedy curators, who often sent letters asking to view is his collection. At none of his abodes did he have a listed phone number, but his Rolodex was a who's who of movers and shakers.

In Hollywood, Korshak emanated more social allure than the biggest stars and most important producers. Though his moves were executed in shadows, he was a monument in the limelight of importance. The A list of Hollywood bigshots were drawn to him as metal filings to a magnet. The annual Christmas parties that Korshak and his wife Bee hosted were the high points of the Hollywood social season. Those who were not invited lamely claimed to have been out of town. Some even claimed to have been in hospitals or recovering from near-death experiences. "Sidney Korshak is probably the most important man socially out here. If you're not invited to his Christmas party, it's a disaster," wrote Joyce Haber in a 1975 column in the *Los Angeles Times*.[11]

Korshak didn't spend all of his time wheeling and dealing; he reserved sufficient time to carry on numerous affairs with some of Hollywood's most beautiful actresses, one of whom was the glamorous star Jill St. John. Though he had brief flings with other stars, Jill St. John was his prize catch. The former Jill Oppenheim was gorgeous, sexy, and smart. Though she was having an affair with then national security adviser Henry Kissinger, she preferred Korshak. Once when Kissinger invited her to a White House party, she told him she had a date with a more important person (i.e., Korshak). When word got back to Korshak, a subtle smile lifted his cheeks. He was extremely generous to St. John: he gave her a $50,000 diamond bracelet and bought her a Rolls-Royce convertible. Unfortunately for St. John, the car, which Korshak had bought while in London, was delivered to Korshak's wife, Bee, who was so impressed by the gift that she said her husband was the most thoughtful sweetheart. He couldn't very well tell his wife that the car was meant for another, and he didn't want to disappoint St. John, so he bought St. John a house in Aspen. The relationship finally ended, however, after Korshak refused to leave his wife and move in with St. John. In addition to all the money and jewels he had given her, Korshak had also gotten her a leading role in the James Bond movie *Diamonds Are Forever*.

"It was common knowledge he was keeping her. Sidney was incredibly powerful, generous, and charming. My opinion is that neither one thought this was going to last forever. I think they were both very real. If I was an attractive young lady, I would see nothing wrong with Sidney," said one of Jill's friends.[12]

Korshak, the ladies' man and power broker, had a friend who exercised as much control of the entertainment business as Korshak did, though he had a higher public profile than Korshak. He was Lew Wasserman, head of MCA. He had been hired by MCA's founder, Jules Stein, who believed that Wasserman was brilliant, creative, and hard working. Wasserman was twenty-three years old when he arrived in Hollywood in 1936. He learned the company's history from Stein, his mentor, who had booked bands into nightclubs owned by Al Capone. He knew that the Outfit's influence had been a significant factor in MCA's early success. Stein knew which bands to book and how much they should be paid. He worked it out with representatives of the Outfit. For MCA and the Outfit, it was a win-win arrangement. As the company grew, it signed big-name bandleaders, such as Guy Lombardo, Artie Shaw, Tommy Dorsey, and Harry James. By the mid-1930s, MCA had signed half the bands in America.

While Wasserman had started out as a theater usher and publicist, Jules Stein was a graduate of medical school, an ophthalmologist with a sharp eye not just for optical problems, but also for talent, deals, and artful negotiators. He was taken by the bright, energetic young Wasserman who had never attended college but who had a quick mind and was a savvy dealmaker and workaholic. Stein groomed him to be his eventual successor.

But Wasserman needed his own power broker, a man who could sweep away bullshit and deliver results. Korshak was his man. If Wasserman couldn't get it done on his own, he called on Korshak, who never failed. The two were a power couple and became the closest of friends. When the two sat down at a table opposite producers, actors, directors, and agents, they were an unbeatable team. By the time their relationship was in full flower, MCA had signed the top talent in Hollywood. There was a lot of money invested in their careers, so if movie stars got into trouble that might ruin their reputations and diminish their popularity, Korshak would be the magician who freed them of the chains of possible notoriety. Korshak, a master puppeteer, pulled strings, whitewashed reputations, and collected favors of those whose careers he saved. It wasn't just actors whose careers he served and studios whose investments in actors he preserved, it was also his extraordinary ability to demolish obstacles that stood in the way of productions being completed on time. For example: "MCA was shooting a movie in a Mafia-dominated neighborhood in Boston; the script was set in the twenties so the TV aerials were a jarring anachronism—but the producer had no success in trying to persuade the residents to take them down. Wasserman called Korshak; within hours the aerials were down."[13] The production was completed on time and within budget.

Korshak also made sure that the Teamsters never struck MCA or any of its clients. Whether it was labor negotiations or contract negotiations with producers, bankers, or investors, Korshak's behind-the-scenes activities were instrumental in helping Wasserman reach his goals. With Korshak's help, Wasserman helped James Stewart reduce his tax liability by becoming a corporation and successfully negotiating points for him in the movie *Winchester '73*. It started a trend for other Hollywood stars. Though Wassserman and Korshak had been extremely valuable to Stewart's career, one of Korshak's more devoted beneficiaries was Ronald Reagan. Korshak and MCA helped Reagan become president of the Screen Actors Guild (SAG). SAG's bylaws had always banned talent agencies like MCA from producing any form of entertainment, such as TV programs and movies. But during Reagan's fifth year as the guild's president, a secret blanket waiver was negotiated with SAG, giving MCA and Wasserman the opportunity not only to act as agents, but also to produce TV programs and movies. As a result, MCA formed MCA Television Limited, which handled syndication, and Review Productions, which made movies for theaters and television. This led to MCA becoming one of the biggest power players in the entertainment industry.

While MCA and Korshak negotiated real estate deals that made Reagan wealthy, MCA Review produced programing for

General Electric Theater, which Reagan hosted. MCA did not act out of disinterested generosity; quid pro quo was the modus operandi of the game for both politicians and mobsters. MCA and Korshak increased their wealth and power as they increased Reagan's wealth and power. It was an arrangement that would last through Reagan's presidency. MCA and the mob could certainly benefit from having an indebted friend in the White House, and to get Reagan there, they first helped to get him elected governor of California. Financing for Reagan's gubernatorial campaign included significant contributions from the entertainment industry and sources in Chicago.

Korshak, though a reliable supporter of Reagan, nevertheless judged him cynically. (A cynic, as Oscar Wilde wrote, "knows the price of everything and the value of nothing.") A prominent LA attorney, Leo Geffner, said of Korshak and Reagan: "Sidney would say, 'Ronnie says he's so pure, he's really phony with this big moralistic platform—he and I used to be with hookers in the same bedroom!' He said they went out screwing together in between Reagan's two marriages."

Geffner went on to state: "[Korshak] was the fixer, the money man, the consigliere to the real big boys. I can't tell you how many times I'd be sitting at the racetrack with him, and someone would bring him a note, and he'd say, 'I'm sorry, I have to go'—and later I'd find out that there had been a private plane waiting for him to take him to Las Vegas, or Chicago, or Miami."[14]

MCA and Korshak expected to benefit from Reagan's executive decisions, and they were not disappointed, especially during a vigorous Department of Justice investigation.

By the time that Reagan became president of the United States, the Department of Justice was investigating MCA's ties to organized crime. The Justice Department–FBI investigation into mob ties within MCA had started fortuitously when the organized crime strike force prosecutor Marvin Rudnick uncovered information that Salvatore Pisello was in the hierarchy of MCA. Sal "the Swindler" Pisello was a mobster whose ostensible career had been that of an ice cream and pizza distributor, but he was also known for smuggling heroin into the United States inside of frozen fish. His relationship with MCA had begun 1983. "Pisello was described in court documents as an alleged international heroin trafficker and high-ranking soldier in the Carlo Gambino crime family of New York who, in 1983 and 1984, engaged in a series of record business deals with Los Angeles-based MCA Records."[15]

Rudnick wanted to know why a high-ranking soldier in the Gambino crime family of New York was doing business with MCA and why he had the run of the MCA's offices in Universal City. He uncovered information that Pisello, who had been sentenced to four years in prison on a tax evasion conviction, was involved in criminal activity within the record industry.

> *Investigators are trying to determine how Pisello—with no previous record business experience—wound up in high-level meetings with MCA officers, including President Irving Azoff, negotiating record deals that earned him a high six-figure income—an amount that would place him among the best-paid executives in the industry.*
>
> *MCA, the giant Los Angeles-based entertainment firm and parent of Universal Studios, has stated that its record executives had no prior knowledge of Pisello's background or alleged organized crime ties. The various parties to the deals can't seem to agree on how Pisello got his foot in MCA's door.*[16]

Not unexpectedly, Pisello denied any involvement in organized crime and declaimed that he would go to prison for twenty years if anyone could prove otherwise. He also noted that he attended church every Sunday and belonged to the Holy Name Society. MCA, like an outraged Victorian virgin accused of sexual peccadilloes, huffed that Pisello would not have been connected to MCA if his criminal past had been known to them. He certainly would not have been permitted a free run of the company's offices.

One MCA employee stated: "Everyone in the office knew Sal. And he stuck out so much, in terms of style and appearance. You know, the diamond rings and gold watch. . . . There was a standing joke around the office that you didn't know whether to shake Sal's hand or kiss it."[17]

Pisello had arranged for MCA to purchase the catalog of Chess Records. He was also engaged in selling cutouts, which are older recordings that no one wanted. "Cutouts (so called because a corner is cut off a cover) are the record industry's remainders and overstock; deleted from a label's catalog, cutouts are sold to dealers for anywhere from 10 cents to a dollar. . . . [T]here were ten million cutouts in MCA's warehouses alone. . . . Cutouts had been sold through sealed bids to the highest per-unit bidder. Pisello had different plans."[18]

He offered to include popular saleable records that distributors and retailers wanted along with the cutouts. When prospective buyers refused the bait, Pisello's thugs beat them. That didn't stop Pisello from being treated as a valuable executive at MCA.

The investigation into MCA was moving forward at a brisk pace, when suddenly it was shut down. Marvin Rudnick was threatened by an MCA lawyer who told him, "we have friends in the courthouse. We can make life very difficult for you." Rudnick was called to Washington and told by Justice Department officials not to cause MCA "any embarrassment." Rudnick's new task force boss, John Newcomer, ordered him "not to conduct any investigation of MCA." Justice Department investigators working the LaMonte/Levy case on the East Coast were forbidden to cooperate with or even talk to Rudnick. (Morris Levy was president of Roulette Records, numerous other labels, owner of eighty-one record stores, nightclubs, and an associate of the Genovese crime family. He died in 1990, two months after losing an appeal of his extortion conviction; he had been found guilty of the attempted extortion of John LaMonte, a record wholesaler.)

Rudnick, however, was as persistent as a beaver. "While he got a conviction in the Pisello case, Rudnick was gradually defanged and was fired in 1989 for 'insubordination and failure to follow orders.'"[19]

Rudnick later commented,

> One week they were going to give me an award for getting the Pisello tax evasion convictions, but as soon as I tried to turn Pisello against the people who paid him off (MCA), they just snuffed it out. They called me a loose cannon. They pushed me out of my job and my career all because they wanted to stop something. What was it? They said it was because MCA was complaining about me. But it was because Wasserman was the connection between Korshak and the higher-ups in Washington. Wasserman was known for his political connections. You have to ask yourself, "Is someone getting paid off somewhere?"[20]

Would someone have attempted to intimidate Rudnick? When he told his bosses that he was being shadowed on the street, he was told to watch his back.

Richard Stavin, a former prosecutor with the DOJ's organized crime strike force in Los Angeles, told an interviewer,

> It's my belief that MCA and its involvement with Mafia individuals, Mafia-dominated companies and our inability to pursue those was not happenstance. I believe it was an organized, orchestrated effort on the part of certain individuals within Washington, D.C. to keep a hands-off policy towards MCA.
>
> At the time, Ronald Reagan was the President of the United States and Edwin Meese was the Attorney General of the United States. A little-known fact was MCA and Lew

Wasserman supported Ronald Reagan when he wanted to become president of the Screen Actors Guild, which was the launch of Mr. Reagan's political career.

I would like to think that the people in the highest levels of this government were not protective of MCA. . . . But I'm not so sure about that.[21]

In addition, FBI Special Agent Thomas G. Gates, said: "The powers trumped what we were trying to do. The players within MCA tried to stay as low-key as they could. I don't know how much influence Wasserman was able to put on President Reagan when he was in office because [Wasserman] was always a backdoor participant, but we knew who he was associating with."[22]

Before the government shut down the investigation of MCA, another mob connection was uncovered: Eugene Giaquinto, who ran MCA's home video division. FBI agent Gates said that Wasserman was Giaquinto's mentor, and Giaquinto had ties to Gambino crime family boss John Gotti. When James Caan wanted to make a movie about Meyer Lansky, Giaquinto (who wanted to make his own Lansky movie) got Gotti to kill the project. It's not surprising that Caan agreed not to make the movie.

The *Los Angeles Times*, in a story headlined "MCA Official Given Leave of Absence As FBI Probes Mob Tie," reported: "Eugene F. Giaquinto, president of MCA Inc.'s home video division, was placed on a leave of absence Thursday after news reports that the FBI suspects him of funneling company money to a reputed East Coast Mafia boss." The story continues:

The affidavits painted a picture of Giaquinto contacts with a reputed boss of a Pennsylvania crime family, Edward M. (The Conductor) Sciandra, to whom MCA cash was allegedly being passed on an annual basis; with the reputed boss of the Gambino crime family of New York, John Gotti, and with a number of

other individuals believed by the FBI to be connected to orga-
nized crime across the country. . . .

    Additionally, in the summer of 1987, when takeover rumors
sent MCA's stock soaring, FBI affidavits allege that Giaquinto
"furnished" information to individuals outside the company
about the health status of MCA's then-hospitalized chairman,
Lew R. Wasserman, and "the status of takeover attempts of
MCA . . . in advance of public disclosures in the media. . . ."

    The FBI affidavits said such dissemination is "a possible
violation" of federal criminal laws on insider stock trading. . . .

    In addition, "a power struggle was going on among differ-
ent Mafia families across the country to muscle in on the Lansky
film's potential profits."[23]

Wasserman and Korshak were certainly the beneficiaries of
having friends in high places. Not only had Reagan's White House
helped to terminate an investigation into MCA, it also helped to
entirely erase the Korshak-Mafia connection. In 1986, the President's Commission on Organized Crime delivered its findings in a
report titled *The Impact: Organized Crime Today*. Although Jimmy
"the Weasel" Fratianno told the Commission that Korshak "prac-
tically runs the Mafia industry,"[24] that information is absent from
the report. And although Roy Williams, president of the Teamsters,
told the commissioners that Korshak was a "member" of the mob,
that information is also absent from the report. When one of the
commissioners was questioned about why Korshak's involvement
in organized crime was not included in the report, he said: "It was
just not meant to be. There were forces that didn't want Korshak
touched. So the commission rounded up the usual suspects."[25]

Though Korshak passed through the investigation as elusive as
a ghost, he wasn't so fortunate when Seymour Hersh and Jeff Gerth
wrote a four-part exposé in the *New York Times*. That exposé was the
result of a six-month investigation into Korshak's activities. Among

the discoveries listed in the *Times* were the blackmailing of Senator Estes Kefauver, payoffs to Chicago judges and politicians, stock fraud that netted Korshak $1 million, a secret $500,000 payment for negotiating a secret deal between an organized crime figure and a public corporation that was kept secret from the Securities and Exchange Commission. Korshak allegedly threatened a client who tried to fire him and warned that another would not have labor peace unless it purchased all of its insurance from a Korshak associate. The Department of Justice rated him as one of the five most powerful underworld figures in America. Yet it never laid a finger on him. To say he was protected would be an understatement. In Los Angeles, he was revered as a top power player who could pull more strings than a dozen political power brokers. As one former Department of Justice official commented: "It's not like Korshak operates in some specific area, like one particular business or labor union. Korshak is unique, because he has the ability to deal with anybody, to fix anything. . . . I honestly believe that their [the Reagan administration] punch is being pulled."[26] And A. O. Richards, the FBI chief of its organized crime section in Los Angeles, stated: "He was almost an untouchable. You couldn't go after him, he was too well protected. Who would *dare* to wiretap Kokshak?"[27] Even when mobsters contacted Korshak on their own initiative, word got back to the Outfit, and those mobsters were warned never again to contact Korshak. "He has been with us thirty years. We don't want him loused up."[28] Indeed, he felt so invulnerable that when he and Robert Evans were walking from the 21 to the Carlyle Hotel one night in New York, Korshak noted that he was carrying $200,000 in cash. Evans exclaimed, "Are you crazy? How can you walk with all that money?" And he said, "Who's gonna take it?"[29]

Following the *New York Times* story, Wasserman began distancing himself from Korshak, though Korshak helped Wasserman arrange for MCA to purchase Universal Studios and Decca

Records. Wasserman then merged both companies into MCA and ran it like a Roman emperor until selling it to Matsushita Electric in 1990 for billions of dollars. From that deal, Wasserman reportedly earned $500 million. No one knows what Korshak's fee was.

Wasserman expanded the distance between himself and Korshak, who found Wasserman's behavior deeply hurtful. He couldn't understand that Wasserman didn't want his own reputation tarred by a broad brush of guilt by association. Not only couldn't Wasserman be seen with Korshak, but he couldn't talk to him on the phone. Who knew who was listening? It was one thing when Korshak existed in the shadows and pulled strings; it was another when he had been outed as part of the mob. It got worse for Korshak: the revelations in the *Times* of numerous of Korshak's shady dealings prompted California Attorney General Evelle Younger to release a report naming Korshak as one of numerous organized crime figures operating in California. The FBI set up a sting operation with a corrupt insurance agent to nail Korshak but failed to entrap the elusive fixer. Nonetheless, Korshak's power in Hollywood began to erode, especially after the murders of Jimmy Hoffa, Sam Giancana (onetime boss of the Chicago Outfit), and Johnny Rosselli. Korshak was becoming an island of bitterness in a roiling sea of troubles.

Paramount Pictures president Frank Yablans noted, "Sidney started to lose his power. He still had influence in Chicago and Vegas, but he lost it in Hollywood. In Chicago and Vegas people respected him for what he had done. But not in Hollywood—Hollywood only respects you for what you can do." Perhaps the hardest pill to swallow was the loss of Wasserman, for whom Korshak had done so much to keep his studio strike free. Yablans said that Korshak's "old-school" style just "brought Lew too much heat. . . . At the end of his life, Sidney was very bitter about Lew, about everything . . . not because he regretted the life he lived, but because he couldn't live the life anymore."[30]

Korshak had a long, prosperous, and exciting life. He died on January 20, 1996, at age eighty-eight. His life had filled him with pride and satisfaction. He was a man of enormous self-confidence who often found an outlet in arrogance. He had risen from poverty to great wealth and influence, the most powerful lawyer in America, according to the FBI. Korshak died of a cerebrovascular event brought on by arteriosclerosis. One wag, who marveled at Korshak's power and influence, commented that he had heard the news of Korshak's death but would still believe in the man's powers until he heard news that the fixer's body had actually been buried. The *Los Angeles Times* headlined its obituary, "Sidney Korshak, Alleged Mafia Liaison to Hollywood, Dies at 88." More than 150 people attended his funeral at the Jewish Hillside Memorial Park. The article failed to note that Korshak's firm represented major American corporations, such as Gulf + Western, Hilton Hotels, Hyatt Hotels, the Los Angeles Dodgers, the San Diego Chargers, and Schenely Industries, all of which are legitimate companies without underworld connections. Korshak's fees were enormous, ranging from $500,000 to $1,000,000 a year in 1976 dollars. He left behind eight cars, a magnificent wine cellar, and a fabulous art collection of impressionist, postimpressionist, and modernist paintings. In life, Korshak not only spent money generously on himself and on his wife and his lovers, but he was also extremely generous to charities. For example, he donated significant sums of money to the Cardinal Stritch School of Medicine at Loyola University. At one of the university's annual awards dinners, Korshak underwrote the entire cost, which was $50,000. The recipient of the award was FBI director J. Edgar Hoover, who sat with Korshak at the head table. In addition, Korshak gave generously to numerous Israeli charities and Jewish organizations in the United States. He and his brother Marshall generated multimillion-dollar sales of Israeli bonds.

Death breeds gossip like worms around a corpse. And so some of the women who counted themselves friends of the widowed Bee Korshak began wagging their tongues that poor Bee was left nothing by her philanderer of a husband. It was unbelievable, they said, that a man as rich as Sidney Korshak had not left behind millions of dollars for Bee. It was worse than a slap to the face. A search of Los Angeles County public records revealed that there was no probate, no visible assets except for the Beverly Hills home, which was part of a family trust. Of course, mobsters are known for not leaving estates that the IRS can examine and tax. Money is passed to heirs from numbered bank accounts and various business fronts. It was similar to what happened to the widows of Frank Costello and Meyer Lansky. They, too, it was said, had been left with nothing. Then, toward year's end, Bee took some work as an interior decorator. One project was the Sinatra home on Foothill. Around this time Bee anonymously auctioned off some jewelry through Christie's in New York. Reached for comment in February 1997, Bee said simply that everything had been left in a family trust. Yes, she said, she had redone the Sinatra home, but this was nothing new: she had worked as a designer for twenty-five years and had done all the Sinatra homes since Frank's marriage to Barbara. And, yes, she had in fact anonymously auctioned her jewelry, but not everything, only pieces she no longer wore. Neither poor nor deprived, Bee Korshak lived the rest of her life in comfort.

Perhaps Sidney Korshak should be remembered in the words of Hollywood columnist Joyce Haber: "Sidney Korshak [was] probably the most important man socially out here. If [you were] not invited to his Christmas party, it [was] a disaster." The party had indeed ended, but for his friends and those who benefitted from his power and influence, the memory ruefully lives on.

Sidney Korshak knew the rules, and as he told Robert Evans, the secret to staying alive was to keep your mouth shut.[31]

NOTES

1. Tim Adler, *Hollywood and the Mob* (London: Bloomsbury, 2008), 162.

2. Connie Bruck, *When Hollywood Had a King* (New York: Random House, 2003), 171.

3. www.commentary.org/articles/barry-gross/yours-sincerely-sinclair-levy/ (accessed December 21, 2022).

4. Gus Russo, *Supermob* (New York: Bloomsbury, 2006), 322–23.

5. https://screenrant.com/al-pacino-godfather-movie-cast-backstory-controversy-explained/ (accessed December 21, 2022).

6. Russo, *Supermob*, 396.

7. Russo, *Supermob*, 397.

8. Russo, *Supermob*, 397.

9. Robert McG. Thomas Jr., "Sidney Korshak, 88, Dies; Fabled Fixer for the Chicago Mob: An Obituary," *New York Times*, January 22, 1996, D10.

10. Dan E. Moldea, *Dark Victory* (New York: Viking, 1986), 138.

11. Moldea, *Dark Victory*, 279.

12. Russo, *Supermob*, 331.

13. Connie Bruck, *When Hollywood Had a King* (New York: Random House, 2003), 172–73.

14. Bruck, *When Hollywood Had a King*, 354–55.

15. www.latimes.com/archives/la-xpm-1986-05-04-fi-3550-story.html (accessed December 22, 2022).

16. www.latimes.com/archives/la-xpm-1986-05-04-fi-3550-story.html (accessed December 26, 2022).

17. www.latimes.com/archives/la-xpm-1986-05-04-fi-3550-story.html (accessed December 22, 2022.

18. www.washingtonpost.com/archive/entertainment/books/1993/04/11/making-music-with-the-mob/615b947e-ef2c-40e7-b53d-9cfe0d56f42f/ (accessed December 22, 2022).

19. www.washingtonpost.com/archive/entertainment/books/1993/04/11/making-music-with-the-mob/615b947e-ef2c-40e7-b53d-9cfe0d56f42f/ (accessed December 22, 2022).

20. Russo, *Supermob*, 504.

21. www.daile-Shocking-documentary-reveals-Mob-connections-catapulted-presidency-probe-thwarted-highest-levels.html (accessed December 26, 2022).

22. www.dail   e-Shocking-documentary-reveals-Mob-connections-cata
pulted-presidency-probe-thwarted-highest-levels.html (accessed December 26,
2022).

23. www.latimes.com/archives/la-xpm-1988-12-16-mn-165-story.html
(accessed December 26, 2022).

24. Russo, *Supermob*, 499.

25. Russo, *Supermob*, 499.

26. Moldea, *Dark Victory*, 336.

27. Bruck, *When Hollywood Had a King*, 351–52.

28. Moldea, *Dark Victory*, 337.

29. Bruck, *When Hollywood Had a King*, 356.

30. Russo, *Supermob*, 497.

31. Seymour Hersh, *New York Times*, June 17, 1976, 1.

CHAPTER NINE

The Cotton Club Murders

MR. SLICK. MR. SUCCESS. MR. HOLLYWOOD. ROBERT EVANS, made for greatness, was all of them. He produced a bonanza of moneymaking hits. His movies earned shelves of awards. He married beautiful women. He was the toast of Hollywood. Handsome, witty, engaging, he was the perfect subject for gossip columnists, TV interviews, and movie characters based on him. He didn't look the part of a typical Hollywood mogul (i.e., soft, balding, conservatively dressed in a three-piece suit); he looked like a movie star or fashion model or, as one magazine wrote, "a mannequin manque." He got his start in Tinseltown after being cast in a few good movies and a few awful ones. He was too ambitious to be a mere movie star and smart enough to know that he was not cut out to be a great actor. He was on-screen because he was handsome, elegant, tanned, and had a chiseled profile. He was certainly not in demand for his thespian abilities. Yet Evans was a genuine Hollywood hotshot. However, one day he would be called on to play a role he had never anticipated: a possible suspect in a murder trial.

Being a Hollywood producer often means being a high-stakes gambler. And if you've been winning for years, you expect to go on winning for the duration of your career. Evans was the man who had produced *The Godfather* movies; he obviously had a golden touch. And now, he wanted to produce *The Cotton Club*, a movie he touted as *The Godfather* with music. Who wouldn't want to invest in it? Perhaps a better question is, who would want to invest in a movie produced by a known cocaine addict whose most recent movies were disappointing and didn't portend future success? Well, not an Arab sheik, a Texas oilman, an investment banker, or a wealthy heir, all whom Evans had tried to sweet-talk. He eventually managed to scrape up a total of $8 million in foreign money, but that was a pittance compared to what his movie would cost. He needed a lot more money: $8 million would be just enough to cover preproduction costs. Evans thought that notorious arms dealer Adnan Khashoggi might come through with the necessary funds. After all, he was worth about $6 billion. Their negotiations resulted in Khashoggi investing $12 million in what the trade papers referred to as an independently produced Evans movie. Evans still needed a lot more money; he decided to sell his Paramount stock and considered the possibility of selling his beloved Hollywood mansion; however, he would hold off on that, at least temporarily. In order to raise additional funds, he knew he would have to retain a top Hollywood director, a screenwriter, and a cast of bankable stars. They would all have to be big names.

Could he do it? He knew he was yesterday's golden boy, and he didn't want to be tomorrow's tarnished failure. Could he, Robert Evans, one of Hollywood's most brilliant and successful producers rise from the flames of failure like the phoenix and be reborn? He believed that *The Cotton Club* would be the foundation upon which he could rebuild his career.

Yet people in the business still spoke of him as having lost his magic touch. As an independent producer, he was regularly dismissed as a failure for a string of box office flops: *Popeye*, *Black Sunday*, and *Players*. It was a trio that cost too much money and returned too little. No studio would give him money to produce more flops. No investor would pour money into a sinking venture. As if his string of failures wasn't enough for studio executives not to return his phone calls, Evans had further dimmed his tarnished star after he was busted in 1980 for cocaine possession and trafficking. He plea-bargained the charge and agreed to make a TV special titled *Get High on Yourself*. Like all such endeavors, it was intended as a form of redemption that would win the sympathy and admiration of viewers. Unfortunately, it was as popular with audiences as his three failed movies. Now no one wanted to take a chance on a man who seemed unable to produce hits and was considered an incorrigible drug addict.

Where to turn? A desperate Evans even asked his limo driver if he knew any rich people who might want to invest in movies. Perhaps wanting to get in on a good thing, his driver suggested that Evans meet a woman named Laney (aka Lanie) Jacobs. She was tall, elegant, beautiful, and presented herself as being enormously wealthy. She claimed that her wealth came from a jewelry business and ownership stakes in successful boutiques. In fact, she was in the cocaine business, and whether Evans knew this before he met her is uncertain. Some people claim he did and wanted to use drug money to finance his movie, while others say he was in the dark about it.

Laney grew up a poor girl in rural Alabama. She had worked as a legal secretary and drove an old Volkswagen bug. That was not the life she envisioned for herself. Her tastes were for luxury goods: cars, clothes, jewelry. She realized that rich men would be her means of escaping her unexciting life. Men and drugs. She used both with a casual willfulness that helped her become a millionaire. Each of her numerous husbands had paved the way for her to become an increasingly more successful drug dealer. (The number of her marriages is uncertain, for after her second marriage, she claimed that each new marriage was only her second.) She distributed drugs, via couriers, from Miami to Los Angeles. At her Sherman Oaks mansion, she received multiple kilos of cocaine, which she sold for $60,000 a kilo, then paid her supplier $45,000 per kilo. Her garage was stacked with kilo upon kilo. She received shipments every ten weeks and worked feverishly to sell the consignments as quickly as the kilos arrived. She was a rich woman, richer than she had ever dreamed of being. But it was never enough. She not only lived in a mansion, but she drove expensive cars and wore jewelry worth hundreds of thousands of dollars. She went to the finest restaurants, partied at exclusive clubs, snorted line after line of coke. She had multiple lovers; with a few exceptions, all were Hispanics involved in the drug business. With one of them she had a son named Dax; a perpetual scammer, she passed off various different lovers as the boy's father. The legal secretary in the old VW bug was a distant memory. Laney had shed that identity as completely as a snake sheds its skin.

After she was introduced to Evans, she thought she could use her millions of dollars to become a Hollywood producer and leave the drug business. Being a movie producer was far classier than being a drug distributor. She wanted a glamorous Hollywood life. She told Evans she could give him $5 million and come up with many more millions from associates in Miami. While selling Evans on her financial wherewithal, she was also supplying him with enough white powder to power both of their dreams of success. She imagined a glamorous Hollywood premier of their first movie, a blockbuster produced by Robert Evans and Laney Jacobs, their names writ in towering letters on a silver screen.

Evans and Laney knew they would need a big investor to round out their plans. Before Evans ever heard about *The Cotton Club*, he was introduced to Roy Radin, who brought *The Cotton Club* as his property to Evans; it was not long before Radin had sold Evans on the idea of producing *The Cotton Club*. They would be coproducers.

Before planting his flag in Hollywood, Radin did not have a career that portended success as a movie producer, but then neither did Evans. Radin had begun his professional life as a publicist for circuses, then graduated to producing vaudeville shows and revival meetings, all of which were sufficiently lucrative for him to buy Ocean Castle, a sixty-six-room mansion in Southampton, New York. Radin's theatrical tastes as manifested in his vaudeville shows were coarse and vulgar; however, he wanted to be respected as a serious Hollywood producer of critically acclaimed movies. He told his friend, the singer Tiny Tim, that he was going to become a successful Hollywood producer. Radin had visions of himself as the toast of Tinseltown. His most valuable property, *The Cotton Club*, would be his passport to fame and fortune. He intended to turn *The Cotton Club* into a great Hollywood musical. In addition to earning him respect, Radin believed the movie would diminish the notoriety that descended on him after a beautiful actress and former *Playboy* model named Melonie Haller had incriminated him after she was raped and beaten at a party in his mansion.

Haller's visit to Ocean Castle "had been arranged by a New York photographer named Ron Sissman who was a friend of Haller's and who told her that Radin might be able to help her."[1]

Her date for the evening was Robert McKeage, a management consultant. The next day, an unconscious, bruised, and bloody Haller was found slumped on a seat of a Long Island Rail Road car heading to Manhattan. A train conductor found her comatose body and called for an ambulance. She was taken to a hospital emergency room and police were called. She told officers that she had been beaten and raped in Radin's home and that Radin had a gun and a large quantity of cocaine. She also claimed that while being raped, she was filmed in Radin's bedroom. (The film in Radin's camera had been erased.) When questioned, Radin claimed that Haller had agreed to participate in sexual games. Apparently, she and Robert McKeage had dressed in sexy leather outfits, put on Nazi hats, then went into Radin's bedroom and began whipping each other. What came next was never elucidated. Nevertheless, after Haller's police interview, criminal charges were leveled against Radin for menacing and illegal drug and gun possession but not for rape. The ensuing notoriety was sufficient to put an end to Radin's traveling vaudeville shows, which had been used to generate funds for local police departments. It didn't matter that all charges against him were ultimately dropped; his reputation was stained. It wasn't removed even after Robert McKeage pleaded guilty to assaulting Haller and was sentenced to thirty days in prison. Sissman, whom Radin blamed for the whole episode, was shot and killed in his New York City apartment six months later. The killer had broken into Sissman's apartment, threw him to the floor, and fired a single bullet into his head. The murder was never solved. After all that, Radin needed a successful venture for his often cocaine-induced hyperenergetic pursuit of money and fame. He heard the siren call of Tinseltown, and he arrived eager to produce *The Cotton Club*.

Radin had always loved movie musicals, and his dream was to produce a musical that would put his name in lights and earn him millions of dollars. It would be *The Cotton Club*, and he would be known as a high-powered Hollywood producer. Soon after arriving in Los Angeles, he contacted Carol Johnston, a travel agent whose father owned a big house. Laney Jacobs was moving out of the house, and it was now for rent. Johnston introduced the two transplants, and all three soon attended a big Hollywood fete. Following the event, Johnston and Jacobs accompanied Radin back to his suite in the Regency Hotel. Radin was smitten with Jacobs, for they not only shared an ambition to be movie producers, but they also loved to snort cocaine. And Radin was impressed by the high quality of the cocaine that Jacobs gave him.

It was not long before Radin was introduced to Evans. Radin was exultant after meeting the producer of the two *Godfather* movies. He now firmly believed he was on a new road to success; that success would be greater than anything he had achieved as a producer of traveling vaudeville and revival shows. He told Evans that he was prepared to finance the production of *The Cotton Club* with $35 million. Whether Evans believed him or not is unclear.

He had been used to hearing wild claims from people who wanted to be in the movie business. Most of what they said evaporated when it came time to write checks. Yet Evans was willing to be convinced. When Radin showed Evans letters from the Puerto Rican government stating that it would sell bonds to fund *The Cotton Club* in exchange for Evans building a movie studio on the island, Evans took the bait. He went from being a skeptic to being a believer. While his belief in Radin's promise of financing remained unshaken, Jacobs was about to explode Radin's world, and Evans would suffer collateral damage.

Jacobs phoned Radin late one night and explosively accused him of stealing ten kilos of cocaine and $270,000 from her home. It was an outrage. She said her life was in danger. Radin listened unbelievingly for a few minutes, then told her she was crazy and hung up the phone. Jacobs was back on the phone within seconds, cursing Radin and demanding to know the whereabouts of her drug courier, Tally Rogers. Radin told her he didn't know, then added that she was irrational, and hung up again. He disconnected his phone.

In Miami, Tally Rogers had been hired as Jacobs's drug supplier by Milan Bellachasses; Rogers was given the responsibility for transporting cocaine from Miami to Los Angeles. He was regularly paid $20,000 for each cross-country drive with kilos of cocaine neatly packed in the trunk of his car. For his last drive, Rogers was promised $30,000 by Bellachasses, but Jacobs refused to pay him that amount. She said she would pay him his usual fee of $20,000. An irate Rogers thought Jacobs was keeping $10,000 for herself and decided to get even; he stole the ten kilos of cocaine and $270,000 from a safe in Jacobs's garage.

Jacobs refused to believe that Rogers acted on his own. Later the next day, she phoned Radin again after he had reconnected his phone. As soon as Radin answered, Jacobs accused him of setting up the heist. An exasperated Radin told her she was imagining such a scenario and hung up his phone before she could respond.

Jacobs's anger then turned to panic: she knew that Bellachasses, one of the biggest suppliers of cocaine in Florida, would kill her if she didn't pay him for the losses. It didn't matter that she and Bellachasses had been lovers. Meanwhile, Rogers moved from one southern state to another, hiding out, knowing that if his whereabouts were discovered, he would not live long. Jacobs phoned Radin again, this time calmly telling him that if Rogers returned the stolen kilos of cocaine, he could keep the $270,000. Again, Radin told her that he knew nothing about it. This time, a frustrated Jacobs hung up on Radin.

Jacobs cooled her anger by snorting a few lines of cocaine and entertaining visions of becoming a movie producer, even if that meant being an equal partner with Radin and Evans in their production company. She expected to make many millions and would easily be able to cover the loss of the money and the cocaine that had been stolen from her garage. However, unbeknown to Jacobs, Radin and Evans had come to an agreement: they would be the sole partners in their new production company. When Jacobs asked about putting together a corporate agreement in which they would all be equal shareholders, Radin and Evans responded by offering Jacobs a $50,000 finder's fee. The offer ignited another round of explosive anger. She screamed at Radin and Evans that the stolen ten kilos of cocaine, like all her other kilos, were provided on consignment: she was responsible for the loss and would have to come up with hundreds of thousands of dollars; otherwise, she could be killed. A $50,000 finder's fee would not save her. Bellachasses did not accept failure and had bragged about all the people he had killed. He would surely have Jacobs killed if she didn't pay him for the losses. Evans said he would be willing to give Jacobs a percentage of their production company, but Radin adamantly refused. As far as Jacobs was concerned, Radin had to be eliminated from *The Cotton Club*.

While Jacobs plotted against Radin for betraying her, Evans hired Francis Ford Coppola to film his musical extravaganza. Richard Gere was hired to play the lead, a musician named Dixie Dwyer, who was to be a member of the Cotton Club band. It didn't matter to producers or director that white musicians didn't perform at the Harlem-based Cotton Club. The Club featured some of the finest black jazz musicians of the twentieth century: Duke Ellington, Louis Armstrong, Billie Holiday, Lena Horne, Count Basie, Fats Waller. On Sunday nights, an exception was made, and white celebrities were invited to perform. They included George Gershwin, Sophie Tucker, Al Jolson, Fanny Brice, and Judy Garland, among various others. It was the hottest nightclub in New York.

The club was originally started in 1920 by heavyweight boxer Jack Johnson. However, in 1923, gangster Owney "the Killer" Madden, recently released from Sing Sing prison, forced Johnson to become the club's manager, while he took it over and made it a nearly insatiable customer for his bootlegged beer, Madden's #1. The club became a whites-only nightspot that featured black musicians and gorgeous young showgirls who (in the club's words) were "tall, tan, and terrific." They were black, but not too black. They had to be closer to tan.

Meanwhile, a lack of payment for the crew and performers generated a growing chorus of dissension that stalled production of *The Cotton Club*. Jacobs's revenge plot, however, was going full speed ahead. She called Radin and, in a calm, friendly voice and her best diplomatic persona, suggested that they get together for a friendly dinner to iron out their problems. Radin agreed, though his friends and his secretary warned him not to go. He would be meeting a ruthless drug dealer who would stop at nothing when it came to getting what she wanted. Radin lacked insight into the character of Jacobs. He believed what he wanted to believe, and he believed that he could charm her into accepting the $50,000 finder's fee. If told that she was planning to have him killed, he would not have believed it.

A few days before the dinner, Jacobs moved from planning to execution of her plot and hired someone to kill Radin. He was Laney's new boyfriend, William Mentzer, a handsome bodybuilder and bodyguard for *Hustler* magazine publisher Larry Flynt. Mentzer recruited his friend, Alex Marti, a man who loved guns and often fantasized about shooting people. Marti, an Argentinian immigrant, also worked as a bodyguard for Flynt. Steve Wick, in *Bad Company*, writes: "Marti loved guns, had a fascination with violence, craved money, and hated lots of people, but particularly Jews. A watercolor portrait of Adolf Hitler adorned one wall of his Los Angeles apartment."[2] After seeing a photo of Radin, Marti thereafter referred to him as a "fat pig." Mentzer and Marti were joined in the plot to kill Radin by Robert Ulmer Lowe, a security guard for *Hustler*, who would drive Jacobs and Radin to dinner in a limo supplied by Marc Fogel, who ran a luxury car rental company. Chauffeured by Lowe on May 13, 1983, Jacobs picked up Radin at his hotel and headed to what Radin thought would be a pleasant dinner at La Scala, a Beverly Hills restaurant popular with Hollywood actors, producers, and directors. In fact,

> the plan called for [Jacobs] to get out of the limousine at some point en route to Beverly Hills and for Mentzer and Marti to get in and force Radin to the floor at gunpoint. Lowe, Mentzer and Marti would drive Radin to the desert, and they would try to get information from Radin regarding the money owed [Jacobs]. Once in the desert the plan was to shoot Radin and blow up his face so his corpse could not be identified.[3]

Before departing for dinner with Jacobs, Radin began to have doubts about the wisdom of getting in a car with her, the warnings of his friends and secretary finally penetrating his naivete. He decided not to venture out alone and asked his friend and client, *Sanford and Son* actor Demond Wilson, to follow the limo. Wilson agreed to do so; however, shortly after he began following the limo, he lost sight of it. The limo had shot through a red light, leaving Wilson stuck behind a line of cars waiting for the light to change.

Days passed and no one heard from Radin. His friends and secretary reported him missing in mid-May. On June 10, 1983, Radin's badly decomposed body was discovered in a dry riverbed near Gorman, California, about sixty-five miles north of Los Angeles. Radin had been shot multiple times through the back of his head with a .22 caliber pistol. A stick of dynamite had been shoved into his mouth, which then exploded, blowing away the front of his face. The killers had wanted to eliminate the possibility of Radin being identified by his dental records. However, the killers failed to chop off his hands, so police succeeded in identifying Radin's rotted, shrunken, bug-infested corpse by his fingerprints.

When Evans heard the news of Radin's death, he naturally worried that he might be next. He knew that Jacobs was tied to violent drug dealers whose transactions often resulted in bloody, gunshot bodies. He locked his Beverly Hills mansion and decamped to Las Vegas, where he was shrouded in the protection of casino owners Edward and Frederick Doumani. Shortly after his arrival, he began discussing his need for money with the brothers. He knew they had many millions to invest, and he told them that the rewards from a hit movie would be substantial. Evans convinced them to replace Radin as investors in *The Cotton Club*. They put in $30 million in exchange for owning 50 percent of the movie. The Doumanis then brought in another investor, Victor Sayrah. Evans was now a minority shareholder. Shooting the movie finally commenced on August 28, 1983. In addition to Richard Gere, the cast of the movie included Gregory Hines, Diane Lane, Lonette McKee, Bob Hoskins, James Remar, Nicolas Cage, Allen Garfield, Gwen Verdon, Fred Gwynne, Laurence Fishburne, and numerous others.

Though a stellar cast of top actors, they were treated like interns in summer stock. They had not been paid and threatened to strike. A chorus of their complaints rose in waves of anger that crashed against the stony silence of investors. However, when it became apparent to the investors that they would indeed go on strike, the cast was finally paid. Director Francis Ford Coppola, one of the most in-demand directors in Hollywood, also had not received his full fee and warned that he would not continue until paid. The machinery of moviemaking could not be allowed to grind to a halt, for the cost to the Doumanis and others would be greater than their investment. So Coppola was paid a portion of his fee.

Yet the production still proved chaotic with much extemporizing, the abandonment and destruction of specially built sets, and frequent script changes. Rumors circulated that mob-connected shylocks were bringing suitcases of money to Evans. The vigorish on those loans would be enough to cause bouts of mental agony. Evans was running faster and faster on a treadmill to nowhere. Production costs continued to mount. No one was happy with the script, so from July 15 to August 22, 1983, writers shot out new scripts as fast as pitched baseballs in a mechanical batting cage, though none were hit back, scoring no runs. Writer Mario Puzo was out; writer William Kennedy was in. Kennedy estimated that between thirty to forty scripts were dashed off. Not even journalists working under punishing deadlines could write so quickly. During one forty-eight-hour period, twelve scripts were written. Finally, on August 22, 1983, a shooting script was polished and accepted. To relieved investors, cameras began rolling. Cast and crew were all on board at the Kaufman Astoria Studios in Queens, New York. That, however, was not the end of the chaos. Costs rocketed to $250,000 a day as more than six hundred craftspeople built and rebuilt sets, designed and produced costumes, and arranged music. To cut costs, crew members were fired. Several weeks later, the movie was so over budget that the producers decided to deduct expenses from

Coppola's fee. It didn't matter to Evans and others that Coppola had received only a portion of his fee. However, it mattered to Coppola, who walked off the set. He refused to continue directing until he was paid the full amount: $4 million. Though the money for Coppola soon would be found, the producers now had second thoughts about the script. Again, it was written and rewritten.

To say that the Doumani brothers were growing frustrated by the mismanagement of their investment would be an understatement. Casino owners regularly make money; they don't invest $30 million to see it flushed down a toilet. As costs on *The Cotton Club* continued to rise, the Doumanis reached out to Orion Pictures and asked for enough money to complete the movie. An agreement was reached, but it was contingent on Evans stepping down as producer. This was a tremendous blow to the producer of *The Godfather* movies and other major Hollywood hits. To guarantee no further cost overruns, the Doumanis brought in a watchdog, their friend Joey Cusumano, who would oversee the production like a lion guarding its next meal. He was a reputed associate of the Chicago Outfit and a friend of notorious hitman Anthony "Tony the Ant" Spilotro (who had been chosen to protect the Outfit's skim at several casinos and was later beaten to death for his failure to meet the goals that had been set for him). Cusumano's calm but menacing presence had the desired effect on the set. He issued an order that could not be countermanded, instructing the entire crew that the majority of the filming had to be completed by December 23, 1983. "Cusumano whom the crew was by now calling 'my favorite gangster,' distributed T-shirts with 'December 23, 1983' printed on the back to keep everybody focused."[4] Several years later, Cusumano was convicted of an insurance scam and sentenced to four years in prison. He also survived an attempted assassination. But on the set, Cusumano was a general overseeing an army of compliant soldiers who followed his orders without so much as a whispered demur.

Evans, though now superfluous, nevertheless became a target for investor complaints. He had originated the chaos, and those he had sweet-talked wanted more than a pound of flesh. He ended his liability (whatever it may have been), accepted a $1 million payoff, and was given back the deed to his beloved Beverly Hills mansion, which he had mortgaged to help finance production of *The Cotton Club*.

The trials and tribulations of the filming of *The Cotton Club* left Evans's reputation tarnished, and it would be further stained by the murder trial of Jacobs and the men she hired to kill Radin. Six years after *The Cotton Club* opened to less-than-rave reviews, Radin finally received justice but not the kind of fame that he had hungered for. Unfortunately for Evans, the murder trial generated more publicity than the movie had.

When called to testify, Evans, upon the advice of famed Hollywood lawyer Robert Shapiro, invoked his Fifth Amendment right. Who in his right mind, after all, would want to incriminate himself in a murder trial? Looking tan and fit as usual, his long dark hair pomaded and perfectly coifed, his eyes shielded by large tinted glasses, he sat before judge and prosecutor as Shapiro asserted that Evans could not be compelled to incriminate himself. As expected, Shapiro's argument prevailed, and Evans—despite appearing tense throughout Shapiro's explanation—ultimately looked relieved. From the start, prosecutors must have known that they were wasting their time when Evans refused to answer whether he knew Radin. He uttered his Fifth Amendment rights with the dismissive air of Hollywood royalty. Though he may not have acquitted himself as being completely innocent in the eyes of cynical reporters, he nevertheless left the courtroom a free man. The prosecutors' frustration was palpable, for they had been unable to obtain testimony that might have generated thousands of words of positive publicity.

Evans, handsome playboy producer, and his putative golden goose, Laney Jacobs, whose real name is Karen Delayne Greenberger, were supposed to be the stars of the trial. But now that

Evan's lawyer freed him from the traps of incrimination, Greenberger would get star billing all by herself. Testimony revealed that she was less a theatrical investment angel than a drug distributor for a major Colombian cocaine network run by Carlos Lehder.

The case against Greenberger and the hitmen she hired was, to a large extent, based on the evidence and testimony of William Rider, former brother-in-law of *Hustler* magazine publisher Larry Flynt. Rider had come forward to offer his cooperation, which propelled the investigation into high gear. Rider was then wired to obtain details that would implicate the defendants. "Asked why it had been necessary to kill [Radin], Mentzer told Rider two different stories. One story was that Radin had been killed because Laney believed he was somehow involved in the theft of cocaine from her house. The second story was that Radin had tried to cut her out of a promising movie deal with Evans."[5] To protect their star witness, authorities provided round-the-clock police protection for Rider. It was not long before prosecutors were able to charge Greenberger, Alex Marti, William Molony Mentzer, and Robert Ulmer Lowe with the murder of Radin.

Another valuable witness was Carl Plzak. The Associated Press reported that "Most details were corroborated last week by Carl Plzak, [who linked] the defendants to the crime. Plzak, a body builder and sometime bodyguard, received immunity from prosecution in the Radin murder for his testimony. He said he heard the others make plans to 'grab a fat pig and take him to the desert.' Later, he said they told him about the murder."[6]

Following the trial's closing arguments, cocaine dealer Karen DeLayne "Laney" Greenberger, age forty-three, was found guilty of second-degree murder. The conviction carried an automatic sentence of life in prison without parole. Evidence proved that she had hired hitmen Alex Marti, William Mentzer, and Robert Ulmer Lowe to carry out the murder. Each of them was convicted of first-degree murder, kidnapping, and six additional charges.

Greenberger's attorney, Edward Shohat, vehemently argued that his client should not be sentenced to life in prison but should serve a reduced term of sixteen years to life in prison with the possibility of parole. "Impose a severe sentence that would grant Mrs. Greenberger a hope, not a promise, but a hope that she may someday return to society." The judge did not buy it: Superior Court Judge Curtis Rappe refused Shohat's request to drop the special circumstance allegation of kidnapping for extortion, which mandates life in prison.

"I find it hard to believe, in fact impossible to believe, that she just thought Mr. Radin was going to be taken for a ride," Rappe said. "The potential for violence loomed large." He added that Greenberger should have known that kidnapping and extortion often end in the death of the victim. He therefore rejected the defense lawyer's argument.

To counter the defense, Kate Radin, eloquently emotional, said that Greenberger should get the maximum sentence of life without possibility of parole. She then held up a photo of her brother and read a poem. "Maybe he isn't a perfect 10, but maybe you'll think before you hire a triggerman again," she said. Speaking from a handwritten note, she tearfully added, "We couldn't look at Roy's body. It was a skeleton with very little of the head intact from gunshots and dynamite."[7]

The Cotton Club was not as fascinating as the bitter arguments, crazy accusations, and murderous plots that preceded its premiere. The movie received poor reviews and was a box office flop. Greenberger would have come out ahead if she had simply accepted the finder's fee of $50,000 and remained free to carry on her drug dealing and scheming. Radin might have avoided his grisly death by simply giving Greenberg a piece of the movie. Evans, of course, could not abandon his reputation as one of Hollywood's great magicians, a producer who had his finger on the pulse of the zeitgeist and created hit after hit. Given the opportunity to be a player in Hollywood, to make a name for oneself or maintain one's place on the top of the heap of A-list celebrities and to reap millions of dollars as tribute to one's talents and sagacity is an irresistible siren call. But what if things had worked out as Radin, Greenberger, and Evans had originally dreamed? None of them had been able to pass up the chance of being celebrated, rich Hollywood producers. No one, not even Hollywood oracles, can predict the future.

In the years after *The Cotton Club* killing, Evans's career crawled slowly along. His movies did not live up to his earlier successes. He no longer was a zeitgeist weathervane. He continued snorting cocaine. However, Hollywood was in his blood. He could not walk away from the arena in which he had been celebrated for his magical ability to produce award-winning hits. He was not one to lounge in self-pity, transfixed on the past. He was a player, and he was going to prove to himself and others that he still had the ability to produce hits. Eventually he rose from a crawl, stretched his legs, and joined the pack of those feverishly running toward success. It would not be an easy race. But Evans was determined to take whatever actions were necessary to reach the finish line. He produced several films for Paramount and released his gossipy, self-aggrandizing autobiography. After losing his house as a result of tanked investments, he regained occupancy with the help of his loyal friend, Jack Nicholson. In a profile in *Vanity Fair* magazine, he vengefully declared: "I'm back on top, and don't you think it doesn't taste sweet."[8]

He may have spoken too soon. But his determination was as strong as a hurricane. He said he was going to produce a sequel to his critically acclaimed and popular movie *Chinatown*. He even considered acting in it, but his acting chops, though never terrific, had rusted over the years. Better to do what he did best: produce it. The *Chinatown* sequel, *The Two Jakes*, was written by Robert Towne, who also had written *Chinatown*. Problems arose, and shortly after production had begun, Evans was fired. It was not only a blow to his ego, but it further contributed to his reputation as a has-been.

With a $25 million budget, production resumed in 1990 with Jack Nicholson directing and starring in it. It didn't matter; the movie was another critical and financial flop, generating box office sales of $10 million. But Evans would not give up. His 1995 project was an erotic thriller titled *Jade*. It starred David Caruso, Linda Fiorentino, Chazz Palminteri, and Richard Crenna. It, like *The Two Jakes*, was another flop. The movie's $50 million budget resulted in meager box office sales of $9.9 million in the United States. In 1997, Evans thought he finally had come up with a project that would be a surefire hit. Planned as a franchise series of movies like 007 and other spy thrillers, *The Saint* starred Val Kilmer. However, the movie didn't do well, and no sequels were produced. Yet by Hollywood blockbuster standards, it enjoyed modest financial success, earning box office sales $169.4 million on a budget of $90 million. Before moving on to his next producing project, Evans narrated the documentary, *The Kid Stays in the Picture*, based on his 1994 autobiography of the same title. Then, whammo: in 2002, he achieved great success with his final movie: *How to Lose a Guy in 10 Days*. On a budget of $50 million, it earned $177.5 million. Evans was now back on top. His celebrity shone brightly; the dark clouds dispersed. He returned as the daring daredevil of dreams in magazine profiles and on TV interview programs. None of the stories failed to mention that he had been married to a series of sexy goddesses: Sharon Hugueny, Camilla Sparv, Ali MacGraw, Phyllis George, and Catherine Oxenberg. That he had been mentioned in the case of notorious Hollywood madam Heidi Fleiss only added further luster to his image as a rogue lover.

Evans returned not only as a celebrated producer, but as a bon vivant and Hollywood legend. He was asked to speak at numerous dinners and award ceremonies. While toasting director Wes Craven at an awards ceremony, he suddenly had a massive stroke and collapsed. He uttered a garbled burble of sound. An ambulance's siren screamed as it rushed Evans to Cedars-Sinai Medical Center. He was almost a goner, having flatlined during the dash to the hospital, but he was soon resuscitated. Like the aftershocks of an earthquake, three additional strokes attacked his body, and he nearly died. Amazingly, he lived, though his right side was paralyzed and he had been robbed of the ability to speak. Nurses, doctors, and therapists ministered to him, working tirelessly to restore Evans to a modicum of health. The man who deserved much credit for helping Evans regain his ability to speak was media mogul and close friend Sumner Redstone, who stayed at Evans's bedside day after day. During that time, Evans learned that Frank Sinatra lay close to death in the next room. Sinatra soon died of a heart attack, and Evans watched as the corpse of the world's greatest pop singer was wheeled away. Rather than filling Evans with pessimistic dread, Sinatra's death provided a strong drive to recover and return to his life as a producer. Through tremendous force of will and with expert help, he regained his ability to speak and learned to walk short distances, albeit with the aid of a cane. He died in Beverly Hills on October 26, 2019, at eighty-nine years old, and was eulogized as one of Hollywood's great producers, the man who produced two of the most celebrated American classics: *The Godfather* pictures.

NOTES

1. Steve Wick, *Bad Company* (New York: Harcourt Brace Jovanovich, 1990), 66.

2. Wick, *Bad Company*, 112.

3. www.leagle.com/decision/incaco20210607006 (accessed February 2, 2023).

4. Tim Adler, *Hollywood and the Mob* (London: Bloomsbury, 2007), 209.

5. Wick, *Bad Company*, 181.

6. https://apnews.com/article/947fe214043d686b164f14353b11fea (accessed February 2, 2023).

7. www.upi.com/Archives/1992/02/07/Mastermind-in-Cotton-Club-kidnap-murder-gets-life-in-prison/5393697438800/ (accessed February 2, 2023).

8. www.vanityfair.com/hollywood/2022/04/robert-evans-the-offer-true-stories (accessed February 2, 2023).

CHAPTER TEN

Lords of Pornography

THE PORNO MOVIE *DEEP THROAT* USHERED IN NOT ONLY THE CON-cept of porno chic, but also the golden age of pornography. Following the opening of *Deep Throat* in June 1972 at the New World theater on West Forty-Ninth Street in Manhattan, five thousand patrons a week viewed the movie. It was a bonanza for the mob. They didn't care whether the patrons were chic or not. The golden age for them meant a cascade of money. And *Deep Throat* was one of the top box office winners, beating out many legitimate Hollywood hits. Of course, the golden age could not last forever; now anyone with an internet connection can freely watch hours of porno videos, including scenes from *Deep Throat*.

Though *Deep Throat* was a turning point for the mob, porno profits for them started long before porno chic. For many years, the mob had been making and distributing "stag films," which produced a steady stream of nontaxable income. But the amounts did not result in luxurious retirements for aging mobsters. In addition to the "stags," (eight-millimeter black-and-white movies of short duration) the mob also produced "loops" (porno movies that were shown in "peep" booths where viewers deposit a quarter or a dollar to watch a few minutes of the movie on a small screen); lines of booths were found in porno stores, such as those that lined the streets of Times Square in the 1970s, 1980s, and 1990s. The stores were owned by the mob and virtually everything in them (e.g., magazines, sex toys, blow-up dolls, video cassettes, and, later, DVDs) were manufactured by the mob, distributed by the mob, or distributed by mob-owned front companies.

The mob's men in porno included Richard Basciano, a property developer, who owned the Show World Center, the biggest sex emporium in Times Square. The center, which was known as the McDonald's of Sex, had porno movies, topless dancers, live sex shows, and peep booths, some of which displayed naked dancers on slowly revolving stages. Horny men inserted quarters or dollars in the slots of peep machines for a few seconds of masturbatory excitement. More than one hundred women performed daily on one of the center's four floors. As a bonus attraction for star-starved fans, porno actresses made personal appearances at the center. They sold and signed photos of themselves performing a variety of sex acts. The media dubbed Basciano the "Porn King of Times Square." If Show World was a many-ringed circus of sex acts, then Basciano—in addition to being its king—was also its ringmaster.

There was another kingdom along porno's glaringly garish, gaudy road of temptations. Michael ("Mickey Z") Zaffarano, a member of the Bonanno crime family, owned numerous buildings in the area that housed porno stores, massage parlors, and movie theaters, including the Pussycat Cinema. The euphemistically named massage parlors were, in fact, brothels, where customers were given menus of variously priced sex acts. The no-frills ones operated along Forty-Second Street (aka the Deuce) and on Eighth Avenue. The more upscale ones operated on the East Side of Manhattan, where they catered to office workers during lunch or after work. Because Zaffarano was smoothly diplomatic, he was often called upon to mediate disputes between various Mafia families over the production of X-rated movies. From distributing movies, the mobs moved quickly into the production of movies, and Zaffarano was often called upon to arrange for the division of profits. Zaffarano was like an old-time movie studio boss, for he had the foresight to see the enormous profits that could be made if the mob controlled the making of movies, the distribution of movies, and even the pirating of movies.

Men like Zaffarano were eager to establish a monopoly. Although the federal government pursued mobsters for a variety of financial crimes and for transporting obscene material, they never prosecuted them for attempting to operate a monopoly. Whereas the Hollywood studios had to divest themselves of their theaters, the mob continued cranking out movies and showing them in their own theaters. The profits were enormous.

And like the Hollywood studios, which wined and dined important critics, the Bonanno family put Al Goldstein, editor and publisher of *Screw* newspaper, on its payroll. They were assured rave reviews. Excerpts of Goldstein's reviews, for example, were featured on the marquee of the Pussycat Cinema. And whereas more legitimate reviewers of Hollywood fare rated movies with a series of stars, ranging from one to five, Goldstein's reviews were highlighted with drawings of erect penises, ranging from one to four. The Bonannos were never awarded anything less than four penises.

The *New York Times* reported on Zaffarano and the Bonanno crime family in a story headlined "Sex Business Linked to Alleged Mobster":

> *Justice Department and city police records describe Mr. Zaffarano as a "captain" in the Carmine Galante crime group [aka Bonanno crime family]. According to law enforcement officials, he has secretly been involved in the pornography trade for almost a decade and he reportedly is so influential that he arbitrates disputes over pornography trafficking and profits.*
>
> *Mr. Zaffarano served a seven-year term in a federal prison for transporting stolen securities. He was known to*

*be the former bodyguard for Joseph Bonanno, who previously
headed the Galante crime organization.*[1]

When Zaffarano was told that he had been indicted for trafficking
pornography and would be arrested, he dropped dead of a heart
attack at the feet of FBI agents. It may have been one of the most
emphatic surrenders in the annals of crime.

Two other mobsters played important roles in the porno industry: Louis "Butchie" Peraino, one of the producers of *Deep Throat*,
and Robert DiBernardo, a member of the Gambino crime family
who was murdered by Salvatore "Sammy the Bull" Gravano on the
orders of John Gotti.

Peraino's father, Anthony "Big Tony" Peraino, and his uncle
Joseph "Joe the Whale" Peraino were members of the Colombo
crime family. Each of the brothers was alleged to weigh at least
three hundred pounds. Though they could not walk through a
doorway together, their combined power was enough to intimidate
anyone who got in their way. One person who worked diligently
to avoid getting in their way and to ingratiate himself with them
was Chuck Traynor, manager and husband of Linda Lovelace.
He either forced or encouraged Lovelace to perform fellatio on
Butchie Peraino to ensure her role in *Deep Throat*. It was not so
much in the tradition of the Hollywood casting couch as it was a
new kind of audition.

Butchie owned two-thirds of the company that produced *Deep
Throat*. The other third was owned by the movie's director, Gerard
Damiano. When the Perainos saw celebrities and middle-class
couples lined up to buy tickets for *Deep Throat*, they knew they
had hit gold. Millions of dollars in ticket sales would pour into the
Colombo coffers. Unfortunately, the movie's stars, Linda Lovelace
(born Linda Boreman), whom Butchie referred to as a sword swal-
lower, and her costar Harry Reems (born Herbert John Streicher),

who performed sex acts like a mechanical rabbit, each earned the measly sum of $1,200 for their filmed sexual antics.

Of all the stars of X-rated movies, Linda Lovelace became the most famous. She rose to fame solely due to the success and notoriety of *Deep Throat* and then increased her fame by becoming a spokesperson for sexually abused women. She appeared on numerous television talk shows, often contradicting herself and altering the facts of her life. Nevertheless, after listening to her laments, one cannot help but feel sympathetic toward this woman whose career consisted of serial abuse and alleged beatings that drove her to submit to dehumanizing sex acts. Her demeanor ranged from sad bravado to coy smiles to self-righteous denial about her past. What seemed undeniable, however, was that her manager-husband, Chuck Traynor, treated her as his sex slave, often beat her into submission, and pimped her for money. Though Lovelace specifically claimed that Traynor had forced her to make porno loops for peep shows, others who knew her said she was more than willing to do so. She also claimed that Traynor had forced her to make a bestiality movie titled *Dograma*. However, the cameraman and another porno actor said that Lovelace was a willing participant. Her later attempt to bridge the worlds of porno and legitimate movies manifested in a starring role in a 1975 comedy titled *Linda Lovelace for President*, in which she played the presidential candidate of the Upright Party. Her slogan was "A vote for Linda is a blow for democracy." The movie, in its X-rated and R-rated versions, was a box office flop. Lovelace lacked the talents and skills to be a respected actress. Audiences only wanted the Linda Lovelace of *Deep Throat*.

Adding to the public's puzzlement about the real Linda Lovelace, she published four contradictory books. Two of the books, *Inside Linda Lovelace* and *The Intimate Diary of Linda Lovelace*, were written to appeal to the lascivious fantasies of male readers.

The third and fourth books, titled *Ordeal* and *Out of Bondage*, in which she portrays herself as a victim of abuse, fed the antipornography movement. As a result, Lovelace was accused of being an opportunist who had thoroughly enjoyed participating in porno movies but then did an about-face after her porno career came to an end. Her new role was that of an ardent feminist and member of a group called Women against Pornography. Lovelace eventually married, had two children, and died at age fifty-three as a result of a horrific car crash.

Her *Deep Throat* costar, Harry Reems, was a sybaritic figure who gave up on his failed acting career to earn a living as a porno star. In addition to appearing in *Deep Throat*, he appeared in another popular porno movie, *The Devil in Miss Jones*, after which he appeared in numerous less popular porno movies. Other than reliably exhibiting his copulative abilities in porno movies, he earned the dubious distinction of being the first American porno star to be prosecuted for performing sex acts in a movie. He commented that at least he wasn't prosecuted for a poor performance: "In the end, I came through." His career nearly made a successful U-turn when he was cast as Coach Calhoun in the 1978 movie, *Grease*. However, after surveying moviegoers in the Bible Belt, the producers decided that the teen musical would be boycotted if Reems were to appear in it. The part then went to Sid Caesar. Eventually Reems abandoned his hopes for a career in mainstream Hollywood movies and became a real estate agent and converted to Christianity. He died at age sixty-five of pancreatic cancer.

Being a director of porno movies was a different story. As a result of the success of *Deep Throat*, Damiano was offered a job as a director with MGM—if his movies contained scenes of hardcore pornography—but neither he nor MGM could come to terms about the length of such scenes and whether stars or standbys would perform. Though Damiano never got to direct legitimate Hollywood movies, he did direct more than fifty porno movies that elevated him to the celebrated position of a porno auteur. After directing *Deep Throat*, he asked the Perainos for his share of the movie's profits. They didn't exactly tell him to get lost, but they told him his salary was $15,000: take it or leave it. He not only took his fee, but he was forced to accept a buyout for his one-third ownership of the *Deep Throat* production company for $25,000. If he had insisted on his rightful share as a one-third owner, he would not have gone on to make other porno movies. He would have been either dead or crippled.

Though the stars and director of *Deep Throat* received less-than-generous salaries, the movie made financial history, out-earning the most popular Hollywood movies of the year. Not bad for a movie filmed primarily in an inexpensive motel on Biscayne Boulevard in North Miami that cost a mere $25,000 to produce. Yet it made more than $600 million worldwide: $127 million in box office sales and $385 million in home video sales in the United States alone.

As a result, the Perainos were swimming in money. They had so much cash they didn't know where to hide all of it. They settled on stashing some money in offshore and Swiss banks and parlaying their success as producers of Deep Throat into making other blockbusters. They decided to open Bryanston Distributing Company, also known as Bryanston Pictures. The company went on to release *Flesh for Frankenstein*, *Dark Star*, *Return of the Dragon*, and *The Texas Chain Saw Massacre*, among various others.

The Perainos became targets not only of the FBI, but also for mobsters who wanted to take over their business and prevent them from possibly turning into prosecutorial witnesses. Following his conviction on six counts of interstate shipment of pornography, Joseph Peraino Sr. was tracked down by gunmen to a quiet residential street in the aptly named Gravesend section of Brooklyn. The gunmen, blasting away with shotguns from a speeding car, shot him in his buttocks. Unfortunately, two innocent people doing laundry were shot full of holes and died at the scene, 432 Lake Street, off Avenue W. A third man, Joseph Peraino Jr., age thirty, was hit several times while running into the apartment of the two dead launderers. There had been several earlier attempts to kill the Perainos, but they had been blessed that those gunmen couldn't shoot straight.

The Perainos not only kept their distance from gunmen, they also never succeeded in getting close to the Mitchell brothers, neither of whom was out to murder the Perainos. The Mitchells did not operate in Hollywood and New York so were often ignored by the mob. The Mitchells had produced and directed *Behind the Green Door*, one of the top-earning porno movies of the golden age. It starred a fresh-faced, blonde, all-American young woman, Marilyn Chambers, who had been pictured on millions of boxes of Ivory Snow soap cuddling an adorable baby, below which a tagline announced the soap—if not the model—was "99 & 44/100 pure." Chambers was the image of idealized young American motherhood. Chambers went on to be managed by Chuck Traynor, the notorious former husband of Linda Lovelace. In addition to the *Green Door* movie, she appeared in another popular porno movie titled *Insatiable* with John "Johnny Wad" Holmes. Later in her career, she was drawn to politics and ran for vice president on the Personal Choice ticket, a libertarian party, and received 946 votes. Her checkered career included acting in a few legitimate movies and several plays. She even recorded a disco record. She died at age fifty-six (ten days short of her fifty-seventh birthday) from a cerebral aneurysm.

After hitting it big with Chambers and *Green Door*, the Mitchells were contacted by members of the Gambino crime family, who finally became aware of another money-making opportunity. The Gambinos offered the producers a multimillion-dollar distribution package. The Mitchells turned them down. And instead of being murdered, they became victims of a massive counterfeiting scheme.

The Gambinos realized they would achieve little by killing the Mitchells, so they produced millions of counterfeit copies of their movies and distributed the copies throughout the world. The Gambinos made unrecorded millions via their own distribution deal.

Among the Gambinos, the man who had the Midas touch in the pornography business was Robert DiBernardo. He started out as a family soldier with the DeCavalcante family in New Jersey but was soon taken in by the Gambinos and served the family boss, Paul Castellano. Not a leather-jacket-and-jeans type, he wore bespoke suits and had a pleasant manner. He appeared more like an investment banker than a mafioso dealer of pornography. He was not a member of a crew; he operated solo and had little power within the family. He was respected for being a great earner and a savvy entrepreneur. His company, Star Distributors, grew to be the main supplier of pornography not just in New York City, but throughout much of the country. He was also responsible for bringing hundreds of pornographers under the control of the Gambinos. In addition to his successful distribution business, he produced cheaply made porno movies, which were distributed to theaters and sold in porno stores.

As early as 1972, the *Wall Street Journal* had identified DiBernardo as a widely known "prominent dealer in pornography." He was less well known as the nation's largest distributor of child pornography. According to FBI documents, DiBernardo was a top lieutenant to Gambino family boss Paul Castellano and was aided and mentored by capo Ettore Zappi, who had sponsored DiBernardo for membership in the Gambino family.

An unwelcome spotlight focused on DiBernardo in 1986 after federal postal inspectors discovered cartons of magazines depicting underage boys engaged in sexually explicit conduct at porno stores in Times Square and Greenwich Village. The magazines, inspectors claimed, had been distributed by DiBernardo. Prior to that, he was regularly surveilled and monitored by the FBI, which raided his offices a few times, confiscating evidence of child pornography and financial records. His first arrest for child pornography had occurred in the late 1960s for distributing a magazine titled *Young Stuff*. The charges against him were dropped as a result of insufficient evidence. For DiBernardo, arrests were the price of doing business, and the price was minimal compared to the vast sums that he and the Gambinos made from pornography.

Worse than the indignation he expressed about being arrested was the anger he expressed to friends about having to pay inordinately large tributes to Castellano, a man known for his greed. DiBernardo grew to despise his boss. In return, Castellano made no secret of his contempt for DiBernardo and the business of pornography, referring to DiBernardo as a smut peddler. Nevertheless, DiBernardo continued to deliver packed briefcases of cash to his boss, who continued to despise him and his rackets. DiBernardo had no choice but to continue.

Castellano would never think of rejecting money from a source he despised. Money was money, and he wanted as much of it as he could get. As the boss, he was entitled to significant sums of the money earned by all family members. From soldiers to capos to the underboss to the boss, money flowed upward, and no one was entitled to dispute the volume of the flow. Whenever DiBernardo complained to friends about the amount of money he was required to turn over to Castellano, his friends wisely cautioned him to cool his anger and suppress his comments. If not, he would be killed and replaced by a more congenial messenger.

As his anger intensified, DiBernardo was happy to see John Gotti becoming increasingly powerful in the family. It was rumored that after Gotti's mentor and family underboss Aniello Dellacroce died, Gotti would make his move and eliminate the hated Castellano. Indeed, after Gotti had arranged for the assassination of Castellano and installed himself as the new boss, DiBernardo expressed his loyalty to Gotti. Gotti, who admired, valued, and expected loyalty from family members, rewarded DiBernardo by promoting him to capo. Yet DiBernardo was still without a crew, so his position as capo carried less weight than other capos had. As a crewless capo, DiBernardo did not have soldiers whom he could command to kill, extort, beat, or commit any of the other crimes in a gangster's repertoire. Had he wanted a crew, he certainly could have organized one. But, for a man who never killed anyone, he didn't have to issue threats to get others to comply with his demands. All he had to do was let it be known that John Gotti was his boss and would act to protect his capo.

One arena in which his position as capo did not help him and managed to hurt others was presidential politics. During the 1984 presidential campaign, the media had been fed rumors about vice presidential candidate Geraldine Ferraro's husband, John Zaccaro, and his possible dealings with the Mafia. Rumors led to DiBernardo, and the media shined a probing spotlight into his shadowy dealings. Zaccaro had rented space to some of DiBernardo's porno operations. A whirlwind of false accusations, innuendo, and insinuations resulted in the narrative that Ferraro was a patsy connected to the Mafia through her husband. The whirlwind grew into a hurricane of nasty rumors that helped to capsize her candidacy and that of her running mate, Walter Mondale. No evidence ever emerged that Zaccaro was involved with the mob. He was just an innocent landlord. But Mondale and Ferraro were trounced by Ronald Reagan and George H. W. Bush, who won every state except Minnesota and the District of Columbia.

DiBernardo was now hated by many Democrats who had previously been unconcerned by the pornography business. Though DiBernardo had been disparaged in the media as a porno entrepreneur and a mob associate, mob reporters asserted that he was not a conventional gangster: he did not become a made member by killing anyone and in fact had never killed anyone. That was no consolation to politicians who went down to defeat. Though he was an embarrassment to some family members who would have liked to take over his businesses, DiBernardo thought he walked on water because of all the money he generated.

In addition to generating torrential rivers of money, DiBernardo was smart enough to know that he could increase the torrent by developing partnerships with other porno entrepreneurs. Three of those characters were Reuben Sturman, Michael Thevis, and Theodore "Teddy" Rothstein.

Sturman, known as the "Walt Disney of Porn," started his career selling comic books then expanded his operation to selling porno magazines and sex toys. His company grew quickly and in short order became the largest distributor of porno magazines in the United States. He soon extended his business operations into Canada, Great Britain, Panama, Liberia, Lichtenstein, and the Netherlands. He carried out the international expansion of his business through General Video of America, one of the largest distributors of sexually explicit video cassettes in the world. In Los Angeles alone, cops discovered that 580 of 765 porno arcade machines were owned by companies that Sturman controlled.

Sturman, like numerous mobsters before him, made himself a target for investigations and prosecution because he had failed to pay income taxes and had laundered more than $7 million through foreign banks. His failure to report and pay taxes resulted in a $2.5 million fine and a ten-year prison term beginning in 1989. Back in 1986, the Attorney General's Commission on Pornography named Sturman the most prolific producer and distributor of pornography and the wealthiest pornographer in the history of the world. He was proud of his position and his accomplishments. The government, however, didn't care whether he was proud or embarrassed. All it wanted was a conviction, which it won in 1992. Sturman was convicted of racketeering and interstate transportation of obscene matter.

Criminality, desperation, and resourcefulness were imbedded in his psyche, so it was not surprising that he had attempted to win an acquittal by bribing a juror. He was caught and convicted, and a merciless judge sentenced him to an additional nineteen years in prison. However, determined to thumb his nose at his judicial fate, a madly determined Sturman escaped from prison, using the darkness of night to evade detection as he fled through fields and forests, across creeks, and under bridges. From Bron, California, his escape route carried him as far as Anaheim, where cuffs were placed on the angrily submissive convict. For his efforts, Sturman was led into small, dark cell, where he cursed his fate in solitary confinement. He died in prison on October 27, 1997, at age seventy-three.

His notoriety, however, did not prevent him from becoming a celebrated martyr in the video porno industry. The Reuben Sturman Lifetime Achievement Award has been presented to leaders in the porno industry at the annual AVN (Adult Video News) Awards Ceremony held in Las Vegas. The event has been compared to the Oscar ceremonies, though it has never aired on network television.

Michael Thevis, in addition to being a pornographer, was also a murderer whose partners included DiBernardo as well as the members of the other four New York Mafia families and the DeCavalcante family of New Jersey. Thevis, a man of expansive ambitions, controlled the distribution of all peep show machines in the United States. His control and uncompromising demands led to his moniker, the "Sultan of Smut." Though millions of dollars poured into his coffers, the sultan's reign didn't last long. He was arrested, tried and convicted. His new title was convict. In prison, he was identified by a series of numbers; his ignominious end was preceded by his conviction for murder and racketeering.

Unlike Sturman, he did not attempt to escape from prison. Instead, as a man who always played the angles, he managed to persuade former US congressman Andrew Young of Georgia, who had been appointed US ambassador to the United Nations, to intervene and contact the head of the Bureau of Prisons so that Thevis could be moved to a facility where he would receive proper medical care. Young's letter had arrived on UN stationery, and its author received the respect due to a high-ranking government official. The ever-resourceful Thevis died in prison on November 20, 2013.

Teddy Rothstein was luckier than Sturman and Thevis. He and DiBernardo, co-owners of KED Productions Inc., were among forty-four others who were indicted following an undercover FBI investigation of publishers and distributors of pornographic movies and magazines. DiBernardo and Rothstein were convicted of transporting and distributing obscene materials across state lines on June 12, 1981. They were each sentenced to five years in prison; however, a federal judge overturned their convictions and ordered their indictments dismissed on grounds that the undercover FBI agent who had investigated them may have lied to a grand jury. The agent was subsequently arrested for shoplifting, and evidence suggested that he suffered from an inability to distinguish between his genuine identity and the identity he assumed when working undercover.

DiBernardo said he had escaped a bullet. But another one was waiting for him. He would be set up by a mob friend whom DiBernardo trusted. DiBernardo never considered that another member of the Gambino family would order his death, for he was a great earner who never threatened the status quo of the family. He was reliable, even tempered, and respectful. Nevertheless, John Gotti ordered that he be murdered.

In his book *Underboss*, Peter Maas quotes Sammy the Bull Gravano stating:

> *Angie [Angelo Ruggiero] is the messenger to communicate what John [Gotti, who is in prison] wants done. In early June, Angie came to me and said John has sent out an order to kill DiB*

*[DiBernardo]. He said DiB was talking behind his back, and
there were other reasons, which Angie didn't say.*

*DiB's a brilliant, wealthy guy. Paul [Castellano] used him
directly with unions, and other business, and he's in with these
Jewish guys as the largest distributor of X-rated films and stuff
in the country. . . . But DiB is no threat. He's got no crew,
no strength.*

*Angelo wants to be underboss. Joe Piney had told me that
DiB said to Angie he had the balls to be underboss, but not the
brains. If anyone should be underboss, DiB said it should be
Sammy. That didn't mean anything to me.*

*I said to Angie that if DiB was saying anything it didn't
mean nothing. Just talk. DiB wasn't dangerous. I asked Angie
to reach John and see if we couldn't hold up on this, and when
John came out, we would discuss it.*

*But Angie immediately responded that it had to be done.
John was steaming. . . .*

*Angie came back to me. He said John was really hot. He
wanted it done right now, he wanted it done right, and he
wanted me to do it. I didn't know what Angie was telling John
about my reservations. I knew Angie was into DiB for two
hundred and fifty thousand. I could imagine that this could've
played a part in everything. But I don't know if John knew that.*

*I told Angie that DiB would be coming to my office for a
construction meeting at five thirty. . . .*

*I sent the girl in my office home at five. Me, my brother-in-
law, Eddie, and Old Man Paruta were there. DiB came in and
said hello. I told Paruta to get him a cup of coffee. In the cabinet,
there was a .380 with a silencer. Paruta took it out, walked over
to DiB and shot him twice in the back of the head.*[2]

Unfortunately for the family, they were never able to untangle
DiBernardo's tightly knit complex of deals in the pornography

industry. As a result, profits that should have flowed to the family dried up like a stream after a severe drought. Gravano, however, did not walk away empty-handed, for he took over DiBernardo's interest in Teamsters Local 282.

Though Gravano and DiBernardo remain important figures in mob history, there were others who rarely made waves and rarely made news. One such was 350-pound "Chick." (His family asked that I not use his name, for it would embarrass members who operate legitimate businesses.) In the 1940s, 50s, and 60s, Chick ran one of the biggest porno movie distribution companies on the East Coast. He grew up in New York's Little Italy and began his movie career by shooting weddings, often at old St. Patrick's Cathedral on Mulberry Street. His nephew, who grew up to be a CPA and a successful financial adviser, told me:

My uncle would get copies of master reels of color super-8 film. There were two copies of film on a reel. One was reversed and had to be slit from the one that was not reversed. My job was to slit the film, separating one side from the other. I was known as a slitter. After the films were separated, I boxed them, and arranged for the boxes to be shipped all over the world.

During the summer, I worked 14 hours a day at his warehouse, and when I was in college I worked there every evening. I was paid four times the normal hourly pay at the time and learned a lot about the industry.

It was strange to see the sexual tastes from different parts of the world. For example, in Mexico and some Eastern European countries there was enormous demand for bestiality movies, and not just women and canines, but also women and farm animals. There was also an interest in scatology in some Asian countries.

Chick expanded his distribution business to producing movies as well. He made a series of porno movies in a girls' college dorm in which students participated, after being told that their identities would be concealed or disguised. He even made a movie in an empty Catholic church in Mexico. It was called Father Casanova. While he was there, he fooled around with a number of hookers who were in the movie, and the director took still photos of Chick. He had the photos in his jacket pocket when he arrived back in Brooklyn. He went to work the following day, and his wife discovered the photos. She took the photos and pasted all them to the front door of their house. When Chick got home that night, he was not only met by the montage of photos, but also by the message his wife had scribbled on the front door: "I hope you had fun you fat bastard!"

Chick had done something that went beyond angering his wife. He had been required to pay the mob a percentage of the profits from each movie he sold. Instead of paying them based on the profits of the two films that I had slit, he pretended that he had made a profit on only one of the slit films. Well, the mob discovered it, and they put a contract out on him. Fortunately for Chick, there was an obese owner of a Greek diner only two blocks from the warehouse. He was mistaken for Chick and shot on the street. After that, Chick met with the mobsters, and they came to an agreement. Chick escaped, but was later arrested in the 1960s. A photo of him was on the front page of the New York Daily News. *His business was called the biggest porno operation in the city. Fortunately for him, he had a great lawyer named Eddie Mishkin, who in a landmark case, won an acquittal based on the illegal search and seizure of material in the warehouse. It was considered a major Fourth Amendment decision. Chick died a few years later of liver cancer. By then the porno business was no longer illegal: there were porno movies playing in Times Square theaters, and the Internet gave the mob new opportunities. It's strange that in the 40s, 50s, and 60s, pornographers could get long jail sentences, just as drug dealers did. Now pornography is ever present and marijuana is sold and smoked openly.*[3]

Indeed, by the mid-1980s, law enforcement no longer harassed the pornography industry. Much of it had moved to California, where studios solely devoted to the production of X-rated movies thrived. The police commissioner of Los Angeles stated that 90 percent of porno movies were made in LA, the movie capital of the world. Organized crime, he claimed, still controlled much of the industry, but what it controlled was completely legal, with the exception of child pornography, snuff films, and other topics declared to be without legal protections.

But just a few years earlier in 1977, the FBI executed the largest investigation of the pornography industry in its history. It was called the MiPorn (i.e., Miami Pornography) investigation. In the MiPorn case, two FBI agents, Patrick Livingston and Bruce Ellavsky, went undercover and formed a pornography business in Miami as a sting operation; the business had bank accounts, checks, credit cards. The FBI agents traveled throughout the United States, meeting and doing business with major pornographers. They knew the porno business was large and thriving, but they were nevertheless surprised at what an octopus it was. Tentacles stretched into so many different spheres that it was hard to track down all the pieces.

And it wasn't just adult porno movies and magazines they came across. There was an abundance of child pornography, stolen property, illegal weapons, money laundering, prostitution, sex trafficking, extortion, and drug dealing. All the pornographic material was shipped to an FBI warehouse in Miami. Cases were made and prosecuted.

What was initially targeted as a six-month probe with a modest budget of $25,000, eventually developed into an extremely dangerous, 2½-year investigation of the Mafia's involvement in obscenity, costing taxpayers almost a half million dollars.

With their crash-course on the pornography industry behind them, the two opened Golde Coaste Distributors in a warehouse

near the Miami airport. Ostensibly a blue jean outlet, the "real"
business operating out of the store was the distribution of adult
films and magazines. Unbeknownst to a number of criminals
who would visit the location, an electronics expert for the
Bureau had wired the building with cameras and microphones.
Much valuable and irrefutable evidence was gathered there
over the coming months.

Livingston and Ellavsky began making contacts with
lower-echelon players, but before long they were able to infiltrate
the close-knit ranks of the country's pornography leadership.[4]

The FBI agents regularly faced danger, but it

was not in the discovery of their true identities. It was if the
gangsters mistook them for informants. An example of the peril
they lived in was manifested in a trip to New York to visit
Robert DiBernardo's operation. They were warned by one of
his associates not to cross him: "There are plenty of people who
would kill for DiB." But whether they were "made" as cops or
not, pornography had become a dangerous business. . . . About
80 players in the business who . . . were either doing at least five
years in prison or had been murdered.

As time went on, the Batman and Robin of obscenity inves-
tigations continued to establish significant contacts with big-
time pornographers. During their time on the case they made 25
first-class flights to various cities around the country—even one
trip to Hawaii to purchase child pornography.

Many of these trips were to porno conventions. Nowadays,
these gatherings have become almost glamorous, but in those
days they had to be presented as get-togethers of legitimate
magazine publishers. Patrick Livingston and Bruce Ellavsky
continued to build their cases against the main pornographers.

Their covert operation was so secretive that even other agents didn't know about the case.

After about a year, prosecutors with the Justice Department opened a Grand Jury investigation and began presenting evidence which the agents continually supplied.

It seems highly unlikely that there will ever be another MiPorn investigation. The F.B.I. continues to pursue obscenity cases but, for the most part, has confined its attention to child pornography. The lack of concern shown by most Americans over the effects of pornography on our culture has stymied any momentum law enforcement previously had.[5]

Indeed, pornography has become such an accepted part of the culture that TV dramas such as *The Deuce* provide scenes that would have—at an earlier time—been banned as obscene. Although pornography, euphemistically called "adult material," has been legal and prevalent, the mob has not withdrawn its tentacles from the industry. The production of all kinds of movies offers a profitable venue for the mob to launder its illegally acquired money and earn huge returns. In addition, the mob controls numerous porno websites that have been known to rip off naive consumers who provide their credit card information only to discover enormous unauthorized charges.

Pornographic movies during the so-called golden age of pornography produced huge profits for the mob, changed the culture, and made celebrities of performers eager to demonstrate their sexual skills before voyeuristic cameras. The competition among mobsters to control the industry resulted in untold numbers of murders, beatings, and threats of violence. The mob's monopoly is gone. Now, exhibitionistic couples and groups of swingers can make videos of themselves performing every sexual act imaginable and post their talents on the internet for the millions of consumers who can't get enough of pornography. Overall, millions of websites, either directly or indirectly, are involved in pornography. They have a market value exceeding $100 billion. Alexa ranked the following porno sites as the most popular on the internet:

- Chaturbate generates more than 19 million visits per month.
- XVideos generates an average of 18.5 million visits per month.
- Pornhub generates an average of 25.4 million visits per month.
- LiveJasmin generates more than 16.2 million visits per month.
- xHamster generates an average of 18.4 million visits per month.
- XNXX generates an average of 16.3 million visits per month.
- OnlyFans generates an average of 39 million visits per month.[6]

As a service to consumers, the *Los Angeles Times* even listed the fifteen safest porno sites for consumers to visit. The old-time mobsters who had controlled the porno industry would be angrily spinning in their graves if they could see the current democratization of pornography and the free access to it on the internet.

NOTES

1. www.nytimes.com/1978/03/05/archives/sex-business-linked-to-alleged-mobster-zaffaranos-listing-nam (accessed February 25, 2023).

2. Peter Maas, *Underboss* (New York: HarperCollins, 1997), 216–17.

3. Interview with author, February 13, 2023.

4. www.purelifeministries.org/blog/the-fbis-secret-battle-with-the-mafia-over-pornography (accessed March 1, 2023).

5. www.purelifeministries.org/blog/the-fbis-secret-battle-with-the-mafia-over-pornography (accessed March 1, 2023).

6. https://earthweb.com/how-many-porn-sites-are-there/ (accessed March 7, 2023).

BIBLIOGRAPHY

BOOKS

Adler, Tim. *Hollywood and the Mob.* London: Bloomsbury, 2007.

Anger, Kenneth. *Hollywood Babylon.* New York: Straight Arrow Books, 1975.

Cohen, Mickey. *In My Own Words.* Englewood Cliffs, NJ: Prentice Hall, 1975.

Collins, Joan. *Her Autobiography and Two Novels.* New York: Random House, 1994.

Bruck, Connie. *When Hollywood Had a King.* New York: Random House, 2003.

Buntin, John. *L. A. Noir.* New York: Harmony Books, 2009.

Croddy, Marshall, and Patrick Jenning. *Testimony of a Death.* Redondo Beach, CA: Bay City Press, 2012.

Demaris, Ovid. *The Last Mafioso.* New York: Times Books, 1981.

Gabler, Neal. *An Empire of Their Own.* New York: Crown Publishers, 1988.

Hecht, Ben. *Child of the Century.* New York: Simon and Schuster, 1954.

Hubner, John. *Bottom Feeders.* New York: Doubleday, 1992.

Jennings, Dean. *We Only Kill Each Other.* Englewood-Cliffs, NJ: Prentice-Hall, 1968.

Kelley, Kitty. *His Way.* New York: Bantam Books, 1986.

Lewis, Brad. *Hollywood's Celebrity Gangster.* New York: Enigma Books, 2007.

Lieberman, Paul. *Gangster Squad.* New York: Thomas Dunne Books, 2012.

Maas, Peter. *Underboss.* New York: HarperCollins Publishers, 1997.

McCumber, David. *X Rated.* New York: Simon and Schuster, 1992.

Morgan, Michelle. *The Ice Cream Blonde.* Chicago: Chicago Review Press, 2016.

Nasaw, David. *The Patriarch.* New York: Penguin Press, 2012.

Rappleye, Charles, and Ed Becker. *All American Mafioso.* New York: Doubleday, 1991.

Russo, Gus. *Supermob.* New York: Bloomsbury, 2006.

Schwarz, Ted. *Hollywood Confidential.* Lanham, MD: Taylor Trade Publishing, 1997.

————. *Joseph Kennedy.* New York: Wiley and Sons, 2003.

Server, Lee. *Handsome Johnny.* New York: St. Martin's Press, 2018.

Stone, Wallace, *George Raft: The Man Who Would Be Bogart.* Albany, GA: Bear-Manor Media, 2008.

Swanson, Gloria. *Swanson on Swanson.* New York: Random House, 1980.

Tereba, Tere. *Mickey Cohen.* Toronto, Canada: ECW Press, 2012.

Wick, Steve. *Bad Company.* New York: Harcourt Brace Jovanovich, 1990.

Wilkerson, W. R. Wilkerson III. *Hollywood Godfather.* Chicago: Chicago Review Press, 2018.

PERIODICALS

Chicago Sun Times
Chicago Tribune
Confidential
Front Page Detective
Hollywood Nite-Life
Los Angeles Examiner
Los Angeles Magazine
Los Angeles Times
Newsweek
New York Daily News
New York Post
New York Times
Photoplay
Ring
San Francisco Chronicle
The Hollywood Reporter
Time
Times Picayune
Variety

INDEX

About the Author

Jeffrey Sussman is the author of seventeen nonfiction books, seven of which have been published by Rowman & Littlefield. In addition to *Tinseltown Gangsters*, Sussman is the author of *Sin City Gangsters: The Rise and Decline of the Mob in Las Vegas*; *Big Apple Gangsters: The Rise and Decline of the Mob in New York*; and *Boxing and the Mob: The Notorious History of the Sweet Science*. He lives in New York City.